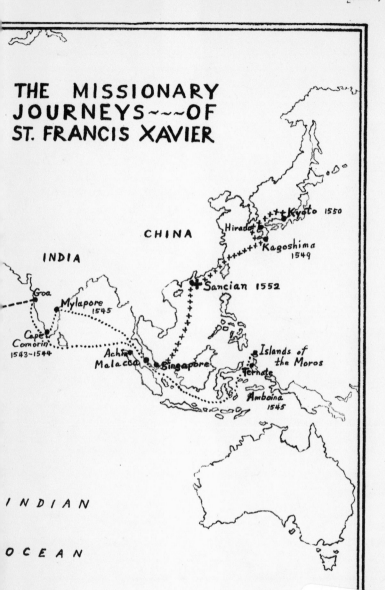

THE MISSIONARY JOURNEYS~~~OF ST. FRANCIS XAVIER

CHINA

INDIA

Kyoto 1550

Hirado

Kagoshima 1549

Sancian 1552

Goa

Mylapore 1545

Cape Comorin 1543-1544

Achin

Malacca Singapore

Islands of the Moros

Ternate

Amboina 1545

INDIAN

OCEAN

D1159793

DON FRANCISCO

by Mary Purcell

The Story of St. Francis Xavier

The Newman Press . . . *Westminster, Maryland*
1954

Nihil Obstat: EDUARDUS GALLEN
Censor Theol. Deput.

Imprimi Potest: ✚ IOANNES CAROLUS
Archiep. Dublinen. Hiberniæ Primas

Dublini, *die 8° Decembris,* anno 1952

Library of Congress Catalog Card Number: 53-5591

AMONG the multitude of chosen souls who have during the centuries embraced the supreme penance —lifelong exile to spread the Gospel—there have been many leaders of distinguished talent. All of them richly deserve the renown which is theirs. "They that are learned shall shine as the brightness of the firmament: and they that instruct many to justice as stars for all eternity" (Daniel 12:3). In this Milky Way of missionary glory, some stars shine with greater brilliance. Among the brightest are Paul, Boniface and Francis Xavier.

In the first century the Apostle of the Gentiles ranged the Mediterranean Sea, on which the Western world of his day was centered, from Jerusalem to Illyria, to Rome, to Spain. Although he founded many bishoprics, none have attached themselves to his name. Paul bore the message of Christ whither others had not ventured. He died in the See of Peter, with whom he is linked as patron of Rome and indeed of the Church.

In the eighth century St. Boniface, the Apostle of Western unity, by founding many of its famous Sees, or-

ganized the Church of Germany. As papal legate, he
reformed the French (Frankish) Church. At the end of
his life, an Archbishop without a See, he returned to
preach the Gospel to pagans in Holland and died there a
martyr.

In 1540 St. Francis Xavier, the Apostle of the Orient,
received from Pope Paul III a unique commission:
"Apostolic Nuncio to the islands of the Red Sea, the
Persian Gulf, and the Indian Ocean, as well as to the
provinces and places of India this side of the Ganges and
the promontory called the Cape of Good Hope and
beyond." No wonder that Blessed Pius X considered
Xavier's call equal to that of the Twelve Apostles—
*"numinis electum in eo reviviscere non secus ac in ipsis
Apostolis videretur."*

God gave Xavier ten years in the East. In that rela-
tively brief period he promoted the Catholic religion in
regions where it had been precariously established:
Mozambique, South India, Malaya, the Spice Islands and
Morotai. He also made the long voyage to Japan and
established a Japanese Church which within a century
was nearly drowned in the blood of myriad martyrs.
When in 1552, death caught up with the intrepid Xavier,
he was waiting on the island of Sancian for a ship to take
him to the nearby coast of China.

Xavier's personality fascinated his contemporaries. For
them he was the Saint of the age and they were eager to
believe all manner of marvelous things about him. During the four centuries since his death, Xavier's fame has

grown in the Church. In many places crowds annually flock to the Novena of Grace, seeking to profit by his intercession with God. When, a few years ago, the reliquary containing Xavier's right arm was carried from Rome to Japan and afterwards on a tour of the United States, and to Ireland, multitudes hastened to venerate it. With St. Thérèse of the Infant Jesus, he is the official patron of Catholic missions. Even outside the Church, Francis Xavier has many devoted friends and admirers. As evidence of this we may point to at least two comparatively recent and laudatory lives in English by non-Catholics, those of Stewart (1917) and Stranks (1933).

Some recent Catholic estimates of the Saint should be mentioned. Paul Claudel, who knew the East, wrote in his *Corona Benignitatis Anni Dei* (1920) some of the finest lines ever penned about Xavier. He sees this one man besieging the whole continent of Asia,

> *L'immense Asie tout entière est cernée par ce petit homme.*
> *Plus pénétrant que la trompette et plus supérieur que le tonnere,*
> *Il a cité la foule enfermée et proclamé la lumière.*

Archbishop Alban Goodier of Bombay in his *Saints for Sinners* (1930), after pointing out that no saint or hero has more enthusiastic admirers than Francis Xavier, studies the reverse of the glorious picture, namely, the failures of the Saint. Xavier did what he did in spite of discouragement from within and from without; he died with his eyes stretched out to a yet more distant horizon and counting all that he had done as nothing. In Father Arthur McGratty's *The Fire of Francis Xavier* (1952) the Saint's joys, trials, defeats and successes are relived. Father James Brodrick's *St. Francis Xavier* (1952) is the work of a man who has devoted many years to research on the early history of the Society of Jesus. In this masterpiece he marshals the fruits of his own investigations and those of many others. Of these the most distinguished is Father George Schurhammer, who not only knows all the printed and manuscript sources of the Saint's life but has inspected every league of land and sea which Xavier, sublimest of globe-trotters, traversed.

Mary Purcell's *Francis Xavier* is a biographical novel. It is, of course, more historical than fictional, yet the author does create incidents while she embroiders on real events and blows up minor characters to more than life size. But basically her work remains true to the saga of Xavier and, beautifully written and easy to read, it may be counted upon to carry the message and the spirit of the Saint to many who might otherwise not know them. To literary men history often, if not always, has the smell of the sepulchre about it. Mary Purcell has banished this dead odor from her book about Xavier where much real history is presented with the scent of the blossoms of spring.

EDWARD A. RYAN, S. J.

Woodstock College
January 26, 1953

PREFACE

I WISH to express my gratitude to all those whose help, so readily and generously given, made it possible to have this book published the year of the fourth centenary of St. Francis Xavier's death.

In particular, I thank His Excellency, the Marquis de Miraflores, Spain's Ambassador to Ireland, and Señor de Córdoba of the Spanish Embassy; the Jesuit Fathers of Ireland and Spain, who had many enquiries made for me and who supplied several books; the Jesuits of Toulouse, who loaned me volumes long out of print; Councillor Conor Cruise O'Brien and other officials of the Department of External Affairs in Dublin and Madrid; the Abbess of the Poor Clares of Gandia, who kindly loaned me a copy of a sixteenth century manuscript life of Doña Madalena, sister of St. Francis Xavier; Monsieur Louis Wei of the Chinese Embassy in Paris; Padre V. Arteta, S.J., historian and custodian of the Saint's birthplace, whose encyclopaedic knowledge was unreservedly placed at my disposal; Padre Ayerra, S.J., who kindly acted as liaison officer and who helped in translation difficulties.

To Padre Pardoe and the Jesuit Fathers of Xavier

ix

Castle; to the Misioneras of Cristo-Jesús, also of Xavier; to Madre Veronica, Señorita Carmen Huarte and the Editor of *Diario de Navarra,* all of Pamplona; to the Canónigo Lago-Cizur of Compostela Cathedral, and to several others in Spain whose kindness and assistance meant so much to me, my best thanks are due.

I am also grateful to the many librarians, in Ireland and abroad, on whose scholarship and advice I freely drew and whose patience I must have severely tested.

Finally, I am much indebted to the Dominican nuns of the Dublin Diocese, to Mr. D. B. Wyndham Lewis, to Miss Betty Crowe, to Mr. Aonghus O Dalaigh and to Mr. Anew McMaster for valuable suggestions.

MARY PURCELL

CHAPTER *1*

THE pilgrims were returning from Compostela. The prancing of reined-in mounts, the trundling of mule wagons, the scuffing of countless feet, some bare, some sandalled, sent the dust upwards in dense swirls that hung—copper-coloured veils—between the verdant landscape and the sun. The rough roads, radiating from Santiago like spokes from an axletree, swarmed with people leaving that "happiest and noblest of all the towns of Spain"—Santiago, last resting-place of the sterner of the two brother Apostles whom Our Lord had named Boanerges, the Sons of Thunder. Occasionally, one or more travellers would stand looking back towards where Saint James' hospitable door, *el Portico de la Gloria,* stood open to the whole world. There they would remain for a while, staring as though they wished to fix forever in their memories the panorama of churches and convents and hospices crowned by the glorious cathedral that rose in ornate Romanesque splendour among them. With its seven entrances, its seven churches, its fountains, its bell towers, its spires that soared heavenward, it made a sight worthy of admiration. And when they finally turned away, loath to leave this remote corner of Spain, this shrine so hallowed and so lovely, the bells rang out in a parting salute. San Lorenzo clanged, San Martin rang its resonant

1

tones right into the door of the Archbishop's palace, San
Domingo chimed its *Hosanna* one minute, its *Gratias* the
next, and all the time a veritable cascade of sound fell
from the Cathedral towers—sweet, clear notes that flew
out over the adjoining valleys like flocks of golden birds,
echoing and re-echoing above the pleasant land of Galicia.
And the pilgrims said, "Ah! Sant Iago's farewell. The
patron of Spain says *'Vaya Usted con Dios*—Go with
God.'"

Two riders, one elderly, one a youth, followed the
example of many others and withdrew from the thronged
roadway. Urging their mounts up a little eminence they,
too, spent several minutes gazing back affectionately at
Compostela, pointing out to one another the various
buildings and landmarks with which they had become
familiar during the days of pilgrimage. They noted, gleaming among green pastures, the waters of the Sar and the
Sarela, which formed two shining curves on either side of
Santiago. To the young man the twin streams suggested
two great scimitars, the bright blades of archangels
placed upon the velvety sward. He voiced his thought to
his companion who—used to his youthful charge's vivid
imaginings—agreed, but begged leave to wonder where
the celestial warriors capable of wielding such tremendous weapons had gone. Pointing to the trails of blue-
grey smoke falling from the honey-coloured towers of the
Cathedral, the older man asked could it be that the archangels were swinging *el Botafumeiro*—the giant, six-foot
censer—helping Saint James to forget how some of the
pilgrims had smelled. Feeling that he was being quietly
laughed at, young Don Francisco de Jassu y Xavier for-
bore to reply, although he had an answer to his tutor's
question; his imaginary archangels would, of course, have
done what was fitting—divested themselves of all

2

armour—before flying further west to pay homage to Our Lady of the Ends of the Earth. With a final salute to Sant Iago and his city, Don Miguel and Don Francisco turned their horses' heads and rejoined the mass of pilgrims that thronged the road leading to Palaz le Rey.

The English, the Welsh, the Scots and the Irish had gone to Corunna and Vigo, where two score ships waited to bear them to their islands in the north. Soon the Portuguese and Andalusians and Estremadurans would break away from the main body of pilgrims and take their several roads to the south. But the thousands upon thousands whose destinations lay in Castile, Murcia and Valencia, in the Asturias, Navarre, Aragon and Catalonia went steadily eastward, as did the multitudes who had come from beyond the Pyrenees. These latter would take twelve or thirteen days to reach Puente de la Reina, a town where the four roads that ran into Spain from the farthest ends of Europe joined to form what the Spaniards called *el camino francés*, the French road. Conditions would be as bad all the way to Triacastella—the end of the second day's journey—the pilgrims told one another, wryly, as they resigned themselves to the jostling, the dust and the slow progress. Despite the milling crowds, *juglares*, *gitanas*, tumblers, tambourine players, guitar strummers, dwarfs, clowns and beggars all managed to ply their various callings. And, here and there, palm readers and charm vendors and horoscope casters did a steady trade, for the devotion of some returning pilgrims evaporated quickly, and curiosity—dormant during the days of prayer —needed but a few shrewd remarks to rouse it.

The seemingly endless column streamed on, past valleys of chestnut and walnut, past oak forests and ridges sentinelled by stone pines, past poplar-fringed streams, past farm lands where fawn-coloured oxen turned mournful eyes on the passing cavalcade, past clearings where charcoal burners worked, past groves where wood-doves cooed, and on and on to Palaz le Rey the first evening, Triacastella the second. There the Hospice *inglés* and the Monastery of St. Gerard had doors open for all. Carved along the cloisters—in case the monks might forget—were the words: "Who receives you, receives Me." And over the lintel of the Hospice ran the inscription: "I was hungry and you fed Me, thirsty and you gave Me to drink, shelterless and you housed Me."

On the third morning the tempo changed. Travellers going north for the Asturias, as well as those bound for central, eastern and southern Spain, betook themselves away, shortly after dawn. Finding the congestion on the main route, *el camino francés,* relieved, the pilgrims who had come from Navarre, Aragon and the lands beyond the Pyrenees made haste to depart. Wallets and gourds were adjusted on waist-belts; pilgrim hats were fastened at the angle affording greatest possible protection from sun and dust; saddle girths were tightened or loosened, axle pins greased. Horses and mules, held in check by their riders during the two previous days, when progress was impeded and speed impossible, were now given rein and spur and the open road. Muleteers shouted to their teams; occupants of the covered wagons—nuns, ailing people, women and girls—prepared for the jolting and discomfort and sweltering heat inseparable from that mode of travel.

The foot-pilgrims, following the example of the professional palmers, began to take long, seemingly slow strides, swinging their five-foot hazelwood staves with a dignified, rhythmic movement that lessened fatigue and made for enduring speed. This steady pacing, difficult to acquire at the start, was an appropriate gait for a Christian returning from a spiritual odyssey. Though he lived in a world that seemed to grow in extent with each passing year, the pilgrim of 1525, like his fathers of the preceding centuries, felt a deep sense of personal achievement on completing a pilgrimage. Whether his goal was one of the three major shrines—Jerusalem, Rome, Compostela—or whether he contented himself with undertaking some secondary pilgrimage at the time of a Great Pardon—such as the Three Kings at Cologne, St. Thomas of Canterbury, Notre Dame at Puy en Velay, the Madeleine at Vezelay, St. Patrick's Purgatory in Ireland—his journey was certain to be penitential in the extreme. But the penance he endured, the vigils, the fastings, the travel weariness, the very garb he donned, the hazards he encountered on the way, all helped to induce in his soul the dispositions needful for its sacramental cleansing. Setting forth with definite goals, spiritual as well as geographical, the Christian who overcame all the intervening difficulties found in his pilgrimage a means of appeasing somewhat the perpetual clamourings of the human heart. The winds of passion were calmed, the waves of desire were stilled; and, returning, such a one came from the sacred mountain with his whole being in perfect control—his soul, one might say, in his hand.

Young Don Francisco Xavier, watering his mount near the Triacastella quarries, watched the pilgrims pass. He sensed this content that possessed them. The same serenity and happiness seemed to emanate from old Don Miguel despite his rather awkward appearance on horseback. But the pilgrimage had not made Francisco's heart less restless, rather had it whetted his appetite for further wanderings. He was impatient now for the coming journey to Paris, for the new university life, so soon to begin for him. Even at Compostela the urge to move elsewhere had plagued him. He had persuaded Don Miguel to forsake Saint James for a few days and ride twenty leagues westward so that they might make their obeisances to Our Lady of the Ends of the Earth. It had been fine to stand there, with the Mother of God, at the gate of Europe; to look out with her over the western sea. It stirred the mind to think of her standing, so calm and fair, on Heaven's bright strand, her maternal gaze on the sea of life, where myriad souls sailed like mariners from the shore of Birth to that of Death. It gladdened the heart to remember that, no matter what tempests or misfortune befell one's frail boat, God's Blessed Mother was watching and hoping and praying on the coast to which all must come. . . . And, at Finisterre, Don Miguel and Francisco had seen a tall ship waiting on the tide, a ship bound for those strange new lands which Christopher Columbus and Hernán Cortés had found for Spain. Late in the evening they had heard the seamen singing *Ave Maris Stella,* as the noble galleon, starting with the turn of the tide and a following breeze, rode into a sunset that touched her sails with flame. Francisco had yearned to be aboard. Beyond that unknown ocean there were lands strange and beautiful—so the mariners said. Gazing at the Atlantic sunset, a marvel the like of which he had never seen in his mountain home, the youth from Navarre could well believe that they who sailed such glorious seas found Paradise on the further shore.

Don Miguel, waiting patiently by the water trough at Triacastella, thought Francisco had had enough of daydreaming and said so. The elderly priest was glad to be getting back to the ordered life of the *abadía* of Xavier. It had been no slight cause of scruple to him, his pilgrimage. Even during the most devotional exercises worldliness had insinuated itself on every side, and he, Don

Miguel, had contributed his own share, riding the horse Doña Maria had insisted that he take. It was no way to start off on a pilgrimage, he told her, giving bad example. Everyone knew that clerics were forbidden to ride horses; the decree of *los Reyes Católicos* setting forth the edict—"mules for clergy and women"—was still very much in force.

Holy man that he was, Don Miguel felt that the flaunting of any authority, obsolete or active, was—for a follower of Christ—something that amounted almost to treachery at a time when all God's laws were being broken. When the wreckers were rallying to overthrow the Church and its Founder, it behoved all the friends of Our Lord to show Him greater love and fidelity. To be sure, young Francisco would not have consented to ride through Spain on a mule: nothing but the best horse in the sadly depleted stables of Xavier for him. So the old priest had bowed to circumstance and the will of others and gone on horseback. He had confessed and repented of such worldliness at Compostela and promised himself a goodly measure of fasts, vigils and disciplines in the months ahead.

"Don Miguel—we have to make Villafranca by nightfall. Let's ride a bit faster."

"There you go again, Francisco, always wanting to make haste. How often have I had to tell you that a steady pace gets there just as surely in the end, and it's easier on the horses. Time enough for hard riding when we come to the lonely forest roads or that stretch near Carrion where bandits lurk to attack pilgrims. This is pleasant country; it would be a pity to gallop through these green valleys. No wonder Sant Iago made it his own; the very name—Galicia—must have reminded him of his native Galilee."

7

"I wish mother had been at Compostela. Every time I passed that quaint old statue of Sant Iago's mother in the right-hand transept of the Capilla Mayor I thought of her and smiled."

"Smiled?"

"Mary Salome reminded me of mother."

"But that statue was Byzantine in style—I saw no resemblance to Doña Maria."

"Oh, the statue didn't resemble mother in appearance —nor mother the statue—*Gracias a Dios!* But, you remember the day Mary Salome asked Our Lord for high places in His kingdom for her sons? I could just imagine mother, if she met Christ on the road, asking Him for the most exalted honours for Juan and Miguel and myself!"

"I see. Yes, that would be Doña Maria. No doubt she has already made some great requests on behalf of her children. I hope her sons would be as ready to answer as were the sons of Mary Salome—not only in word but in deed."

"Well, for my part, I hope mother doesn't aim as high as Salome. I don't think I could live up to such a request as would require me to suffer and die. Juan and Miguel, perhaps, could face death and torture; they are used to bloodshed, having fought in the wars. But I have other ideas."

They rode ahead silently after that, each occupied with his own thoughts. It was a good journey to Mount Cebrero, where the next hospice stood; there they would spend the afternoon, enjoying a meal and a siesta before pressing on for Villafranca. As they rode, Don Miguel's thoughts went back, as the thoughts of all aging people tend to go, over the span of the years. He recalled his previous pilgrimage to Compostela, thirty-three years before, the year of his ordination—1492.

It was an easy year to remember—1492. The year good Cristóbal Colón sailed west to discover new kingdoms for Queen Isabel the beloved. The very year Boabdil, the Moorish king, delivered the keys of Granada to the Queen and her consort—Boabdil, who had shed tears over his defeat, while his mother and wives taunted him with weeping like a woman for what he had failed to defend like a man. It was the year, too, when Don Miguel had first gone to live at Xavier, where his young cousin, Doña Maria, and her husband, Dr. Juan de Jassu, lived. The three little girls had been quite young then, Juan and Miguel as yet unborn; Don Miguel had been fully fourteen years at Xavier before Francisco, the child of his parents' later years, was born. By that Holy Week of 1506, the week of Francisco's birth, Don Miguel and the other priests who had come to Xavier had been quite a long time living according to rule in the *abadía* on the little hill beyond the castle.

What troubled times Xavier had been through since last Don Miguel had ridden to Compostela! It was almost a dream now, those quiet days when the girls had to be taught their first lessons: Latin and *castellano,* reading and writing, a knowledge of figures, astronomy and the use of the globes. He recalled Madalena, the loveliest of the three, the morning she left for the court of Queen Isabel to be a maid of honour. He remembered the day, not so many years later, when a Queen's messenger had come posting to Navarre with a letter for Doña Maria— the letter bearing the news that Madalena would never return to Xavier Castle, the Queen's favourite maid of honour having taken her fair face to a court other than Isabel's. Madalena had asked permission and received it— not without regret on the part of her royal mistress—to enter the monastery of the Poor Clares at Gandia, a small

9

fishing town some miles south of Valencia. The courier who brought the news reported that Her Highness, Queen Isabel, was ailing; he had ridden from Medina del Campo, where the first lady of Spain lay abed, her friends having entreated her to retire to her favourite residence and rest until Pentecost. Medina was a pleasant town in Maytime; the young wheat and saffron laid bright carpets on the countryside all about, and the plains of Castile were white with flocks of sheep being driven to the great wool fairs, where merchants from far and near came to buy; the Queen would recover in Medina, people said. But, six months later, word arrived in Xavier that Isabel of Castile was dead, that Spain was left desolate. Doña Maria assembled the household and reread, with tears, the gracious letter received from the deceased lady half a year previously, and all repaired to the *abadía* to chant the Office for the Dead and assist at the Requiem Mass offered by Don Martin Azpilcueta, the learned canonist, cousin of Doña Maria and Don Miguel. Dr. Juan de Jassu had been in attendance on the Bishop of Pamplona when the latter rode south to accompany the Queen's cortege on the three-week journey from Medina to Granada, where she had asked to be buried. Neither the Bishop nor the Lord of Xavier had ever been to such a funeral. Three weeks' hard riding, under skies that were steel-grey by day, jet-black by night; winds, rains, blizzards, the like of which they had never experienced. In Italy *el Gran Capitan* mourned her passing. From San Lucar came Columbus, recently returned from his fourth voyage. Each would have died for the noble-hearted Isabel. Each was to suffer dismissal and ingratitude at the hands of Ferdinand. Columbus gave the Queen her finest epitaph; in a letter to his son he wrote:

Don Francisco

The principal thing to do is to commend the soul
of Nuestra Señora, the Queen, to God. Her life was
ever Catholic and holy; and in all things she served
God promptly; for this reason we may rest assured
that she has been received into His glory—beyond
the care of this harsh and weary world.

No, it was not for nothing, the dead Queen's bereaved
subjects told one another, that the terrible earthquake
had shaken Castile on the Good Friday preceding that
much-lamented death. Troubles came on Spain from the
day of Isabel's demise. All along, her own excellence as
a ruler and her love for Ferdinand cloaked the latter's
faults; she had readily given her husband credit for much
of the good she herself accomplished. On her removal
from the earthly scene his incompetence as a king soon
came to notice, his egoism and craftiness well-nigh destroy-
ing all that his consort's genius for sovereignty had
achieved. His covetous eye marked Navarre, that little
realm sitting astride the Pyrenees—that border-province
of the Basques, with one foot in France and the other in
Spain. From coveting he passed to demanding, from
demanding to taking, from taking to keeping. Ferdinand
made other blunders; he alienated Castile and Valladolid;
only that his captains upheld Spanish prestige by waging
successful wars abroad it would have gone ill with him
and with Spain. But, from the point of view of Don
Miguel and the family with whom his life was inextricably
bound, no disaster of all those made imminent or precipi-
tated by Ferdinand compared with the attack on independent Navarre—resulting as it did in the outlawing of
the master of Xavier Castle and the two older boys.

As he rode along now behind young Francisco, Don
Miguel recalled that the boy had been only six when the

fighting began. Ana, the second daughter of the house, had been married in the springtime and by autumn Dr. Jassu and his two older sons were fugitives. They in Xavier did not see the head of the household again until one sad evening about two years later when he came, unannounced, unexpected, to his home. Juan de Jassu had returned to die. Despite Doña Maria's devoted care, the fever swept him away.

People thought that the events of 1516 would mean better days for Navarre. In January the old bell of Velilla in Aragon began to toll, though no hand pulled the bell-rope. Men reminded one another, with awe, what such tolling portended. Into the casting of that bell had gone one of the thirty pieces of silver paid to Judas Iscariot— the price of God's Son. When an invisible hand rang the bell of Velilla, the death of some great one was infallibly presaged. Ferdinand of Aragon, who had been persuading himself that his physicians were wrong and *la Beata* of Barco—who had foretold that he would yet conquer Jerusalem—right, heard that the bell of Velilla was tolling. He at once sent for his confessor, whom he had banished in favour of *la Beata,* made his peace with God, and died. Pending the arrival of the heir, the austere, eighty-year-old Franciscan, Cardinal Ximenes, ruled Spain as Regent. But Navarre was in worse state than ever; the pawn of France and Spain, the province drew on itself the displeasure of the Regent, who was determined to hand over to Isabel's successor a strong, united nation. Ximenes would not tolerate rebellion in Navarre; he sent his captains thither with orders to stamp out all disloyalty with a heavy hand. All rebel fortresses were to be razed to the ground; rebels were to be executed and their families dispossessed. In the general subjugation of Navarre demolition squads visited Xavier and proceeded to mutilate its towers and walls until scarcely more than the living quarters were left intact.

In 1517 Isabel's Hapsburg grandson, Charles, left Flanders to rule the Kingdoms of Spain, shortly afterwards being elected Emperor of that huge slice of Europe known as the Holy Roman Empire. Four years later, revolts in Castile and Valencia forcing the Emperor to withdraw his garrisons from Navarre, the Navarrese, taking heart anew, rose again in rebellion. They besieged the town of Pamplona, gallantly defended for Spain by a brave and distinguished Basque *hidalgo*, Ignatius Loyola. The courage of this captain so impressed the besiegers that, when the town fell to them, they had the wounded Loyola sent by litter to his brother's castle, some distance to the west of Pamplona.

The guerilla war lasted for three years, when an amnesty was proclaimed. Juan and Miguel, no longer boys but men in their late twenties, were amongst those granted the Imperial pardon; after long years of virtual banishment, Doña Maria's sons were free to return to Xavier. Their homecoming, alas, was not to that Xavier they had left in 1512, for there were many who had taken advantage of their prolonged absence. Shepherds, bound for the fairs of Castile, had remained for days on end in the precincts of the castle, grazing their flocks with impunity on Doña Maria's lands. Drover told drover that it paid to drive one's sheep by Xavier, Maria Azpilcueta's toll-gates being guarded only by a couple of old men. As there was a price on the head of her menfolk, the lady of the castle would get scant justice—if she got a hearing at all—should she haul any trespassers or toll evaders before the judge in Sangüesa. Yes, even if it meant making a detour, it was well worth one's while to go by Xavier—it was so much toll money saved. In the woods, the axes of thieves sounded, first on moonlit nights only, then in broad daylight; the marauders merely laughed at Doña Maria's protests and threats as they hauled away loads of valuable timber right past the castle itself. Poachers waited at the weirs and hunted in the woods; fields, gardens and orchards were raided; even the dairies and cellars did not escape the general depredations.

But in this year of Our Lord, 1525, Juan and Miguel had come home to Xavier. Doña Maria had been overjoyed at their return and had insisted that Don Miguel and Francisco make the Compostela pilgrimage in thanksgiving for the peace and to beg God's blessing on the three upon whom the future of the family depended. Don Miguel had been glad of the opportunity to visit Santiago again. If only Doña Maria had not insisted on his riding that horse. . . . What was that strange story Juan and Miguel had told about the wounded Basque captain—the captain from Loyola? . . . Something about his conversion while he was recovering from his wound. The fellow was now serving God with as much zeal as he had formerly served the Emperor. Ah, well, that was nothing new in Spain . . . Don Miguel himself would have been truly converted at Compostela—only for that horse Doña Maria had bidden him ride!

Unlike Don Miguel, eighteen-year-old Francisco felt little delight at the prospect of returning to the remote. isolated dwelling called Xavier. He wished his home were not so lonely, not so dilapidated. It squatted at the end of a sloping ridge of foothills that, jutting south from the Sierra Leyre, sentinelled the borders of Navarre and Aragon. At its best Xavier was not much of a building, compared with those fine castles they had seen on the road to Santiago. In the razing of Navarrese fortresses by Ximenes' captains, it had come off better than many others, perhaps, but it was now a sorry sight. Juan and Miguel had raged on their return, when they beheld the round towers and the drawbridge tower reduced to little more than stumps of masonry. And when they saw the great central tower of San Miguel, now pulled down to half its original height, the great gaps made in the battlements, the wrecked drawbridge, the stone and rubble blocking the moat and lying in heaps on the top terraces and the stairways, they had been furious. And they had been angry with Francisco because he did not share their rage. Although he deplored the destruction, Francisco's main fault with his home was that it was a dull old place at the very back of beyond; now that he had seen a bit further afield he was almost glad at the prospect of leaving Xavier for Paris.

He wondered if his mother had remembered all the instructions for the tailor regarding the clothes for going away. It would be galling to cut a shabby figure when riding north in September with those other students who were to call for him. Had the green suit of merino wool been ready in time he would have liked to wear it to Compostela; he had no liking for the rough serge pilgrim gown that Don Miguel had made him don for the journey. The only compensation had been the magnificent white satin cloak with the red sword of Sant Iago on the shoulder, which he, as representative of the Azpilcueta family, had been entitled to wear. His mother's forebears, noted for their charity to pilgrims and for their alacrity in defending Compostela-bound travellers against the lawless and rapacious who waited to attack them, had qualified to become Knights of Sant Iago. Don Francisco de Jassu y Xavier—tall, lithe, handsome and more than a little vain of his figure and bearing—sported with enthusiasm the insignia of the silver scallop, and carried his

15

fine shoulders so that the white cloak with the crimson sword swung with a flourish as he walked. It had been conspicuous at Compostela, that satin cloak. True, there were other knights of Sant Iago here and there amid the crowds, but they had been men withered and old, their cloaks—in most cases—being as worn and faded as themselves. Thanks to Doña Maria and that excellent needle-woman, Aunt Violante, Francisco had cut a dash at the pilgrimage. He had been glad of his finery when he met the company with whom he was to ride to Paris: Flemings and English boys, all rather soberly clad; German and Scandinavian landgraves and landsknechts, wearing accoutrement eminently suitable, no doubt, in their own cold countries, but neither sensible nor fashionable in Spain; a few gorgeously attired fellows—French counts and a Lombard banker—were amongst those strangely assorted students of Paris University but, even beside such elegance, the cloak of Bruges satin had held its own.

Don Miguel broke the long silence: "You are sure the students will call at Xavier on their return journey?"

"Yes. They said they'd be glad to come. The English and the Danes are gone to buy blades in Toledo. If the money in their saddle-bags suffices, they will go on to Córdoba to buy riding gear."

"And probably be as poor as students the world over when they return," commented Don Miguel. "You may be sure they'll be glad to avail themselves of Doña Maria's hospitality for a few days."

"Do you think they'll notice that we in Xavier are poor? Our castle will seem a very broken-down place to some of those wealthy fellows." Anxiety was evident in Francisco Xavier's face. Don Miguel hastened to reassure him.

"Students don't notice poverty. They are well acquainted with it. And when did poverty become dishonourable? As for the scars your home bears, when these young men hear your brothers tell of the wars and of how Xavier suffered for Navarre, they will reverence the ruined towers and battlements. Your mother will see to it that their food and lodging are of the best. Besides, if they are coming before the *fiesta,* as they said, you will be able to take them to the *pelota* game and the *feria* at Sangüesa."

They lapsed into silence again. Francisco found his thoughts speeding onwards. Unlike his companion he found the future far more interesting than the past. He saw himself, as he hoped to be in a month's time, one of a band of youths, debonair and handsome, riding eagerly towards Paris. Ambitions which he did not attempt to stifle stirred in him and he yearned for the new life ahead. His brothers would probably settle down now—having won some renown with the sword, they would try to retrieve their ruined estates. Not for Francisco such a pedestrian, humdrum life. Juan and Miguel had been fools to waste the best years of their lives in hiding—fugitives with a price upon their heads. And for what, in the end? Power was passing from the soldiers and warriors to the schoolmen and the thinkers. A new era was dawning; Francisco himself was conscious of being at its birth. Wars would still be waged, but with minds not with hands. For this fray the old weapons were useless, outmoded—science and learning were the steels one needed to hold sharp and ready in the intellect's scabbard.

As he put spurs to his horse, Francisco exulted to think that he would be in that battle; and not a raw recruit either, thanks to patient Don Miguel. His brothers had returned defeated from the wars, but he would not come back beaten from *his* encounters—never, with the help of God and Sant Iago. Only in Paris—so Don Martin Azpilcueta, mother's learned cousin, who was spending the

summer in Xavier, before taking a professor's chair in
Coimbra, said—only in Paris could one be perfected in the
mental parry and thrust so essential for the arguments of
scholars. Paris was the university "not of one town but of
all the world." There one mingled with the best brains of
Europe. Don Martin Azpilcueta—affable, witty, altogether
charming—was in himself an example of what scholarship
and travel made of a man. It was beyond Francisco to
fathom how so great a man of learning had contented
himself to spend a whole summer in Xavier. But there he
had remained, living in the *abadía* with the other priests,
giving Francisco the advantage of his company, occasionally taking over the teaching from Don Miguel—
proving himself a boon during those recent weeks when
the entrance examinations for the College of Ste. Barbe,
which was the establishment in Paris University attended
by the Navarrese, had to be prepared for.

. . . It was Villafranca that night, and Rabanat the
next, and then Leon. "Oviedo the holy, Toledo the rich,
Seville the great, Salamanca the strong, Leon the lovely"
—ran the litany of the cathedrals of Spain. But the travellers had seen all they wished to see on the journey to
Compostela; now they only wished to press home quickly.
After a good night's rest they rode eastward again, on and
on, day after day, coming to Carrion one evening, Burgos
the next. Burgos itself, like a tawny lion couched on an
eminence in a melancholy, sterile plain, needed all its
romantic links with the Cid to raise the travellers' flagging
spirits.

From Burgos, on by the forest of Oca, and over the
mountains to Najera; on the next day to Estella and the
next again to Pamplona and the familiar stretch of road
between that and Xavier. Though their horses were jaded
and they themselves weary of the saddle, the two trav-

ellers felt their hearts rise as they sighted the grey hills of home.

"Doña Madalena will be disappointed when she receives the letter telling her that you will not have time to visit her in Gandia," remarked Don Miguel. "It must be strange for her having a grown brother whom she has never seen. She was almost three years in Gandia that Holy Week in 1506 when you were born."

Francisco did not think that this unknown sister would be disappointed. She would understand—knowing of their changed circumstances in Xavier—about the horse having to be rested well before leaving for Paris. Compostela and back, Gandia and back, and then Xavier to Paris was too much to expect from one mount, even though it was a blooded animal, with a strong Arab strain. He himself felt no great urge to visit Doña Madalena. Last year it might have been different. This year, what with the return of Juan and Miguel, the pilgrimage, and now the preparations for Paris, a visit to his sister in Gandia held no great attraction for him. He had no doubt but that the Abbess of Gandia was so fully occupied with her devotions and the administration of community affairs that she cared not a whit whether he visited her or not. He seldom thought of her, although he was, of course, grateful to Madalena for having written that letter insisting that he be sent to Paris—not to any lesser seat of learning. In a few years' time, when he hoped to emerge from his University's many examinations as victorious as *el Gran Capitan*, as successful in his quest for learning as Columbus and Cortés for lands, then he would go to Gandia, he told Don Miguel. The latter sighed.

"Yes. Probably Doña Madalena will accept your decision to defer your visit as the will of God. But she was always one with a warm, human heart; and the human

19

heart has not yet been created that is immune to disappointment; even the Heart of Christ felt it . . . However, after twenty years in religion she has doubtless reached the stage where trials and disappointments are to her as so many flavourings to a tasty dish."

"Don Miguel! How could she leave the court? It wasn't a corrupt one; Queen Isabel was good. How was it Madalena left to bury herself in a Poor Clare convent in an unimportant, faraway town like Gandia? Could she not easily have entered the Cistercian Monastery—*Las Huelgas*—you remember that royal convent we passed near Burgos, where we stopped for High Mass, and watched the hundred nuns, all of noble birth, and the mitred abbess?"

"Yes. I remember. The Abbess of *Las Huelgas* is a princess-palatine, yielding precedence to no lady in Spain —save the Queen. She has powers of life and death. The cloisters of *Las Huelgas* are a most magnificent example of Moorish art. But Madalena would have none of that. She had seen all the world has to show of beauty and magnificence; she had lived in the Alhambra; she had visited *Las Huelgas* with Queen Isabel. No; Madalena was for greater things. God seemed to have set her apart from the very cradle. She was the saint of the family."

"Probably she heard herself so described again and again, and finally she became convinced that she would have to live up to what everyone expected of her. Then, having taken the step, she wouldn't go back on it."

"God calls people in different ways. She is a long time in religion now, and shows no signs of having ever regretted her decision. And she is no indifferent nun either —her letters all breathe the spirit of St. Clare and St. Colette."

"Well, I am glad God has not called me that way. The

austerities—*Válgame Dios!* Mother says that they get up in the night to pray; that they live on a meatless diet, with long fastings, vigils and disciplines. The path of learning is more attractive than the path of penance."

"Maybe, maybe, Francisco, but there are more stumbling blocks on the scholar's road. Learning is a maze where souls can easily go astray. Madalena's path is narrow and thorny perhaps, and a flinty one for delicate feet to tread, but it goes straight to God and that is what Madalena has been doing all her life—going straight to God."

They were silent as they walked their weary mounts along the Calle Mayor in Sangüesa. This evening there would be no time to call at the Ortiz house, Doña Maria's paternal home; nor to Miguel Anues, who had been the *gran amigo* of Dr. Juan de Jassu. They had to get to Xavier before dark. At Santa Maria la Real they made a short halt, offering thanks for their safe return, lighting a taper before Nuestra Señora de Rocamador, while Francisco wondered, for the twentieth time, how it came about that it was a French representation of Our Lady, not that of Our Lady of Pilar, which was venerated in Sangüesa. When they remounted, the tired horses, scenting the heady air of their native hills, gathered a final spurt of energy for the five-mile climb to Xavier. They had to be led past the more dangerous parts of the mule-track that wound so capriciously in and out along the ridge of hills. It was late evening and the tinkle of bells told that the sheep were coming home; shouts of muleteers and the rumble of wagon wheels on the road to Yesa meant that some travellers hoped to reach Leyre before nightfall— the Cistercian monks would give bed and board to all who knocked on the doors of their mountain monastery. At last the two riders sighted the *abadía* perched on the hill

above Xavier castle, its clear silhouette—standing out
sharply against the pearly sky—contrasting sharply with
the ungainly outline of the fortress. Don Francisco felt his
heart go out to those unsightly towers—maimed stumps
now, where once the Santo Cristo, the tall San Miguel and
the Homage towers had reared themselves towards
Heaven. He hoped Juan and Miguel would rebuild the
towers before anything else, he told Don Miguel. But Don
Miguel hardly heard; he was too overjoyed to find that
they had come to journey's end. The road, which had
climbed so many hills and dipped into so many valleys
since leaving Compostela, had finally wound past the
olive orchard and the vineyard to lose itself under the
doorway of the courtyard of Xavier.

CHAPTER 2

THE poor Clares of Gandia had a saint for Abbess. Like all saints Doña Madalena considered herself to be of sinners the chief. She hoped that her name, the same in religion as in Baptism, proclaimed her status before God and man. It was seldom, however, that the Abbess of Gandia indulged in vain reflections. A Poor Clare, she told her novices, should look forward, never back; and one who was Christ's had no thoughts or time to waste upon the passing pageant of this world; neither did it become a nun to dally—admiring herself in the unreliable mirror of self-esteem—while hastening to her heavenly Espousals. As she advised others, so she endeavoured to live herself. Yet, there were times when Doña Madalena came upon herself, almost unawares, lost amid other scenes and other days—times when she crossed and recrossed Spain in a matter of moments, her mind playing among the years like a hand lifting and letting fall bright gems. Just such a mood of retrospection seized her on an August evening in 1525 when she sat in the shade of the sunken garden behind the convent, wondering if young Francisco would come to visit her before he left for Paris University.

She remembered Xavier, that northern home so different from this sun-loved province of Valencia, at the other

23

end of Spain; Xavier, so desolate when, on winter nights, the winds from the Pyrenees rode mercilessly over Navarre in their mad rush on Castile, shrieking like ten thousand demons as they hurled themselves down the valley of the Aragon; Xavier, so parched in summer. She remembered her mother, Doña Maria, so valiant and good; Doña Maria—whose "works praised her in the gates"—to whom, if to any woman, could be applied the words of the Book of Proverbs. She remembered her sister, Maria, now a nun in Pamplona; and her other sister, Ana, now married and rearing a family; her brothers Juan and Miguel, much younger than herself; Aunt Violante, nearer in age to her nieces than to her sister, Doña Maria; her father, Dr. Juan de Jassu, so seldom at home, so constantly employed in his legal work at the court of Navarre and in Pamplona. She remembered their old nurse, Guillerma, with her nut-brown skin and her ample and apt stock of Basque proverbs. She remembered Don Miguel, so holy and good, so patient to teach, so wise to advise.

She remembered the years at the court, the Alhambra gardens beautiful with white jasmine and blood-red oleanders, the air laden with scent of myrtle and musk-rose, the Queen walking in the Hall of the Ambassadors or the Court of the Lions, reading the letters newly arrived from Christopher Columbus—letters with the most exciting news of strange lands and stranger peoples. She remembered her own dread lest she be sent to faraway England in the retinue of the Infanta Catalina when the latter went to wed the heir of Henry VII; the old English king had stipulated that all the Maids of Honour should be beautiful, and Madalena had had to confide in the Queen—had to tell, sooner than she intended to, her intention of becoming a Poor Clare—lest she be included in the company of 150 preparing for exile in England. She remembered the distress and humiliation of Isabel when the second Infanta, Juana, heiress to Castila, began to earn for herself the sobriquet of *la Loca*—the Mad One. Juana had spent a winter's night clinging, half-naked, to the gates of Burgos, screaming for freedom to range Europe in the wake of her faithless husband, Philip, the heir to Maximilian the Emperor. And the Queen, hearing that no one, not even the Archbishop, could do anything with the frenzied creature, had risen in the night and galloped the forty miles to Burgos. There, a motley crowd turned from the diverting spectacle of mad Juana to gape at their Queen as she pulled up her froth-flecked, steaming mount and walked to the crazed, snarling woman whom none dared approach. She must have had need, then, of all her will power, all the grace that was hers by right of her anointed sovereignty. "Is this how an Archduchess receives guests?"—her eyebrows asked. "Come and get dressed and welcome the Queen of Spain according to court ceremonial." And, from the sullen but cowed Juana, the woman who was every inch a Queen had wrested obedience without uttering a word . . . Sighing, Doña Madalena remembered her own farewell to the court and the great lady who had made Spain, and the whole Christian world, a better place because of her wise rule and the example of her noble life. Madalena de Jassu y Xavier had knelt for a blessing and, unexpectedly, Isabel relaxed her rigid self-control and wept for a few moments. "Your beautiful hair," she said. Madalena understood, or thought she did. The Queen was thinking, no doubt, of Juana's latest bout of insanity, when she had so far forgotten her lineage and upbringing as to belabour and berate one of the Duke's mistresses before the Flemish court, ending by cutting off the girl's hair. But the Queen did not speak of Juana. "The Magdalen wiped Christ's feet with her hair.

25

So will you. You will sacrifice it for Him. You will sacrifice yourself. Pray for me in Gandia . . ." She remembered— and then, suddenly conscious that her memories were making breaches in the walls of that inner enclosure where came none but God, the Abbess of Gandia brusquely pulled herself back to the present and began walking up and down the sanded path, examining herself on how she had spent the day.

It had passed quickly, like most days. She slept on her straw pallet from two until five that morning; she came down in the cool of dawn for Prime, Tierce and the conventual Mass; then she tidied her cell, before partaking of the *frustulum* of goat's milk, thickened with a little meal. Later she had attended to letters, had seen the workman who was to repair the outer gates, had met and conveyed the chaplain to two ailing nuns, and had joined the community in the common room where some embroidered vestments, others repaired or sewed altar linens, while a few painted devotional objects or strung rosaries. Then came the eleven o'clock meal. One had long since become accustomed to the wooden platters and bowls, the vegetables cooked in an inferior oil, the occasional egg or fruit, the lack of meat and wine—"that they might," as the Rule said, "have the benediction of Our Lord on the table of their poverty and for salt and tastiness the divine love." Harder to bear was the regulation that insisted upon no singularity—each one having to eat what was left at her place, no one more or less than her neighbour.

Then there were Psalms and reading and praying and private devotions for that difficult period from one o'clock to three o'clock when sleep had to be fought against—a really hard task in summer. At three o'clock there was manual work for two hours again—laundering, gardening, making altar breads—tasks which could be done in common. At five o'clock there were the prayers for the deceased benefactors, afterwards a scanty collation of bread and water—on feasts a little fruit. And then Compline, after which the Great Silence commenced. Compline sung, one was free to pray, read or walk in the gardens or cloisters. At eight o'clock night prayers would be said and each Poor Clare would go to her cell to lie down, fully clothed in her rough serge habit, ready to rise again at midnight for the Matins, spiritual reading and hour of watching with God that was the privilege of her vocation.

A nun approached, bowed without speaking and signed to the Abbess that her presence was required at the grille. As she went to answer the summons she passed various nuns in the passages and hall, each intent upon some occupation, yet not so intent but that work could be joined to and interspersed with prayer. The novices were walking in the cloisters, their bare feet seeming to slide along; it was one of the things that most delighted Madalena—the silence not only of speech but of movement in the life of a Poor Clare. It was like the seamless robe woven for the Lord by His Mother; each nun helped to weave the garment of quiet and, in the evenings, when the Great Silence began, it was as though the entire community wrapped itself and its Beloved in some vesture not of earth.

In the parlour there were visitors—Juan de Borgia, second Duke of Gandia, and fifteen-year-old Francis, the Duke's eldest son.

"You will pardon us for calling at this late hour," said the Duke, "but Francis leaves for Zaragossa in the morning and he wishes to say farewell to you, Doña Abbess, and to his grandmother, Sor Gabriela and his aunt, Sor Francis of Jesus."

"But certainly, your Highness. Indeed, all the nuns will want to bid young Don Francis Godspeed. For tonight and for such an occasion we will relax the rule of silence and have everyone here for a few moments." She called a passing nun and gave a whispered order. "How the boy grows!" she commented, looking at Francis. "It seems but the other day when he used to toddle into the refectory to 'preach' to the community. Ah, here come your mother and sister," she continued, as two nuns entered the grille-parlour. "Family farewells are best said in the family. I will come back again with the other nuns."

"But wait, Doña Abbess, one moment," called the Duke. "I had almost forgotten. I bear a message from your brother, Don Francisco de Xavier—two men of my household have just returned from Compostela. They met your brother there and he gave them this letter for you."

The Abbess took the letter, promised to come back in a little while with a keepsake for the young Duke, and padded away to the oratory to cut a little piece of the convent's most prized possession—the now-ravelled rope that had served St. Francis of Assisi for a girdle. She cut an inch off the relic, rapidly stitched the detached fragment into a little case—she had had such a case in readiness against the coming of her own brother, Francisco. They could make another one tomorrow for him, she decided. This one should go to the motherless Borgia boy.

She thought that she had better read the letter, in case her brother were already on the way and perhaps arriving at any moment, with no place bespoken for his lodging. She broke the seal and read rapidly; the letter was short and to the point. Francisco was not coming to Gandia. The horse had to be rested before leaving for Paris. In a few years, when his studies were done, he would come to see his sister. In the meantime he asked her prayers. All in Xavier were well. He hoped that this letter would not be a cause of disappointment.

So. It was not to be. She was not to see this brother for
whom she had prayed even before his birth—the only one
of her family whose face she had never seen, whose voice
she had never heard. For some unknown reason, she
yearned towards this stranger-brother; she hoped it was
not a fault, this longing to set eyes upon the youngest of
the six children God gave her parents. Well, God had not
willed that her wish be gratified. Bowing her head, she
acquiesced. What will had she now, save that of Him to
whom she had pledged her troth? One's own will, one's
desires great and small, realised the only dowry poor
human nature had to bring to such a bridal as hers. In her
Lord's unchanging realms, wealth, beauty, talent and all
this world's ephemeral riches were but dust; only the
heart counted with the Creator—the heart where burned
unceasingly the sacrificial fire, where stood the secret altar
on which one laid, bit by bit, the holocaust of self. Doña
Madalena sighed a little as she added her wish to see her
brother to all that she had already surrendered. Some day,
when she became holy, she would, she told herself, find
her will so locked in—so identified with—the will of God
that she would come to know great peace. "In His will lies
our peace," had written the Florentine, Dante, whose
writings had been having quite a vogue in Isabel's court
when Madalena left it. How right Dante had been. It had
taken twenty years for one nun to fathom the truth of his
words. There was a difference between the acceptance of
ill health, poor fare, austerities, as one's just portion, and
the receiving—nay, welcoming—of such trials as mani-
festations of the will of Someone dearer than life, dearer
than self. Only because one loved could one rise above
such disappointments as this one she had just received
regarding her brother. She put Francisco resolutely out of
mind. But, being a warmhearted woman, as she went to

29

call the nuns to the grille to meet their benefactor, the Duke, tears coursed down her face and on to her serge robes.

.   .   .   .   .

Guillerma stood, leaning on her stick, watching Doña Maria fold and pack the cambric shirts, the hose, the student gowns, and all the rest of the belongings that Don Francisco needed for Paris. The old nurse's gnomish face puckered even more than usual; she strongly disapproved of foreign countries, and was highly indignant at the thought of young Francisco being allowed to go and live there uncared for by any relative. "Guillerma," learned Don Martin was wont to say, "speaketh in proverbs, and without proverbs she openeth not her mouth." For this occasion she produced a fresh store which no one had heard before. The mistress of Xavier, bending over her checking and packing, sighed and smiled as the old Basque woman rattled on, at one moment recalling past events, at another making gloomy prophecies. "A foreign land is a land of wolves," announced Guillerma. In a few moments she followed up with "Heavy is the hand of foreigners."

"Fetch me the ruffs Violante finished last night," ordered Doña Maria. "They are in my bedroom." She was glad to be rid of Guillerma for a little; though the old retainer was one in a thousand, sometimes her ceaseless chatter and domineering ways grated on one. Those ruffs, now; after all the trouble starching the muslin ones and stitching the stiff satin ones, it appeared that such fabrics were going out of fashion. Francisco said that the Florentines at Compostela had all favoured lace ruffs—everyone in Italy was wearing lace ruffs this year, it seemed. Naturally, being but a boy, Francisco could not be expected to know just how one made a lace ruff; if she or Violante could have seen or handled some of that stylish neckwear called "Medici," they would have been able to provide him with it.

Guillerma pottered back with the ruffs, yet another proverb on her lips: "He makes a good pilgrimage," she observed, "who stays in peace at home."

"Nonsense," retorted Doña Maria. "It did Francisco good to go to Compostela. He grew up in a few weeks. He doesn't have that nightmare—where he has to carry an Indian—any more. The pilgrimage helped to prepare him—soul and body—for Paris."

Guillerma pursed her lips; she would have continued to express her opinions, proverb-framed, on foreign persons, places and things, and the undesirability of exposing Don Francisco to such influences; but it was obvious that Doña Maria would hear no more of such talk. The old woman, by this time in the mood for railing at everything, began to contrast the tables set out in the hall with banquets they of Xavier had known in better days.

Doña Maria sighed as she wrapped a few cheeses in clean cloths. Guillerma recalled the day when the Queen of Navarre, with the Infantas, had ridden from Olite to Xavier, to spend an afternoon there. Doctor Juan de Jassu, the Counsellor of Navarre, had told his wife, Doña Maria, and her household, to make ready for a hundred guests; but, between courtiers, caballeros, muleteers and the usual poor people and widows invited to share in such festivities, there had been almost two hundred.

It put Guillerma into good humour again to recount the amount of food that had to be prepared on that occasion. Sixteen sheep, seven calves and a suckling pig were slaughtered; Doña Maria herself had cooked the ten great gosling pies and the five dozen fat chickens served on

steaming platters of creamy rice. Guillerma had seen to
the bran bread and rye bread for the muleteers; from
Sangüesa had come the six score of fine white loaves for
the grandees and the sweet wafers for the Infantas. The
royal children made a lot of cooking—syrups beaten with
eggs, almond and apple pasties and all sorts of sweet-
meats. And some of the guests had to be pampered with
special dainties—oranges all the way from the Tudela
orange-groves for the maids in waiting, sardines for the
Bishop of Pamplona, partridge pie for the Abbot of Irachi,
eels in a hot sauce for the Señor de Luxa and, surprisingly,
nothing for the Queen but bread and cheese.

"Go down and see to the tables. The kid for roasting
should be on the spit by now; and set out the melons and
beat the eggs for the tortillas. The almond tarts are to be
brought to table," ordered Doña Maria.

When Guillerma was gone, she rose from her knees,
and went into the oratory. *El Cristo,* the great crucifix of
Xavier, hung there. She knelt and prayed; prayed for her
two boys home from the wars, for the future fortunes of
Xavier, for Ana and her children; for Maria in her Pamplona convent and Madalena in Gandia, for her youngest
—her Francisco—the one who had been with her all during
the years of sadness and ill fortune, the one who, now
that he was about to go away, seemed dearer than all.

Soon he and the students would be back from the *pelota*
game. She would not spoil his last evening by weeping;
he would be keeping cheerful before the other boys and
she would do likewise. Had she not kept her grief beneath
the surface in more difficult circumstances? When the
King of Spain's captains had come to demolish Xavier,
had she not begged them to desist? Was she not herself of
the same ancestry as the kings of Aragon and Navarre?
Their own shame at attacking a fortress manned by a

brave woman and a handful of clerics and elderly re-
tainers testified that Doña Maria's dignified silence had
been more effective than the most eloquent protest. When
her husband had died and her sons—fugitives in the
mountains—were under sentence of death, she had held
her grief in check for the sake of her youngest son. She
would do the same tonight, though it might well be that
she would never see him again . . . she was aging rapidly
and of late a constant pain tormented her.

As she turned to go, she looked long at the crucifix, an
unspoken prayer for Francisco on her lips. The *Cristo* of
Xavier, a finely carved life-size figure, vividly showed that
crucifixion was a most bitter and agonising death. Not for
the first time, Doña Maria found herself realising, in some
way, what the Mother of the Saviour suffered in behold-
ing her Son on Calvary. She beheld Him wounded and
was unable to aid Him; she saw Him bleed and she could
neither staunch nor wash away that precious Blood; she
saw His eyes bloodshot and inflamed and she could not
bathe them; she knew that He thirsted, yet she could not
give Him to drink; she saw His head droop—the same
sacred head that she had so often held to her heart in His
childhood—and she could not lift or rest it; she heard men
curse and blaspheme Him, yet she could not defend Him;
she knew that His Father had forsaken Him, but into that
utter desolation she could not enter to succour Him; she
saw Him about to depart and could not embrace Him; she
saw Him die and she could not die with Him . . . Doña
Maria stood for a few minutes before the crucifix, thinking
with and compassionating the Mother of God, and repeating the *Stabat Mater.*

> *Stabat Mater, dolorosa,*
> *Juxta crucem lacrymosa,*
> *Dum pendebat Filius.*

Then, slowly, she went to the hall to see that all was in order for Francisco's farewell dinner.

Don Martin closed his Boethius and turned to his cousin. She was getting on in years, he reflected, a little sadly; her hair was still black as was his own—none of the Azpilcuetas went grey or white; even in old age they retained the sloe-black hair that was a family trait—but the skin on her high cheekbones was drawn and bloodless, her shoulders a little stooped. Well, she was not young, Doña Maria, and sorrow had laid heavy hands on her; and, though she would show no sign, the parting with her young lad was an ordeal for her.

"They have not returned yet?" she asked.

"No. But good news came before them. Francisco won the challenge match."

"The challenge from the Puente de la Reina players?"

"Yes, indeed. Juan and Miguel were there; Juan came home early to see to the shepherds. He says the lad excelled himself. He played a game that will be talked of throughout the valleys for many a day. The students from Paris are delighted with him."

"I hope he won't do anything foolish now—eat too many watermelons to quench his thirst and perhaps bring on a colic, or catch an ague or chill after such sweaty exertions."

"Not Francisco. He has a body made of whipcord—and a constitution of iron. Not but that he'll need good health for the years of studying ahead."

"Don Martin, I wonder is it right to let him go; he has led so sheltered a life here; those students seem so sophisticated—men of the world—beside him."

"You couldn't have held him at your apron strings for ever, my good cousin. Besides, he shows great promise; he has one of the keenest minds I ever met with in one of his age. I know that you worry—hearing some of the talk of the students—that he may get into bad ways. But he is naturally reserved—a bit proud perhaps, but that same reserve and hauteur may save him from worse evils. And he has had a good start and the help of your prayers and Doña Madalena's—not to mention all the Masses being offered for him in the *abadía*. No, Doña Maria; you have done your duty by the lad; keep on praying and leave him to God."

"Here they come, mistress!" old Guillerma called excitedly from the large low-ceilinged room where the dinner table was laid. Horses came clattering under the archway and soon the three young men of the Xavier family ushered in about a dozen guests.

Not only had Francisco won the challenge game against the most noted *pelota*-player of the Pyreneean valleys, he had also cast the javelin farther than any thrower there, and in the barefoot race he had given his rivals a start and beaten them easily. He certainly would leave a name behind him as the finest athlete in the seven Basque provinces, the students told Doña Maria. But Navarre's loss would be a gain for Paris: Francisco would be very popular when the Colleges turned out for games and sports on the Pré-aux-Clercs; on Tuesdays and Thursdays he would be able to put his prowess as a vaulter and runner to good use. On those days all the students gathered in the fields on the left bank of the Seine just below the city, and there was great rivalry between the different Colleges. The Ste. Barbe men would be insufferable now that they could count on fielding a first-class fellow like Francisco, an all-round athlete.

Francisco, unused to such praise, stood back a little from the crowd about his mother. He eyed the table. Trust mother to rise to an occasion—she had not failed to put the best side out for these strangers! The young German margrave, who was always talking about the Rhineland lager and wines, could find no fault with the Rioja wines, with the home made ales and cider—all set out in the crystal flagons and lustre jugs that had been family heirlooms. The son of the Lombard banker, who waxed so eloquent about the cook his family sent to Paris with him—so that he might not have to stomach the abominable messes the college servants produced in the name of cookery—he would not look askance on the pickled veal, the roast kid, the well-flavoured *olla* in which simmered early partridges and dwarf peas. The freshly baked loaves, the gingerbreads and almond tarts were a credit to Aunt Violante and no one could say but that they in Xavier had snowy linens to their tables, sweet-smelling, resinous pines for their firing, deft and courteous folk to wait on guests, and a household which, for all its poverty, showed its nobility in its members. Mother and Aunt Violante were wearing their finest clothes for this, the last little family festivity Francis would grace for a long time. Aunt Violante looked gentle and lovely; and mother looked like a queen. Don Martin, in his most urbane and courteous mood, was charming as ever, while Ana and her tall husband, Don Diego de Ezpeleta, made a handsome pair; Juan and Miguel, whose Latin had become rusty during their long time away in the border wars, turned now to Francis, now to Don Martin for a translation of some phrase that had escaped them. As few of the students spoke *castellano*, all the company spoke Latin—and again Francisco felt proud of his mother and aunt and Ana, all three of whom not only understood Latin but spoke it easily and well. Guillerma bustled about, quoting Basque proverbs, as usual; and there was much merriment as now

one, now another of the company tried to translate her
sayings into Latin.

There was so much to speak of that no one mentioned
their departure in the morning. Don Martin was keenly
interested in the news of international importance—it seldom happened that one met with company so representative of the leading European nations; and these young
men were all capable of giving a first-hand account of
how things were in their various countries. The fact that
they were, for the most part, young men, did not make
their observations any the less interesting; though the
young were sometimes intolerant, and often swayed by
the heart rather than the head, time had not allowed them
to become encrusted with the cynicism that accumulates
with the years—not yet had they acquired the habit of
dissimulation that infected so many of their elders. From
one to another Don Martin tossed the conversational ball
—now to the rather stodgy and not too mannerly German
margrave, now to the young Lombard, again to the
middle-aged Frenchman or to the taciturn English pair.
Two Spaniards—already studying at Ste. Barbe—enthralled
the company with the tale of what they had heard and
seen at Madrid. Magnificent presents sent by the mighty
Cortés to the Emperor, to show what kind of countries
were in the New Spain beyond the seas; a culverin of
silver, the metal in which cost over 24,000 golden pesos. It
was a pity, of course, that Cortés had put that inscription
on the gift. What was that inscription? Don Martin had
not heard about that. The culverin had been made in the
shape of a phoenix and Cortés had bidden his engraver
write

> Peerless is this bird by birth
> Peerless you are on the Earth
> Peerless is my service's worth.

That last line was considered too proud in one who, twenty years before, had been haunting the quays of Seville and Cadiz, wheedling the master mariners to take him on the next journey to the Indies. Yes, poor Cortés had been effectively snubbed. The Emperor had handed the luckless culverin to his Secretary-Treasurer, who had promptly smelted it, pocketing a fortune in gold and silver ducats from the sale of the precious metal. It just showed what happened to those who put their trust in princes! Despite all he had won for Spain, the gallant conquistador was now getting the cold shoulder. *Por Dios!* when one thought of all the rich treasure Cortés sent home—of all the ports of Andalusia swarming with wealth! The returning caravels came in weighted with gold and gems; the quays were crowded with pilots and seamen, with swordsmen and captains, with Indian *caciques* in their bizarre headdresses; with gorgeously attired grandees who, only a few months previously, had left Spain, penniless adventurers, and were now home, fabulously rich. And there was merchandise never heard of before this side of the Atlantic, cloth wrought from the plumage of the bright-coloured birds that flew in these faraway climes, bodkins and daggers of tiger-bone and lion-bone, chests of eagle-wood and other strange aromatic timbers. From the Indies, west and east, came curios of every sort, priceless jewels, gold and silver ornaments wondrously fashioned, furnishings and fabrics and spices in great quantities.

Everyone listened, spellbound; and Francisco remembered the ship they had seen sailing out from Finisterre only a few weeks before; it would be in those strange lands by now, perhaps . . . Don Martin, fearing that the Spaniards might usurp the conversation (which would be a grave breach of courtesy), asked the Frenchman if his

travels in Spain had taken him far. The Frenchman had,
indeed, got as far as Madrid and had been lucky to get
back alive. He had not realised that, in the summer of
1525, every Frenchman approaching Madrid was suspect
—a possible spy coming to get in touch with the Emperor's
royal prisoner, the King of France, then chafing in the
Alcazar. Even if one were so foolhardy as to try to get a
message through to François, the gay Valois, what chance
had one, when the gloomy Charles kept the captive in a
small room a hundred feet from the ground in that impregnable fortress, the Alcazar? After seeing the sights of
Seville, the Frenchman had, indeed, wandered near the
Alcazar—just to be able to tell at home in Nantes that he
had seen the prison where France's king languished. To
be sure, he had hoped to get a glimpse of the imprisoned
monarch; he had been told that the Spanish guards took
him out for a mule-back ride, when he needed exercise. It
was highly unfortunate that, when challenged unexpectedly in Spanish, he had answered in his own tongue; he
had been unceremoniously hauled before the Captain of
the Alcazar and subjected to a long interrogation. It was
well for him that he had his Compostela certificate and
cockleshell to show; he was let off with a caution, and the
guards made sure that he betook himself north right
speedily, following him out of the city and beyond the
orange-groves, and for an hour along the road to Guada-
lajara, threatening to set the Emperor's Irish wolf-hounds
at his heels; he would not soon forget the hours of weary
trudging as he put the long miles between him and
Madrid. Of course, if he had known that Madrid's Alcazar
was the French king's place of imprisonment he would
not have ventured within miles of the city . . . Francisco
noticed Juan and Miguel exchange glances: the man could
hardly have been telling the truth; why, in Compostela

the imprisonment of François in the Alcazar was talked of on all sides; the Salamanca students could talk of nothing else . . .

Sensing an air of general embarrassment, Don Martin hastened to get the English boys speaking about their country and their King, the eighth Henry. Spain had always been interested in Henry—was he not wed to their own Catalina, daughter of the beloved Isabel? She had been a young widow, a forlorn young soul in that strange land; some said that after his elder brother Arthur's untimely death, the poor Infanta had not fared so well; her miserly old father-in-law, the upstart Tudor who had seized the throne in 1485, would neither return her and her dowry to Spain, nor support the Infanta as befitted her station. The English boys were shy; on their tongues the familiar Latin had strange, rasping sounds; and they seemed unwilling to speak much of their sovereign. Don Martin did not know that all London was buzzing with the talk of the liaison between the king and Mary Boleyn; and rumour said that young Northumberland, admirer of the second Boleyn girl, had been told by Cardinal Wolsey to choose himself another sweetheart—and quickly to pursue his courtship to its matrimonial end; otherwise, it might go ill with him. The English boys said nothing of this in Spain; they did not like to make known the humiliation of Catherine of Aragon, the Queen whose inability to bear an heir was spoken of contemptuously by her husband, as he fondled the six-year-old Duke of Richmond, the illegitimate son borne him by Bessie Blount. Nine times Catherine had raised his hopes and the hopes of England, and with what results? A sickly boy, who had died in infancy; a whey-faced daughter, Mary, just now jilted by the Emperor of Spain, who had, no doubt, a better alliance in view; and a mournful succession of miscarriages—stillborn children. Yes, all England knew that their King was repudiating his Queen. But the students would not speak of this to their hosts in Navarre. They murmured commonplaces, failed hopelessly to take the different conversational openings given them by Don Martin, and eventually stammered themselves into a silence from which they did not emerge for the remainder of the night.

Don Martin did not encourage the German margrave to speak of the events taking place in Germany. He had heard, in a recent letter from Coimbra, of the Peasants' Revolt and of the marriage of Luther to Catherine Bora. And, earlier that same week, he had heard a dispute among the young men, the German and the sons of the Swedish landgrave hotly supporting the heretics, while the rich Italian and his compatriots, two Florentines, took the side of orthodoxy. Don Martin was glad to note that Francisco Xavier saw the flaws in the arguments of the Italians; it was appalling, he told his young cousin afterwards, how lads so young had become so infected with the principles of their fellow Florentine, Machiavelli, cynically averring that expedience, not justice, should decide what course a man should follow at all times and in all circumstances. He was glad that Doña Maria had not heard that discussion; had she been present she would certainly never allow Francisco to leave his home in the company of these young men; she would absolutely forbid him to go to Paris. Don Martin could not agree to that; the lad had a good grounding and a keen intelligence and a robust piety. In such times one did not need to go to Paris to meet heresy and heretics; since the printed word had become common to all, there were false teachers on every hand—pamphlets were circulating on all sides; even in Spain, the latest teachings of Luther, Zwingli and the rest of the reformers, who would reform others first and them-

selves last, were being spread. It was a testing time. And
Francisco would have to face a tough test in Paris where,
if rumour were true, masters in some of the leading Colleges were, if not on the side of the heretics, so con-
temptuous of the ancient Church—fallen, alas, on evil
days—that some made no move to defend her, while others
started heresies of their own, relying on their students to
become their disciples.

Doña Maria, rising, remarked that, as the travellers
would be starting early, Mass would be said at dawn. As
it was their last evening in Xavier, there would be Vespers
and the *Salve* in the *abadía* as soon as all were ready. Don
Martin and Don Miguel and the other Don Martin hastened ahead, while Francisco followed to light the candles
and ring the *abadía* bell. The three women walked together, speaking but little. Ana and Violante knew that
Doña Maria was making a noble effort to pretend that
this evening was no different from others. They respected
her sorrow and the wall she had built about it; they lent
her their own unspoken comfort and encouragement.

The students came in a noisy crowd with Juan and
Miguel and Don Diego. Some would not have gone to
Vespers in their own homes or in Paris; but, in Xavier,
one tried to please the gracious lady whose word was law
there. Soon, all were kneeling in the dark stalls of the
abadía. Francisco was lighting the candles; as the flare of
the lifted taper fell on his upturned face his mother
thought: "I shall never see him like this again; when I
see him again his youth will be over . . . I will never see
Francisco again." And, placing her worn hands against
her face, she let the slow, hot tears trickle through her
fingers till they hung and glistened upon her rings.

In honour of the *fiesta*, Our Lady's Birthday, Aunt
Violante, the chandler of Xavier, had put out the best

beeswax candles instead of the everyday tallow ones. Francisco, touching the tall candles one by one with his taper-flame, was reminded of how the sun, God's acolyte, had tipped with fire the gleaming mast heads and snowy sails of that galleon he had seen at Finisterre. The candles lit, he proceeded to the choir stall in front of Don Miguel's, and stood with the others as Don Martin intoned the Antiphon of the feast:

> This is the birthday of the glorious Virgin Mary, of the seed of Abraham, born of the tribe of Juda, of the noble race of David. This day is the birthday of the holy Virgin Mary.

All took up the response:

> Whose glorious life sheddeth lustre on all the churches.

The words "sheddeth lustre" drew Francisco's attention to the candles, and again the Finisterre galleon came, unbidden, sailing up before his mind's eye. He tried to banish the intruding thought, remembering the instruction learned in *Arte para servir a Dios*—to make of an obstinate distraction a link between oneself and God. But it was difficult to find any connection between a galleon—especially one sailing for the kingdoms of New Spain—and God. He made valiant efforts to steer his ship towards the kingdom of Heaven; he tried to recall a line from St. Augustine's *Soliloquies* to which Don Martin had drawn his attention the previous day—an evasive line that said something about sails and something about God . . .

Don Miguel looked reproachfully at his charge. That was the second slip the lad had made since Vespers started; before all the strange students, too; it was unlike

43

Francisco, usually so recollected at prayers, so exact when it was a question of rubrics. Probably the thought of tomorrow's departure made the boy a bit abstracted; he looked as though his mind were concentrated on some faraway, elusive prospect. In a sense Don Miguel was right. St. Augustine's line having at last been recalled, Francisco found himself, his active mind momentarily halted, contemplating unfamiliar but enchanting horizons. "God," said St. Augustine, "to whom we come by love and not by sail . . ."

Turning the phrase over and over, Francisco told himself that, for this time, it was sufficient to memorise it and set it aside. Later on one could think about it, although it sounded the sort of sentence one could repeat and ponder for a lifetime and yet not fully plumb its depths of meaning, not savour it completely. Don Miguel, who had already coughed twice to attract the boy's attention, now leaned over from his stall and gave him a sharp nudge. For the rest of Vespers Francisco Xavier rose and sat, sang and prayed at the proper times; but St. Augustine's strange words made a wonderful echo in his mind: "We come to God by love and not by sail."

When Vespers were over, all stood to sing the *Salve:*

Hail, Holy Queen, Mother of Mercy,
Our life, our sweetness and our hope, Hail!
To thee do we cry, poor banished children of Eve,
To thee do we send up our sighs,
Mourning and weeping in this vale of tears.
Therefore, Most Gracious Advocate, O turn
Thine eyes of mercy towards us;
And after this, our exile,
Show unto us the blessed fruit of thy womb,
Jesus.
O clement,

44

Don Francisco

O loving,
O sweet Virgin Mary.

After the final invocation the priest sang:

Pray for us, O Holy Mother of God,

And all took up the response:

That we may be made worthy of the promises of
Christ.

Doña Maria, usually the last to leave the little chapel,
rose and led the way out. When the others came out she
was composed and dignified as ever; but she showed that
she expected everyone to retire early. "Go with God!" she
said, as each little group came along. Francisco, who had
waited to extinguish the candles and prepare the altars
for the morning Mass, came last. The others had gone on
and his mother was waiting. They walked in silence towards the castle. There was nothing to say. Francisco was
realising, almost with surprise, that he had a mother of
incomparable worth, a mother suddenly grown inexpress-
ibly dear. They were undemonstrative, the Xavier family;
he could only look at her dumbly, unable to find any
words to tell his thanks, his love, his pride in her. He
knew she would not weep or embrace him in the morning
when the moment of farewell came; she would let him go
with his friends as though he were no more to her than
they. And if she wept, it would be when the riders were
well out of sight. She was a mother among mothers—and
he was leaving her, and for God knew how long. This
night, as every night of his life, he knelt for her blessing.
And that night, as though it were an ordinary night, Doña
Maria said, clearly and calmly, "Go with God, my son."

CHAPTER 3

THE sentinels, standing on the high platforms of the Louvre tower, sounded their trumpets, and the city awoke to a new day. A thin wind teased and tweaked the Spinning Sow, the Three Kings of Cologne, the Tin Plate, the Mule, the Nun-Shoeing-the-Goose, the Wooden Sword, the Scarlet Hat and other well-known tavern signs that flapped and creaked and rattled the while they tugged unavailingly at their iron moorings. Sleepy-eyed wine shop owners turned in their beds and felt beneath their pallets to make sure that the previous night's takings had not been tampered with—late roisterers having been known to return and rob. In the three hundred convents and churches of Paris, bell ringers set about their task with a vigour that was half resentment against all who might lie abed while ringers of bells had to toil up steep bell-towers in the early hours.

Above the clamouring tongues of lesser metals two bells—the bell of the Abbey of St. Germain des Prés and the bell of the Sorbonne—seemed to contend for supremacy. If the bell of the Abbey sounded more mellow, that of the Sorbonne had the more sonorous echo. At the first stroke of the Abbey bell the devout among the monks bestirred themselves with a *Benedicamus Domino* or a *Deo Gratias*. At the last stroke of the Sorbonne bell the students, grumbling and muttering, cursing, not in the obligatory Latin of the Colleges but in their various *linguae maternae,* hastened to betake themselves to their studies. Among the many colleges clustered about that hill made holy forever by Sainte Geneviève was the Ste. Barbe. In a little attic room to the rear of the building the occupants were dressing rapidly. It was not yet five o'clock, but, as the first lecture would be given at that hour, there was no time to be lost. Suddenly Francisco Xavier remembered that this was no ordinary lecture day. This was the day he and Favre—good old Peter, already on his knees, himself and the Pilgrim!—this was the day Peter Favre and Francisco Xavier would receive their diplomas in philosophy. Today they would march in procession to the church of St. Denis and there receive authority to teach the arts "in Paris and in all the earth." Surely the Pilgrim would cut short the devotions this morning—these meditations and colloquies and what-not that he and Peter went through as thoroughly and exactly as swordsmen their wrist, foot and body exercises. But no, they were proceeding, as usual, from point to point, from consideration to consideration, with military precision. Francis moved past them, and, leaving the room, went on to a little landing. There, looking out from a dormer window on the sloping roofs of older Colleges adjoining the Ste. Barbe, he began to say his rosary. Although he had been as careless, perhaps, as the next about his prayers for his first year or two at College, since his mother's death the previous year he had begun to pray more and with greater fervour.

Thank Heavens, there would be no huddling in straw-strewn halls this morning, no need to concentrate hearing and attention on the droning of the masters. It was to be hoped that Michael the Navarrese, the servant Francisco had brought to Paris with him, would bestir himself soon and mull the wine and buy a few fresh rolls—the bread was mouldy and the butter rancid for the past fortnight. At this rate they in the Ste. Barbe would soon fare as ill as those in the Montaigu—the most squalidly kept, the most poorly appointed of all the colleges, yet the one that had a reputation for consistently turning out the best men. Erasmus had been a master there thirty years before, professing theology in spite of the Montaigu diet of stinking herrings and addled eggs. Calvin, that thoughtful, unsmiling heretic, had been there up to a year or two ago. The students of the Beauvais, who were always boiling for a fight with the Montaigu men, would, if they could have suspected his future success as an opponent of Catholicism, have used him as a pretext for starting a riot. And, of course, the Pilgrim, Ignatius Loyola, the same who was still praying in the room Francisco had left, he also had been to the Montaigu. Francisco could not see how the impoverished Basque captain had profited by his sojourn there; although he was more than a dozen years senior to Favre and Francisco, they had to coach him—at least, Peter Favre did; Francisco had grown tired of so dull a work in a short time.

It was exciting to think that the King and his sister would be at the conferring in St. Denis. Last year and the previous year had been rather dull occasions. Nothing more unusual than a hanging at Montfaucon and evening excursions to the Cemetery of the Innocents. It was more exciting to remember that the King's sister, Marguerite, had taken for her second husband none other than Henri d'Albret, Henri II, son of that King of Navarre for whom Francisco Xavier's father and brothers had fought and suffered. It might well happen that when the name "Don Francisco de Jassu y Xavier" was called out in St. Denis, King Henri would remember what his family owed the family of Xavier. Then he and Queen Marguerite, who was said to be all-powerful in her influence on her brother, King François, would secure for the young graduate some high post in the Harcourt or the Ste. Barbe; or they might mention him to their brother, the French King, for the next vacancy in the Sorbonne or the College de Navarre—or maybe the Montaigu itself. Or better still—for Xavier had no intention of spending his life with books—some post in Church or State which would insure him a glorious future.

Uneven footsteps sounded on the landing. Francisco wheeled around to find the Pilgrim beside him, smiling, humming an old Basque song. He was getting to be a bit of a nuisance, this Ignatius Loyola; wherever Francisco turned the fellow was under his feet. Though a bit annoyed, Francisco, being naturally gay and good-tempered, made room for his fellow Basque at the little window.

"No six o'clock Mass this morning," he observed, "we could have taken an hour or two longer in bed, had we remembered. But, there will be plenty of fun shortly, when the big procession starts forming up. And Peter and myself will need to spend some time turning ourselves out properly. Juan de Pena, the Rector, would think nothing of sending a scholar down at the last moment, for some trivial fault like disgracing Ste. Barbe with a grimy face or slovenly gown."

Ignatius smiled. He could not imagine Francisco being taken to task on this score; Xavier was most exact about his appearance.

"Will you wear that gown?" he enquired, indicating the one Francisco was wearing.

"At the conferring! That old thing! Good Heavens, no!

My sister Ana sent me a new gown last Michaelmas, and I have been saving it against this day. The gown was a bit too big, too baggy—I suppose we all get a bit thin while in college—and I had Michael the Navarrese leave it with the tailor on the Rue du Fouarre the other day, with instructions to take it in. I expect that's where the Navarrese is now, instead of mulling our wine. I hope he hurries back with it. One would wish to be dressed and get down to where the students assemble early, to know exactly what's happening."

"I'll go and hurry him up," offered Ignatius; "possibly he stopped at some wine shop and forgot our breakfast and your gown."

Francisco stood watching as his roommate, hop-trotting with his now short leg, hastened down the stairs and out onto the street. He was a strange one, that captain from Loyola. He never seemed ashamed to be down in the lowest class, and, if he noticed his young classmates' amused glances at his slow, plodding progress, he never took offence. He was a slow-coach at philosophy; no one but Favre had the patience to help him. Yet, he had not always been so placid; when Peter and Francisco had asked him about his leg, he told them that he had been wounded in the siege of Pamplona—maybe by Miguel or Jean Xavier, Francisco had hastened to add!—and afterwards, hearing that his leg had been badly set, he had ordered the surgeons to break and reset it again. Twice he had suffered this, hoping to find himself straight-limbed afterwards, but all to no avail. He had been so vain of his appearance, he told them, that he was willing to suffer to save it. "Would I had suffered half as much for God," he had added. Well . . . he wasn't very vain now.

A shuffling on the stairs told that Michael the Navarrese was returning. He entered, scowling, a hang-dog expression in his eyes. Ignatius, who had met him in the street, returned on his heels.

"Where is my gown?" demanded Francis.

The other shook his head but said nothing.

"We have waited an hour for the wine you were to mull for breakfast," said Don Xavier, remembering that he was soon to be a graduate of the greatest university in Europe and assuming a tone in keeping with his approaching dignity. "We can manage to mull the wine ourselves— that's if you haven't drunk it all. But, my gown—where's my gown, man?"

"No money," said Michael the Navarrese, sullenly.

"No money!" cried Francisco, aghast. "But I gave you the money to pay for it." He did not need to be told the tale—he knew the habits of the servant whom all at home had warned him against bringing, but whom he had insisted on having with him to uphold his prestige as a Spanish *hidalgo*.

Ignatius, standing by, heard and understood. Other students would have belaboured the fellow to within an inch of his life, but Xavier was not such a one.

"What am I to do?" he said to Ignatius, reddening slowly, as he remembered that he already owed the Pilgrim four *écus*.

But his friend was already in their room, searching among his meagre effects.

"I had a little money last night," he said, sadly, as he came back onto the landing; looking reproachfully at the doubly guilty servant he added, "It isn't there now. But I'll see if I can get that gown for you, Don Francisco," and he hop-footed downstairs again and out. Francisco, ashamed of his unpaid debt, ashamed of his serving-man who robbed both himself and his friends, went back to the window and looked down the street. It was now the hour when the wealthy students—that son of the Lombard banker and that German margrave who had been so hospitably received in Xavier a few years before—would descend into the streets; if he knew where they were likely to be, it would be a good plan to go down and stop them and tell of his dilemma—surely they would offer to come to his rescue. Twice he attempted to sally forth; twice he returned to his window. The last time, he noticed the Pilgrim at the street corner behaving rather strangely. What on earth was the fellow doing? Great heavens! Begging! A nobleman of Navarre begging in the Paris gutters, like any common wretch. A Basque—a captain of Spain—begging! Hardly had he got over the shock when Ignatius came, dot-and-carry-one, up the stairs. He had the gown, all finished and ready to wear. Francisco took it, stammered his thanks and flushed hotly. He could not tell his friend that he had spied on him begging. But some remark seemed called for.

"That's more money I owe you," he said.

"No, nothing at all," said Ignatius. "That was money given me for the love of God. I give it to you on the same score. Here, let me fix your gown. This way, fastened to the side. And, be sure to walk with your thumbs in your belt, and the hood pulled well over your eyes."

Francisco, unable to bear the thought that another should have humbled himself to beggary to do him a service, could only mutter his thanks. By this time Peter Favre, who was already gowned, belted and hooded, was calling them to breakfast. Favre had not left the rolls and wine for so important a morning as that of conferring day to the indifferent care of Michael the Navarrese. No, he had carefully set aside a *sou* now and a *sou* again for such an occasion as this. Guessing from the sulky demeanour of Francisco's servant that Ignatius was again coming to the

52

rescue of Xavier, Favre had not asked the Navarrese to help him to prepare the meal, but had himself mulled the wine and set out the bread.

After the meal the licentiates in philosophy hastened to join the long procession forming outside the Ste. Barbe. The banners, drums and trumpets were well up in the van of the procession; at the rear the beadles and mace-bearers waited to escort the Rector; in the distance the violet gowns of the bursars and under-masters of the Collège de Beauvais caught Francisco's eye. Soon he hoped to become a master in that College; already a friend of Don Martin Azpilcueta had bespoken a regency for him; once he got his Master's bonnet, it would only be a matter of time until he, too, would wear one of those violet gowns and expound Aristotle in the halls of the Beauvais. That ubiquitous Pilgrim was by his side again, with his talk of holy things. Well, a fellow could afford to ignore him on a day like this——though Peter Favre seemed to hang on his every word. One would not mind if the man were a scholar, but his Latin—atrocious, as halt and limping as himself!

The procession moved off—each College singing its own hymns and anthems; the Lisieux, the Navarre, the Ecossais, with its wild-looking Scots; the Narbonne, the du Plessis, the Lombards (Francisco wondered if the banker's son had got his diploma); the various Scandinavian Colleges; the Cluny, the Picardy, and all the lesser Colleges, and just ahead of the Ste. Barbe in the procession, the dirty fellows from the Montaigu—even on conferring day their gowns, their banners, like themselves, seemed bent on presenting a grubby, unkempt appearance.

So long was the procession that the head was at St. Denis while the beadles and the Rector were still passing the Mathurins' Hospice in the Rue St. Jacques. At last all

were at the Abbey and the various Colleges took their
places in the nave and aisles, awaiting the arrival of the
great personages. The court party came on the stroke of
noon; Francisco Xavier turned with his companions to
watch the King walk up the centre aisle. Ruffs were out of
favour now, and François I, who prided himself on his
wardrobe, wore one of the new low-necked doublets, with
huge black and white sleeves, banded with gold and silver embroidery. In his heavily ringed right hand he carried a flat hat of embroidered velvet, trimmed with a
feather. Behind came Henri of Navarre and his Queen,
sister of the King of France. All the students stood on tip-
toe to see this lady who was reputed to be a heretic and a
friend of heretics; she and some of the Sorbonne church-
men were known to be at daggers drawn. To while away
her boredom in Pau, when the court of Navarre was in
residence there, she had written a book, the *Mirror of the
Sinful Soul;* but all Europe knew that she was the patroness and protectress of the ex-monk, Solon, who—now
turned Calvinist—was marrying and burying wives at a
most unholy speed. All France knew that her latest plays
and sonnets had a peculiar tinge. And had she not appointed the reformer, Roussel, her private chaplain?
Marguerite de Valois outshone every Queen in Europe—
no other lady could boast brocades, silks, laces or furs like
hers. Today, as she sailed into the Abbey, she wore two
robes of satin, an under one of white embroidered with
gold, and an over-gown of sky-blue, fastened to the other
with diamond hooks. By contrast, her maids in waiting
looked sombre in their nun-like plum-coloured dresses,
with white frillings at the throat and plum-silk bonnets
with little white plumes. Such a gorgeously attired entourage Francisco had never seen before. He was so intent
on the sight that he found it difficult to attend to the Mass

—he could not help thinking how strange it was that Queen Marguerite, an all but avowed heretic, was present at the Holy Sacrifice as though she were one in good faith.

When Mass was over and the conferring in full swing, he was on pins and needles waiting for his name—wondering if the name of Xavier would awaken memories in Henri d'Albret. When the crier called aloud "Don Francisco de Jassu y Xavier," Francisco walked to the Rector's dais to receive his diploma; as he bowed before the King, he heard Marguerite whisper in the Bearnais *patois,* as well understood on the Xavier side of the Pyrenees as on the French side, "A Basque ball-player if ever there was one; what *is* Paris University coming to when mountainy shepherds can become licentiates of philosophy!" Colouring hotly, Francisco returned to his place. He had lost heart in the proceedings and looked no more at the elegant company from the court. After a while he thrust aside the slight to his family pride, the shattering of his slenderly built hopes. The day was not over yet. In the evening there would be sports on the Pré-aux-Clercs. Perhaps he would get a chance to demonstrate his skill at the *jeu de paume.*

There *were* sports on the Pré-aux-Clercs—tennis and wrestling and bowling. Having patiently waited for the rounders and other games to end, Francis was just preparing for *jeu de paume* when one of the usual rows between the monks of St. Germain and the students broke out. The monks had always claimed the Pré as their property; the College men said that long custom had made these meadows by the river their playground. The monks told one another that, this being conferring day, most of the students would have remained roistering out at St. Denis or, perhaps, gone to the Louvre, to gape at the courtiers as they walked in the gardens, or to watch the Queen of

Navarre feed the peacocks on the terraces. It was an opportune time to make a surprise sally on those insolent graduates and undergraduates who so impudently usurped Abbey property. Armed with cudgels and supported by a troop of horse-soldiers—the escort of an important visitor, who was even then being confessed by the Abbot—the monks of St. Germain came down the meadows. At another time the students would have sent scouts to their various colleges for reinforcements while they themselves skirmished until aid arrived. On this occasion, there was no use sending for help; heaven knew where the occupants of the different Colleges were dispersed. The choruses of those in the Mule tavern could be heard even out on the Pré—the sight of so many great ones had doubtless inspired them to sing the Villon ballade:

> Claquin of Brittany, where's he gone?
> Where's Auvergne's lord, the Conte Dauphin,
> And the late lamented Alençon?
> But where, ah, where's brave Charlemagne?

No use sending for student aid on conferring day. And the band of horsemen conscripted by the monks seemed just spoiling for a fight—already there were bloodied heads among the group of students at the farthest end of the Pré. Nothing to be done but run for it. The evening fun had not yet begun; not one of the sports-loving students on the meadows wished to miss that; there was no sense in getting oneself a split poll or a sore back for nothing. So the remainder of the students took to their heels. Francisco was glad that his roommates had not come out to see him play; the poor old Pilgrim would never have been able to get away in time.

The Pilgrim and Peter Favre were deep in conversation in the room at Ste. Barbe. They laughed at Francisco's account of the students' ignominious rout on the Pré-aux-Clercs. "He who fights and runs away . . ." quoted Loyola. "What are you doing for the rest of the evening, Don Francisco?" He was always careful to give Xavier his full title.

"The others are going to the Innocents. And already some are gone to Montfaucon, to a hanging."

Although he had not said as much, Ignatius and Favre knew that Francisco would not go either to the Innocents' Charnel or to the gibbets just outside the walls. The Cemetery of the Innocents was a squalid railed-off space by the Halles, the old markets. Around the sides of the square ran charnel-galleries, packed tightly with skulls and bones from the cemetery beneath. The spirit of unrest that was abroad in Europe would not allow even the dead to rest in peace—their skeletons had to be disinterred to make room for the passing generations, who also had to descend into earth for that corruption which is the lot of mortal man; then they, in their turn, were uprooted and flung, holus-bolus, among their ancestors. Apart from these grisly attractions, what most drew the crowds to the Innocents was the *Danse Macabre,* the Dance of Death, a series of frescoes—each with appropriate verses beneath —that ran all along the southern wall of the charnel-house. There Death wove in and out, treading a ghastly minuet, leading the lawyer from the law-court, the farmer from the field, the priest from his pulpit, the housewife from her hearth. Only two went willingly with such a partner —the tired labourer who had found no rest in the days of his earthly toil, and the little child, who had no cause for fear.

On evenings of important occasions, like conferring days, the more gallant of the students would repair—with their girls—to the Cemetery. There were practical jokes, and moonlight sprees—and worse. Francisco Xavier was no prude. He had gone with the others, time and again; but something in him revolted against the surroundings, the incongruity, the promiscuity. And there was always the memory of the death of that master whose teaching had been in such high repute in Ste. Barbe in the first year of Francisco's term there. Not only had he helped the scholars to break bounds at night, not only had he encouraged them to debauchery in the bordel-houses of the dark streets across the river—he had accompanied his pupils, applauding and commending the bolder spirits, scoffing at stay-at-homes like Peter Favre, constantly carping at the one or two like Francisco, whose thus-far-and-no-further attitude he rightly attributed to be due more to fear than to virtue. Francisco could not forget the untimely death of that master, that awful pestiferous death, so lacking in hope; those despairing bouts of delirium when the dying man saw himself as the one to whom grinning Death was beckoning; his screams as he raved, searching in vain to escape the demons who waited for the master who had led others astray. Never since had Francisco gone near the Innocents. Never after had he attempted to accompany the roisterers who went out by the Pont St. Michel to the Pet-au-Diable and the other houses of the *femmes amoureuses*. Fear, the beginning of wisdom, held him back.

Montfaucon, the great gibbet by the Porte St. Denis, was another rendezvous of the students. Sometimes, one followed the carts wherein the condemned were roped and tied; passers-by yelled advice to the Provost of Paris, the Sergeants and the executioner; the nuns of the Filles-Dieu convent at the city gate waited with manchets of bread and stoups of wine to comfort the unfortunates in the carts. Then all moved on to the gibbet, the Provost in his scarlet robes and fur-trimmed cloak whipping back the crowds, the attendant friar reciting the last prayers, the Sergeants and hangman busy with ropes and beams and chains. And the crowd would roar and cheer when, finally, the carts moved on, empty, their late loads dangling heavily from the gibbet, spinning and twisting grotesquely when the wind rose. In the summer evenings, when the soldiery of the garrisons and the street bullies, in a spirit of bravado, took flagons and pasties and girls to Montfaucon, there to make a night of it, the *escholiers* asked no better fun than to descend upon these revellers at midnight, sometimes having a hand-to-hand battle or a bout of stone-throwing, sometimes stealing along, disguised as demons, frightening the guests away and themselves falling upon the abandoned wine and pasties.

Francisco had no liking for Montfaucon. Still, on conferring day, one was almost obliged to celebrate. But how go anywhere with empty pockets? He was as short of money as ever. He had, two months ago, sent a letter to his brother Juan at Xavier, asking for money—explaining that on occasions like conferring day students needed more spending money than usual. But, since Doña Maria's death the previous summer, Don Juan had not been over-liberal. He sent his brother what he considered sufficient for college fees and maintenance—but there never seemed to be anything over. His mother, Francisco reflected, were she alive, would have understood how important it was to be in good standing with one's elders and one's equals on a day like this. His brother Juan—married to a Pamplona lady of wealth—might have sent him a few *sueldos*. Ignatius, as always, came to the rescue.

"There's the *Foire au Pain d'Epices*—the Gingerbread Fair—and a contest in archery and running," said the Pilgrim. "I would be honoured if the two learned licentiates in philosophy, Don Francisco de Jassu y Xavier and Peter Favre, the Savoyard, would come with me to the Fair."

It was a pleasant afternoon. The Pilgrim set himself to entertain his companions with tales of his wanderings: in the summer vacations he went to the Lowlands—this year he hoped to go to England; thus he earned sufficient by working and begging to pay for his maintenance and education at Paris during the remainder of the year.

They strolled through the Fair booths, now stopping for a draught of wine spiced with cinnamon and a crumbly piece of gingerbread, again halting to look at the hawkers' wares—lute strings, writing tablets, pocket knives, glass beads, sheafs of the newest ballads, Reformers' pamphlets, ribands, gloves and gauds of all sorts. There were buckles, chains, needles, purses, little pictures and statues of the saints—St. Barbara to guard one in war and in thunder-storms, St. Apollinaria against the toothache, St. Victor against the falling sickness; and there was St. Julian for the tavern-keepers and St. Christopher for travellers.

As they came out of the Fair grounds a fanfare of trumpets sounded, and the King with his royal guests from Navarre drove by. The three Ste. Barbe scholars stood staring after them.

"I was hoping," said Francisco, slowly, "that our King Henri might have remembered the name of Xavier when I was called by the Rector today."

Ignatius knew the ambitions that lay behind that blighted hope. He, who had fought on the opposing side in the civil war in Navarre, understood how the Xavier family felt about the d'Albret dynasty to whom they had given their loyalties and for whom they had lost so much.

"Never mind," he said, "when you get your master's bonnet, I will see to it that you do not lack for pupils. You

will get that vacancy in the Beauvais next year. And
Peter here and myself will advertise you, even if we have
to cry your name through the streets. Wait a while! You
will yet find yourself the most sought-after master in the
Beauvais."

The spring evening shrilled with the echo of the King's
trumpeters as the gay cavalcade again drove by. A chill
breeze sprang up beyond the city walls, evil-sounding
birds wheeled about the now still corpses that threw dark
shadows on Montfaucon. From the Mule and the *Pomme
de Pin* came rowdy strains. The students were singing
another Villon ballade:

> Where are the bonny lads and brave,
> Good comrades mine of long ago,
> Whose witty word and merry stave
> And derring-do set heart aglow?
> Some, stiff and cold in death, lie low,
> No echo answers from the grave;
> May God on them His peace bestow,
> And may He us in mercy save!
>
> Others, praise God! have forged ahead
> And now they're lords and great grandees
> While many another begs the bread
> He only in shop-windows sees.
> Some to Carthusian monasteries,
> Some to the Celestins are fled,
> Booted, like oystermen, in frieze.
> What divers destinies we wed!

The sad little song hung on the air as the three Ste.
Barbe men went back to their College. The honour of
receiving the diploma, the pleasant afternoon, the grand
sights—all had the effect of inducing in Xavier an after-

math of melancholy. He was tired. He hoped he would not be troubled with the nightmare—that one where he had to carry an Indian forever. Now, if it were Ignatius who were troubled with such a dream, one could understand it—the Pilgrim, whose heart was so set on spreading the kingdom of God; or Favre—holy Favre who prayed for the most benighted souls on earth, including even Soliman, Luther and Henry VIII. It was a strange dream. Now that he was a licentiate in philosophy, it was to be hoped that he had done with that nightmare forever.

CHAPTER 4

In JANUARY, 1533, the fishing boats of Gandia seldom went far from the shore. Often, that winter, the sails of the "sea-wolves of the Mediterranean," the pirate galleys commanded by the brothers Barbarossa, had been sighted far too near for peace of mind; and every Christian dwelling along the coast from the Adriatic to the Atlantic, quailed at news that the crescent flag had been seen on the horizon. The Duke of Gandia decided to ask the Poor Clare community to move to some inland town. Should the infidels make a night raid, the Duke's duty would be to fight for the protection of his people and his city—it would be impossible for him, in the event of such a sudden swoop on the part of the pirates, to see to the safety of the nuns, among whom were his sister and his mother.

But when the Duke called at the convent, Doña Gabriela, recently elected Abbess, informed her son that, for the time being, the nuns would have to remain in Gandia. The former Abbess, Sor Madalena de Jassu y Xavier, and another nun, Sor Salvadora, were both at death's door. It was but a matter of days for either, the physician said. When these two holy ones had completed the important business of dying, then—and not until then

63

—the Abbess would consider the question of moving the nuns to a safer place.

Closing the grille, Doña Gabriela returned to the sickroom. It was strange, she told herself for the hundredth time that day, how the two invalids seemed to have changed ailments. Up to yesterday, Sor Madalena had been, to all appearances, dying a tranquil, painless death; indeed, it looked as though her immense desire for God was causing the former Abbess to burn out quickly, like a candle caught in a steady draught. And, up to yesterday, poor Sor Salvadora suffered intensely in all her members. But today Sor Salvadora lay calm, released from pain, her life coursing gently on to its close, while Sor Madalena— though she uttered neither word nor cry to betray her agony—was obviously suffering intensely; the physician had noted how her hands were so tightly clenched that the nails bled the palms; and Doña Gabriela had had to wipe away sweats of anguish that bathed the brow of "the little Madalena," as the nun from Navarre had been known since the first day she had come to Gandia. But the Abbess asked no questions. A Poor Clare regarded suffering much as other women did new gowns or jewels; not that suffering in itself was to be wished for, but because, like poverty, it was a misery of our poor human nature that the Son of God had chosen for His portion.

Kneeling by the sufferer, Doña Gabriela wondered . . . It looked as though Sor Madalena had requested God to give her the pains that had been Sor Salvadora's. Why? For whom did she suffer? Perhaps for that young brother of hers at Paris University. Not very creditable reports had been bruited about Paris and carried home to Xavier Castle about Don Francisco—now a regent in the Beauvais College. Juan and Miguel Xavier had written their sister in Gandia, hinting at the stories they had heard, grumbling at the expense Francisco was to them. They had thought that when he got a professor's chair, he would be self-supporting—but no, as his academic status grew so did his expenses, it seemed. They thought he should be fetched home from Paris, whether he liked it or not. Juan intended to bespeak a benefice for his brother in Pamplona Cathedral; a canon's stall there would ensure him a steady income; they had written Don Francisco telling him their plans and advising him to take some Minor Orders, in preparation for Pamplona. They were heartily tired of pouring out money on Francisco, who was nothing if not extravagant, they told Madalena; and now that they themselves were settled down and endeavouring to build up their impoverished estates, they considered that they had to look to themselves and let Francisco fend for himself; they had done their duty by him.

But Sor Madalena had written her brothers in Xavier, pleading that Francisco be allowed to finish his full term in Paris University. "God," she wrote Juan and Miguel, "has great designs on our brother Francisco, and will yet do great things for the Church through him." The Abbess had reproved Sor Madalena for such a rash venture into the realms of prophecy; a Poor Clare's duty to an errant brother was, obviously, to pray for him and to suffer for him. Madalena was commanded to write to her brother in Paris, giving him some counsel for the good of his soul.

Madalena was immersed in a veritable sea of pain. Now and again her faculties failed her. In moments between, her thoughts focussed once on her three years at court, once on her childhood home in Xavier, several times on the various events of her thirty years in the royal convent of Santa Clara at Gandia. She remembered the great temptations that beset her as a young nun. Discouragement and misery had assailed her when the early novelty of convent life faded; the austerities seemed unbearable, the monotony an endless vista of irksomeness; the rough serge, the straw pallet, the meagre, tasteless fare, the scant hours of sleep, the hairshirt and discipline for the body and the no less prickling and painful curb of mind and soul, the rules—all suddenly became unendurable. She had thought of retracing her steps, not back to court but to the quiet of Xavier, where Aunt Violante, herself a nun in all but name and habit, would surely understand. At the height of the temptation she had a dream—a dream in which she saw all the nuns of Gandia, robed in most splendid garments of cramoisie and gold, walking in processional order. On enquiring from a bystander why the nuns went in such fine raiment she had been told that they were proceeding to receive the rewards prepared for them; since they had, in this life, observed so strict a rule with resoluteness and patience for Christ's sake, there awaited them a recompense beyond all human imagining; their glowing vesture was but a symbol of the love and joy with which the nuns of Gandia were received into the heavenly mansions.

For several years after that vivid dream she had only to recall it when temptation made fresh onslaughts. In her later years in religion a different temptation to discouragement insinuated itself; this time she did not feel her life and circumstances unbearable—she found herself a burden; she never seemed to advance in holiness, like other nuns; she was forever falling and stumbling, forever covering the same ground. "I shall never reach God; I spend my days stumbling and falling; I never seem to make any progress," she complained one day in her prayers. "Falling and rising again, that is how one reaches Him," came the reply.

But the thirty years in Gandia were almost over now.

66

Nothing remained but this pain that gnawed the vitals; the pain which she had asked God to take from Sor Salvadora and give to her. She clenched her hands and bit her tongue when it got too much for her; she did not wish anyone to know that she was bearing another's pain. Soon it would pass. Soon she would be where she had long desired to be . . . out of the body and in those realms of light where her dearly Beloved waited. Before she departed this world she had one last request to make of Him. A request not for herself, nor for anyone known to her; a last prayer for that brother, Francisco, whom she had never met—that he might be preserved from the snares of the world, the flesh and the devil, from heresy and from evil living, that he might yet do for God the great things Madalena would have done, had her deeds kept pace with her love . . .

The pain returned with greater force. Why were the nuns all crowding into her little cell with their choir cloaks on and lighted tapers in their hands—in broad noon-day? And the prayers for the dying—Sor Salvadora must be passing away. Yet, it was her bed—Madalena's—they encircled, the Abbess holding the crucifix before eyes that could no longer focus. The prayers became at one minute the play of the fountains in the Court of the Myrtles, at another the evening breeze sighing in the cypress lanes of the Moorish gardens, again snow-swollen mountain torrents rushing past Xavier to join the Aragon . . . The Abbess prayed:

> Depart, O Christian soul, out of this sinful world, in the name of God the Father Almighty, who created thee; in the name of Jesus Christ, the Son of the Living God, who suffered and died for thee; in the name of the Holy Ghost, who sanctified thee; in the name of the Glorious and Blessed Virgin Mary,

Mother of God; in the name of the blessed Joseph,
the illustrious Spouse of the same Virgin; in the name
of the Angels and Archangels; of the Thrones and
Dominations; of the Principalities and Powers, and
Virtues; of the Cherubim and Seraphim; in the name
of the Patriarchs and Prophets; in the name of the
holy Apostles and Evangelists; in the name of the
holy Martyrs and Confessors; of the holy Monks and
Hermits; of the holy Virgins and of all the Saints of
God. . . . Let peace come to thee this day and let
thy abode be in holy Sion. Through the same Christ
Our Lord, Amen.

To Sor Madalena, wholly withdrawn into the innermost
regions of her soul, waiting, wondering, the prayers of
those whom she was leaving seemed mingled with the
melody of a new song that grew clearer as her human
hearing grew weaker.

May the holy Company of Angels meet thy soul
at its departure. May the court of the Apostles receive thee. May the triumphant army of glorious
martyrs conduct thee——

"She is going," said Doña Gabriela, interrupting the
prayers to place a lighted candle in Sor Madalena's hands.

"Into Thy hands I commend my spirit. O Lord Jesus
Christ, receive my soul," prayed the Poor Clares of
Gandia.

For Madalena de Jassu y Xavier winter was over and
past. Spring had appeared in her land. The eternal day
was breaking and the shadows of time receding. Since the
last bout of pain she had been conscious of nothing but
the cold; snowdrifts encompassed her; ice weighted her
every member and confined her in a small—in far too
small a space.

"Lord Jesus, receive my soul."

Suddenly there came a great thaw and her spirit, like a long pent-up torrent swiftly flowing into a sunlit sea, went to Him in whose image and likeness it was created.

"It is all over," said the Abbess, rising to close the dead nun's eyes and fold her hands.

The nuns stood in a circle waiting to intone the *De Profundis*. During the prayer the Abbess, who had never before made such a mistake, somehow wandered from Psalm 129 to Psalm 115:

> I will pay my vows to the Lord before all His people. Precious in the sight of the Lord is the death of His saints. O Lord, for I am Thy servant . . . Thou hast broken my bonds.

Sor Madalena's sisters in religion smiled happily. The death of a bride of Christ was not a sorrowful occasion but a time of rejoicing; it was fitting that they hold a *fiesta* —an extra fig or two for supper; a *tortilla* for dinner on the morrow; some ballads, perhaps, afterwards—*The Lament of the Moor for Valencia,* or *The Five Maravedis* and, of course, the favourite ballad of Doña Gabriela, *Count Arnaldo.* They would miss the little Madalena; she used to sing *The Loss of Alhama* and *The Bishop, Don Gonzalo* so touchingly. Ah, well, she was doubtless singing in Heaven by now. Her face was peaceful—lovely. One by one the nuns approached the pallet; they clasped her cold hands or touched her brow or straightened the folds of her habit; then they left, their bare feet making no sound on the stone floors, and went about their various duties, rejoicing for their sister, gone to God.

· · · · ·

In the attic room at the Ste. Barbe, Peter Favre and

Master Francisco Xavier, Regent of the Beauvais College, sat listening to Ignatius Loyola. The young Master of Arts was fidgety; he twisted the quill in his green velvet bonnet, setting it at different angles; he fingered his Medici lace ruff, twirled his ring with the great amethyst, slapped at his *fauves botas*—his elegant fawn-coloured boots of soft Córdoba leather. For a long time he had gone abroad of evenings in the violet gown that proclaimed him as one of the faculty of the Beauvais, but this week the good news from Pamplona demanded that he be seen in public in richer, newer clothes. Juan, the captain of Xavier, had written saying that all his efforts on his brother's behalf—and he had left no stone unturned—had been successful; a Canon's stall awaited Francisco in the Cathedral of Pamplona. He could expect official notice any day from the Cathedral Chapter, and had better be ready to travel south when the summons came. Once settled in his canonry, Francisco would have no more money worries, which would be, no doubt, as great a relief to the popular but underpaid Regent of Beauvais as to his brother. Francisco fidgeted because he was conscious of a vague dissatisfaction. A few years before, a regent's chair in the Beauvais seemed to be a first step towards the realisation of his ambitions; but, as soon as the novelty began to wear off, it seemed highly desirable that a generous-hearted, open-handed man should be able to move among his fellows without having to worry about such trivialities as income, expenditure and the like, and he had been very glad when he heard that his brother was exerting himself to secure him a benefice in Pamplona. Now that word had come that his second ambition was realised he found himself wondering at the strange disquiet that possessed him. Checking himself for his discourteousness in fidgeting and being inattentive while

Ignatius was speaking, he set himself to listen with interest.

And, *por Sant Iago!* the old Pilgrim could be interesting when he gave his tongue free rein, like tonight. The older man had embarked on a series of reminiscences; Francisco had missed much of what he had been telling Favre of his days as a page at the court of *los Reyes Católicos;* but he was just in time to hear of what life had been like for a captain trained in the hard but glorious school of *el Gran Capitan*—in time to hear Ignatius speak of two men he had known, Christopher Columbus and Gonzalo de Córdoba, the greatest captain Spain had reared since the Cid.

Yes, Ignatius Loyola—as a boy—had seen Columbus leave on his fourth voyage west; the finder of New Spain had been hopeful of finding a water-route through Cuba, which all had supposed to be a continent. Poor Columbus! He had been lifted up, cast down, lifted up and cast down again. At a much later date, Ignatius had been shown the house in Valladolid where, in obscurity and neglect—his patroness dead, King Ferdinand forgetful—Columbus died. Such were the rewards meted out by men to those to whom they most owed gratitude. It had been the same story with *el Gran Capitan.* Ignatius could remember how, when he himself had been a mere stripling at the court of Castile, the great soldier had been the hero of every youth in Spain.

Francisco Xavier, too, remembered having heard his brothers speak of Gonzalo de Córdoba; Miguel swore by the man. Did Ignatius really think Córdoba the military genius men said he was? Frenchmen and Englishmen were inclined to belittle his prowess; they said that in Spain, more than elsewhere, the profession of arms had been invested with a halo of romance; that in Castile the very babes were hushed with lullabies that told of how Spain had been victorious in the battles with the Moors. Could it be that *el Gran Capitan* had happened to be lifted, opportunely, on the crest of the great wave of bravery and chivalry that, rising with Roland, bore the Cid? Was he great because he had been born at the right time and into the profession of arms? Ignatius did not think anything of the sort. The *Capitan* had been one of the greatest military geniuses of all time; he had brought Spanish soldiering to such a pitch of perfection that, for longer than any man could remember, no army of Spain had been defeated in a pitched battle. He had welded his country's fighting material into a wonderful machine.

Xavier and Favre listened, enthralled, as Ignatius recalled his own army days. De Córdoba had welcomed men from the Basque provinces; the Basques were men of iron, he said; men with constitutions capable of enduring long marches, of withstanding the fevers bred in the malarial swamps of Italy—fevers that decimated the French troops. The military training included abstemiousness in food and drink; *el Capitan* said that, apart from being a useful habit to have acquired against the day of short rations, such a rein on the appetites made for a self-disciplined soldier, and a self-disciplined soldier was, as all knew, one more amenable to the commands of superior officers. The Pilgrim sang—as he and his men had sung in the old campaigning days—the soldiers' ballad which began:

> My cloak, the clanging armour,
> My pastime, endless war,
> My couch, the cold and wintry wold,
> My love, a far-off star.

How exactly had de Córdoba so revolutionised the profession of soldiering that Spain was superior to any country in Europe in the battle-field, Xavier asked—not that he really wished to know but because it was most enjoyable to listen to Ignatius once he began speaking of the science of war, a subject of which he seemed to have an inexhaustible knowledge.

The Pilgrim was only too ready to explain. First of all, Córdoba—realising that in a land like Spain, where mule-travel was so general, cavalry regiments were hard to raise—had concentrated on the infantry. He had aimed at increasing the foot soldier's defensive armour to give him a greater power of resistance, but had not made the armour so heavy and unwieldy that it hampered a man's speed and mobility.

Taking his stick, Ignatius began drawing in the ashes to illustrate other aspects of the science he had learned so well from *el Gran Capitan,* in particular the marvellous genius of Córdoba at placing the right men in the right places. He would have half his men armed with long pikes; these he would use to form the outside ranks of squares. In the centre of these squares would be a third of the available forces—the short-sword men and the javelin-throwers. And, drawn up separately in the avenues crisscrossing the squares—which squares the Pilgrim, once again Captain Loyola, indicated by lines drawn through the ashes—were the remaining sixth of the fighting men. Xavier and Favre would surely see how right Córdoba had been to place that sixth—the *arquebusiers*—in those avenues; he had them in the very position from which they could take aim to the best advantage and wreak havoc in the tightly packed ranks of an advancing foe. If the enemy decided to attack with pikes athrust, the short-sword and javelin men were in the best position for fighting at close quarters; dreadful destruction could be inflicted on the attackers, who would be rendered practically defenceless through having to use both hands to manoeuvre their pikes. Córdoba was a genius. Spain would not see his like again. Ignatius, for one, was more than thankful for having learned the art of war according to the principles of so fine a soldier. From *el Gran Capitan* he had learned lessons that had been useful to him in his army days and which would come in more useful now, when he had plans in which all this knowledge could be utilised, but in a different sphere. Here the Pilgrim fell silent and his listeners knew that he was thinking of the future. They had come to know him well enough to realise that he possessed the secrets of successful spiritual warfare. He was nothing if not thorough. His preparations for the battles of his life were being as carefully thought out as though he were back again fighting for Ferdinand, for Ximenes, for the Emperor.

Peter Favre stared into the embers. Thus far, he was the only man ready to take service under the flag Ignatius was destined to raise. But he was a willing and a docile recruit; and Ignatius liked leading the kind of soldier who could be trusted to obey. They had had hopes of Xavier. They, Ignatius and Favre, had prayed that he might join them in their holy campaign. But, so far, Xavier had shown little sign of wishing to throw in his lot with them. Lainez and Salmeron from Alcala, that hotheaded Spaniard, Bobadilla, and the Portuguese, Simon Rodriguez, had agreed, as had Favre, to do the Spiritual Exercises drawn up by Ignatius. These Exercises corresponded, in Loyola's methodical mind, to the intensive training given a soldier preparatory to sending him into battle. After that there would be discussions as to what vows they should take and what work they should do for God's greater honour and glory.

Francisco, likewise, stared into the embers. Were they three at the parting of the ways? Now that his ambition regarding the Pamplona benefice had been realised, it came almost as a shock to find that Ignatius and Favre were just as much in earnest regarding their futures. They, too, had ambitions—tremendous ones; they were preparing to take, not a Pamplona canonry, but Heaven, the kingdom that suffereth violence and which only the violent bear away.

Rising, he went out on the little landing and looked through the dormer window on the sleeping city. He felt suddenly isolated—a man without a cause. His companions, men he loved dearly, would soon go one way and he another. Ignatius had once jestingly rallied him, telling him that he was one of those men who set little store on home, relatives and country, tending to give to strange people and places the love most men reserved for family and *patria*. And the Pilgrim had been right. Francisco loved Paris as he had never loved Navarre; between his roommates and himself were stronger bonds than had ever bound him to his brothers. All unbidden, a text of Scripture came into his mind: "Go forth out of thy country, and from thy kindred, and out of thy father's house, and come into the land which I shall show thee . . ." And, as he stood on the attic landing, gazing at the stars, he set himself to recall further words which the Lord God had addressed to Abraham: "Look up to heaven, and number the stars, if thou canst. So shall thy seed be."

The Pamplona post was waiting; no more pinching and paring; no more worry for the future. But what of the future's future? What of that time beyond time when the Canon's bones would lie in the Cathedral crypt, when another than Francisco Xavier would occupy the stall and draw the revenues? It was an unsettling thought . . .

And, would there be in Pamplona friends as true and tried as his two boon companions of the Ste. Barbe? His heart went out to them: the Pilgrim, with his short leg, his dynamic energy, his great soul that seemed—within his small frame—like the four winds of heaven imprisoned in a gourd! Favre, so quiet and holy and transparent. Xavier had been happy that they had been his friends, the best friends he had ever known. And now he had to decide whether to stay with them, the only two real reformers in a reform-mad world.

He recalled the many conversations they had held on Luther's so-called reform. Ignatius had said that when the Augustinian friar burned Pope Leo's Bull, *Exsurge,* in the presence of the Wittenberg students, he had started a conflagration greater than he knew. They would yet see, Ignatius surmised, the fair land of Christendom laid waste by this fire. Fields that had once been fertile for the good seed of the Gospel would one day be strewn with the charred debris of a hundred heresies, would be caked with the scarifying ash of error.

In a few short years, they of the Ste. Barbe, in common with most of Europe, had heard the tocsin of reform sounded again and again. Calvin, who had been a student in Ignatius' old college—the unwashed, high-minded Montaigu—had been known to them. They had listened to Erasmus. Friends and proteges of the Queen of Navarre were teaching false doctrines in more than one college of Paris University. Loudly decrying the crimes of others while minimising or excusing their own, Luther, Zwingli, Melanchthon, Calvin, Knox and others made a great din; each kept roaring the word REFORM until the very air echoed with it, until it was bandied from mouth to mouth, taking on, as it travelled, a variety of meanings—the commonest being that it was necessary to reform all men, oneself excepted.

The world was witnessing the spectacle of rulers like Henry VIII of England and Christian of Denmark, egged on by pride, greed and lust, interpreting reform as revolt from the common authority bequeathed by Christ to His followers. Worse even than their rebellion, was the secession of these sovereigns into schism, whither they were followed by great masses of their subjects.

Xavier recalled a night when the Pilgrim had drawn for them a military diagram illustrating the many menaces that faced the Church. In the Germanies and in Scandinavia, as in England, there were the heretics. But there was a far worse menace. Islam, successfully defeated in Spain in the days of great Isabel, had again begun to attack. The cohorts of the Ottoman Sultan, Soliman the Magnificent, advancing steadily from the southeast, had not halted until the crescent flag flew on the plains outside Vienna. And in the Mediterranean all shipping foolhardy enough to hoist sail, was harried by Soliman's underlings, the dreaded Barbarossas. And, worst of all, Ignatius had said, was the danger within the camp—the fact that the Papacy, that most holy and august of human offices, had become in the eyes of rapacious Italian families like the Borgias, the Medici, the Farnese and the Colonnas, a preserve round which they could prowl and intrigue at will.

Good Christians were agreed that there was need for reform. But good Christians felt, instinctively, that the disruptive and destructive tactics employed by the would-be reformers was not the way to improve matters. Ignatius told Xavier and Favre that he had an excellent plan for reforming the world—a plan both simple and foolproof.

"I will begin with myself," he said. "Let you, Favre, do likewise, and there are two reformed Christians. If every man and his friend did as much there would be a real reform. And if Xavier and our other friends joined with us and each set out to get as many more, soon the world would be a happier and better place."

Though he had said this half in jest, Ignatius had been deadly in earnest. And already he and Peter Favre were two truly reformed Christians—men utterly and irrevocably dedicated to God. As he stood apart on the attic landing while his friends remained in their little room, Xavier was conscious of being also a little apart from them in this matter of reform.

Why was it, he asked himself. Was he not as generous as they? Had not Ignatius reproved him again and again for his generosity—which tended to extravagance? If Ignatius, a lame little Captain, with the best part of his life behind him, could attempt great things for God, what held back Don Francisco, the Regent of Beauvais, the best *pelota* player in the valleys of the Sierra Leyre, the fleetest runner in Navarre?

Suddenly he knew the reason for his discontent with his regentship, with the Pamplona canonry. Such triumphs did not satisfy the soul. The two men in the attic room behind him had known far more happiness in giving than he had found in gaining; and they gave that which cost them most—they gave themselves. Wholly and with generous hearts they had given to God their bodies and souls, their hearts and minds, their capabilities and limitations; they had held nothing back. Xavier had heard Ignatius explaining to Bobadilla and those others who were inclined to join himself and Favre the complete surrender that had to be made. One came forward willingly, a volunteer, no conscript, Ignatius said—trust the one-time Captain Loyola to have military terms for even spiritual matters!—a generous love for God spurred one

78

on; one gave without reckoning—the nothing one had to give; one paid no heed to the wounds received fighting under Christ's banner; one toiled on and on, seeking no rest—for a man's time for doing good was shorter than he knew; one served without thought of reward; one constantly strove to give, not less but more, to God.

Almost in spite of himself, Xavier began to say that prayer Ignatius was so fond of repeating:

> O My God! Teach me to be generous; to give and not to count the cost; to fight and not to heed the wounds; to toil and not to seek for rest; to labour and not to seek for any reward save that of doing Thy blessed will.

From some tavern down the Rue de la Juiverie the choruses of roistering bands of students rang out. Xavier had spent many an evening drinking and singing with the others in the *Pomme de Pin;* he had tried his luck with the dice in the *Trou Perrette,* played pranks on the masters, on the tavern-keepers, on the street musicians and showmen, on the fishwives and the bath-house keepers. Since he had risen to the rank of Regent he had thought it due to his position to hold himself somewhat apart from the undergraduates' amusements, but he had been recompensed, in part, in being promoted to the discussions that took place between the various masters. As in former years, but on a different stage and with other players, he spoke and acted as vehemently as the best, when occasion offered. Yet, he had not been altogether unaware of his inner self; sometimes he had visited the secret shrines in his soul's temple. And, somehow, he had kept clean and inviolate that sanctuary where came none but God.

Now, as he listened to Ignatius' and Favre's murmured prayers and thought of the great enterprise on which they were about to embark, he was conscious of a great gladness that—should the Lord come knocking at his door—He would find the latch unfastened, the lamp lit, the dwelling clean though bare. Xavier was already standing with listening ears and outstretched hands, waiting for a call that he knew would come, soon or late. He resolved that when Christ came to tarry on his threshold, to enter his inner room, he would be ready, waiting to dedicate himself to a service greater than that of any college or cathedral. But—suppose God did not come. How did one go to God?

"What do you think of, Francisco, amigo?" asked Ignatius, coming from the room.

"A strange thing; one that I doubt any philosopher has ever answered or been able to answer. How does a man come to God?"

"Is it possible that the Regent of Beauvais does not reckon Augustine among the philosophers? Augustine answered that one centuries ago. He said: 'We come to God by love and not by sail.' "

Francisco made no reply. He was back again in Xavier, lighting the beeswax candles, back again on that evening when his mind had tried to make some connection between God and a galleon sailing for New Spain. It was the same line of St. Augustine's, just quoted by Ignatius, that had held him then. It held him again. To go to God, a man needed but to love. And the essence of loving was giving; the true lover gave goods, life, self. That was how one went to God; giving, though one gave nought but what had been already received.

Ignatius, quick of apperception, knew that his friend had begun to capitulate to God. He was touched, as any soldier would be, to witness the surrender of a brave and noble nature; he was profoundly moved at the thought that this dear friend, this fellow Basque, was already lowering the flags of his ambitions, preparatory to giving his all to God; from worldly standards, Xavier was forfeiting more, far more, than his companions, and the Pilgrim loved him for his generosity.

He knew that it was no time for words and was preparing to withdraw from the landing when Xavier laid a detaining hand on his arm. He gestured towards the town and Ignatius heard a familiar chorus ringing out from a nearby tavern:

> Claquin of Brittany, where's he gone?
> Where's Auvergne's lord, the Conte Dauphin,
> And the late lamented Alençon?
> But where, ah, where's brave Charlemagne?

Though there was a catch in his voice, Francisco chimed in with the last line. Then he smiled, and Ignatius knew that God's long siege of this soul was ended. There were three men for the reform. Now, he would give the Spiritual Exercises to Xavier.

5

IN THE mid-August of 1535, Barbarossa, the corsair captain of Soliman the Magnificent's fleet, swept unchallenged up and down the Mediterranean with his hundred galleys. Plundering both by land and by sea, outwitting Emperor and Pope, beating any opponents bold enough to engage or harry him, spying and turning the tables upon the many secret agents anxious to obtain a rich reward for poisoning or stabbing him, this wily old pirate menaced all south Europe. Ignatius Loyola, Master of Arts of the University of Paris, found it difficult to get transport from Valencia to Genoa; though sailors would venture west to the Indies and would sail right round Africa to get to the Orient, few wished to encounter Barbarossa's galleys on that inland sea which was no more than a lake to the dreaded pirate.

Loyola had gone home to Spain the previous spring, to recover from an indisposition which threatened to become chronic; he also wished to visit the families of the Spanish members of his little company—the seven who, on the previous feast of the Assumption, had gone to the chapel of St. Denis the Martyr, on Montmartre, and bound themselves to life-long chastity, since they were going to be priests, and to evangelical poverty as soon as their studies were completed. They had also vowed a pilgrimage to Jerusalem. Now, Ignatius was anxious to get to Genoa and from thence to Venice, where his companions were to join him on the conclusion of their studies. He would arrive in Venice before them, so as to have some time to think and pray about their future work. And he would have to look about and see where his Company could be lodged, or what they were to turn their hands to before proceeding to the Pope for approbation and directions as to the activities in which the Holy Father would wish them to engage.

While their friend and father was searching Valencia for transport to Italy, Francis Xavier, Peter Favre and four others were wending their way towards Montmartre to renew the vows they had taken a year previously. The chapel of St. Denis was half-way up the hill, a rather lonely little place, well removed from the bustle of the city. There the Benedictine nuns had their Abbey, and Mère Perrette was waiting, just as she had waited the previous year, to hand them the key of the crypt. The very walls of St. Denis, if they could speak, could tell of many holy ones who, in their time, had come there to pray. To St. Denis had come Bernard, the beloved of God; there had come St. Thomas, the Martyr of Canterbury, and that other Thomas, Aquinas. In a dark corner rusted a suit of armour—that bright armour forged a hundred years before in Tours for Jeanne d'Arc; there it hung where the Maid had unharnessed herself forever, shedding hot tears as she laid it, piece by piece, on the Lady altar. If those walls could prophesy they would tell of how others in the years to come—as though attracted by fragrant memories of the holy presences that had hallowed the little church—would visit St. Denis in preference to any church in Paris. They would foretell Francis de Sales, Vincent de Paul, John Eudes, Berulle and Olier, and the last Abbess of Montmartre who, with her fifteen Benedictine nuns, was to die by the guillotine.

But the followers of Ignatius looked neither to the centuries behind nor to those yet unborn. They rejoiced to be of their own time; they rejoiced that they, of all the men on earth, had been led by God into the heavenly platoon captained by Loyola. Francis, in particular, felt a special surge of exaltation and joy. Of all the group, he alone had held out against Ignatius; but of all the surrenders none had been so complete as his. What did it matter to him now, that chair in the Beauvais, the crowds of eager students that he hoped would fill his hall, the spontaneous applause that he hoped would follow his lectures? How little it counted for now, that parchment attestation of his noble ancestry, sent from Navarre and bearing not only the seals of that realm but the seal of the Emperor himself? "Don Francisco de Jassu y Xavier," ran the document, "nobleman, *hidalgo,* and gentleman of ancient origin and lineage" and the signature at the end was "*Yo, el Rey.* I, the King." The news contained in that last letter from his kinsman, Don Martin, that shortly he was to be made a Canon of Pamplona Cathedral was as unwelcome now as, in former days, it would have been a welcome stroke of fortune. For Francis felt himself to be rich beyond measure in being both the beloved and the lover of God. He felt immensely honoured in having been chosen to be one of the souls to whom God Our Lord had said "You have not chosen Me, but I have chosen you." In the nights since the Pilgrim left for Spain, while Favre and Michael the Navarrese slept, he often went out to stand at the little landing window, brooding over Paris— as more than a thousand years before Ste. Geneviève had looked out upon and prayed for the moonlit city. There he kept vigil, holding back the Basque songs—the old love songs of Bas-Navarre—that rose so readily to his lips. There he had wept, prayed, communed silently with God. There, whispering into the darkness, he told—stammeringly—his love. There he hid his joy, lest it transport him, and the sleeping College Ste. Barbe wake to the scandal of a master of Beauvais doing a Basque sword-dance, alone, on an attic landing.

They renewed their vows at the Mass Favre offered in the crypt. They held, as on the previous year, a little picnic in the nearby grove. They wondered how Ignatius was, or where. They hoped that he would not start too soon for Italy, but would give himself time to recover from that stomach illness. They would need another year, at least, to finish their studies and proceed to Venice to join him, as arranged. Heaven knew what might happen within that year. A month before, England had witnessed the execution of her Chancellor, Thomas More, and John Fisher, the Bishop of Rochester. King Henry had declared himself Head of the English Church and broken with Rome; and, while Queen Catherine—discarded and isolated—languished from sheer misery in Kimbolton, Nan Bullen (as the populace called the new wife) queened it in York Palace and Whitehall.

On the following feast of the Assumption the companions of Ignatius, now nine in number, were again at Montmartre, renewing their vows. The intervening year had been a bad one for Christendom but, for men on fire with the love of God, no year was bad.

The year 1536 had brought from England the news of Catherine's death—a death such as one might expect of the daughter of Isabel. If she had suffered humiliations untold in the last twenty years of her life, she departed from England and the world a Queen, with her last ounce of strength signing the letter to her husband—which her

Ambassador Chapuys had written at her dictation—"Catherine, Queene of England." Later in the same year, Nan Bullen's head rolled off the block. In the same year, too, a graduate of the Montaigu, John Calvin, published his *Institutio*, affirmed his doctrine of predestination, and took shelter behind the Queen of Navarre, while her brother, the French king, had heretics executed outside Notre Dame. The building of the palace of Fontainebleau in the heart of the loveliest forest in France and the raising of the château of Chambord in the Loire valley did not cease when, in 1536, war broke out afresh between France and Spain. Ignatius Loyola, who had reached Venice—after many trials and vicissitudes—several months before the war started, waited patiently, if anxiously, for news of his little flock. But no news came. And he had no means of being sure that the letters and messages he sent got through to them. He wrote to the Dominican confessor of Queen Eleanor of France, asking that help might be forthcoming for Favre and the others; with a long and dangerous journey before them, they would need money, safe conducts, passports and directions as to the safest route to take. Having done this, Ignatius resumed his self-imposed task of attending upon the sick in the Incurables Hospital in Venice, while in the evenings he continued his study of theology; and here, as elsewhere, God sent him further recruits.

For a year Loyola waited and hoped and prayed. On the second day of the octave of the Epiphany, 1537, going his night rounds of the hospital, he was told that nine strangers awaited him in the courtyard. Nine! It could not be possible that the others had come—through embattled armies, through winter snows, through heretic country—and had arrived, all nine, safe and sound! Hastening to the courtyard, his short leg almost failing him once or twice on the stairway, he found them—Xavier and Favre, the first and dearest of his sons in God, and the seven others.

He embraced each one, weeping as he noted their sodden, mud-caked gowns, their bandages, their thin bodies, their gaunt faces, their light luggage—Bible, breviary, rosary and little wallet containing passport, diplomas, and other personal papers. The administrator of the hospital, a churchman friendly to Ignatius, having been informed by the servants that Master Loyola's Company had arrived unexpectedly, hastened to welcome these strangers who had come, as it seemed, under the protection of the Magi. A room and a meal were provided and washing water, towels and some dry clothing. It was a happy Company that sat down to supper in the Incurables. Ignatius had to hear of the fifty-four days' journey and all that befell them on the way. Favre told of how, on November 15th, they had visited Notre Dame, bidding farewell to Paris through the Queen and Mother who was, as it were, the very heart of the city. Francis, listening, remembered that farewell. With the others he had knelt before the fourteenth-century statue that stood at the angle to the right of the choir, just where the south transept joined the nave. Against the blue background, flanked with *fleur-de-lis*, she seemed to incline gently to those who looked up to her, smiling tenderly at the Child and on them—the Company formed under the name of her Son. Francis had laid his old self and his old life right there at the feet of Notre Dame de Paris.

Peter Favre had warmed to the tale, telling Ignatius of how, when they met Spanish forces, the Spaniards among them did the speaking and explaining and passport-showing; when they met French soldiers, Favre and the other French-speaking members of the party had had their say.

At the start Rodriguez had been smitten with a fever; a few days after that, Rodriguez' brother followed them with a band of horsemen, trying to get them to return "to Paris and sanity." Then there was the awful business of Xavier's cords. Francis reddened as Ignatius demanded to be told all about that. It appeared that nothing would do Master Francis but to punish his limbs for their former swiftness in the races and ball games—a swiftness in which he thought he took too much pride in earlier years. So, before starting on the road to Italy, he bound his legs tightly with rough cords and, when his companions discovered the cause of his limping and lagging behind, it was nearly too late to do anything for him. They had a bad night and a bad fright, all of them, because of Master Francis' untimely attempt to mortify himself.

It had rained all the way through Lorraine, such rain that the people of Metz thought that the travellers must have come down with the torrents, the countryside was so impassable and the fighting so widespread. Then on to Nancy. The snow began just as they crossed the French frontier. At Basle they met the Calvinists, further on the Anabaptists, near Constance the Lutherans; they had held debates with the heretics, and had one particularly enlivening but profitless encounter with an ex-priest who, having changed his religion, made haste to change his celibate state, take a wife and surround himself with a family. The only thing they regretted was having to cut short their courses at Paris University. Francis and Favre were due to sit for their finals—another few months would have seen them graduates in divinity. But they had been warned to go before the roads were closed to civilians; and anyway here they were, with Ignatius—the Company of Jesus.

For the next three years Francis led a life no different

from the others of the Company. Indeed, they acted as one, not as many. All save Ignatius, who had reason to think he had enemies in Rome, went to Pope Paul III, placing themselves at his disposal. Returning, they devoted their time and energies to the care of the sick poor in the Venetian hospitals. At that time Venice, long supreme mistress of the Adriatic, was in decline. Her galleys, once the symbol of her power on the Mediterranean, now rode listlessly in the crammed harbour. Since the discovery of the Americas, the importance of Venice diminished rapidly. Her sailors, used to swaggering in strange ports, lolled about the quays and wharves, wondering what had become of the captains of older days, who would have manned the galleys, sailed out, and given chase to Barbarossa.

Mention of Barbarossa brought thoughts of the power behind the bold pirate—Soliman, that most powerful of the Turkish Sultans, whose resources were so immense that he could muster 7,000 ships, and blockade and take the hitherto impregnable Isle of Rhodes, stronghold of the Knights of Malta. Was he not advancing northward, this infidel despot! Belgrade was his and rumour said that his ambition did not end with the taking of that town. And, with France and Spain locked in conflict, central and Northern Europe embroiled in religious disputes and quarrels, England ruled by a king whose passions ruled him, Italy a conglomeration of rival city-states, and the Papacy's temporal power a shadow of what it had been, things looked black for Venice. The city faced east—the east, out of which came danger, as Europe, in the course of her history, had had reason to know. Venetians shrugged their shoulders and said to one another: "Let us eat, drink and be merry, for tomorrow we die." In the midst of this *danse macabre*, there moved quietly, pur-

posefully, a few men in black robes, men who made it
their business to bring hope where despair reigned, to set
charity flowering in the wastes of lovelessness and selfish-
ness, to prove that though Soliman menaced Christendom while it was divided against itself, God was still in
His Heaven and would yet prove to them that believed in
Him how all things—even the Barbarossas of this world—
work out His perfect will.

Francis Xavier, in the June of 1537, was ordained priest.
After his ordination he and another newly ordained went
into the desert—the desert, in their case, being an old
ruin on a desolate height above Padua. There, in solitude
and silence, in cold and hunger, the master of Beauvais
College spent forty days preparing for his first Mass.
There he was tempted by the devil. In the first days of his
retreat the enemy did not cease to remind him of his
hunger-pangs, his wretched lodging, his total lack of ease
and comfort; such attacks were repelled easily enough.
Later on, when, during the sultry summer nights, the
sounds of music and merry-making were wafted up from
the town, the tempter spoke again: "What harm to go
down for an hour and join in the revelry? Youth is short.
Not for ever will there remain to you the fleetness of foot
and litheness of frame that won you renown as an athlete
. . . Or, at least, go down and give the Paduan youths
the opportunity of being taught by a master from Paris.
Expound Aristotle to them . . . Being secure now in the
grace of God, He will protect your soul . . . Cast thyself
down . . . the angels will safeguard thee . . ." But it
was during the last ten days of meditation and prayer that
there beset him a yet more insidious temptation. "Ignatius
may be wrong. This new idea of his—sending his priests
into the heart of religious combat everywhere—is but a
snare. It is a new heresy. In prayer and silence thou shalt

possess thy soul. Behold the happiness and peace of these days on the mountain. Fly to the Grande Chartreuse or to Haute Combe or the Abbey of Asti. Why fritter away life and intellect on a hundred works when one thing only is necessary? The life of contemplation is as old as the Church—see where new-fangled ideas have brought so many. In a Charterhouse or among the Cistercians you might well become another Bernard, another Bruno. Nowhere is true reform so needed as in the monasteries . . . you could restore the great houses of prayer to their original fervour . . ."

The last temptation lasted up to the very eve of the day when he and his friend Salmeron quitted their little huts, leaving their Thebaid for the town of Vicenza, where Ignatius had said that all were to meet by the September equinox. They met their companions, all strangely subdued and silent after their several retreats, in the ruins of the old convent of St. Peter's. Everyone had managed to arrive as arranged except Ignatius himself. Favre and Lainez, who with Ignatius had had their hermitage during the forty days of retreat in different quarters of the same old ruin wherein all had now assembled, explained that Loyola was gone to Venice. False stories were going about; people had been busy spreading word that Ignatius Loyola was a dangerous person—one to be suspected of heresy. It was reported that he had been hounded out of the universities of Spain; that he had set Alcala by the heels, been imprisoned in Toledo, and in Salamanca had been examined by the Grand Vicar of the Inquisition. Worse still—witnesses were not wanting, even now and here in Italy to tell all and sundry that Ignatius had had to make himself scarce in Spain as far back as 1528, when he was seen to leave Barcelona one winter's evening, driving before him his donkey on which he had strapped

his books and his scanty wardrobe. Others, late come from
Paris University, were telling of how, in 1529, there had
been quite a furore there about the same Master Ignatius.
He had been before the Grand Inquisitor of Paris in 1529
and again in a later year.

The reports were so many and so malicious that Ignatius had judged it prudent, for sake of the Company's
future, to demand a complete investigation into the wild
slanders being circulated. So he had gone to Venice, to
the Papal Nuncio, to put himself and his case in the hands
of that prelate. He would return when he had secured
that which he hoped for—a formally executed and signed
attestation of his innocence. Meanwhile he left word that
the Fathers were to go and preach in the adjoining villages, while awaiting his return. When he got back he
would see to the arrangements for their first Masses. The
general concern for their Father and leader loosened
tongues, and soon they were telling of their various retreats. Le Jay and Rodriguez had been in a cave near Bassano, Broet and Bobadilla in a wood near Verona, Codure
and Hozes at Treviso. The forty days had gone by all too
quickly, they agreed. They hoped that Ignatius, when he
returned, would have some news of that pilgrimage to
Jerusalem which they had all vowed at Montmartre.

Rodriguez had fallen very ill in the cave near Bassano,
and a holy old hermit living nearby took him in and
looked after him; but the fever got so violent that Le Jay
rose in the night and made haste to Vicenza to inform
Ignatius. The latter, though ill of a tertian ague himself,
hurried to Bassano, and from the moment of his arrival
Rodriguez began to mend. But worse had happened.
When Ignatius had returned to resume his interrupted
retreat, Rodriguez, back in Le Jay's poor quarters, found
himself sighing for the hermit life; and he fell into a great

melancholy that gave him no peace until finally he resolved to leave Ignatius and the Company and build
himself a little hermitage near to that cave in which he
had received such care during his illness; there he, too,
like the holy hermit who had been so good to him, would
live and die. But, when Rodriguez set off to carry out his
decision, an armed figure with a fierce countenance stood
in the path and barred his way with a sword. Three times
Rodriguez had tried to go to the hermit; three times the
figure stood, blocking his way. Finally, feeling great terror
at the sight of this silent, towering stranger, Rodriguez
fled back to Le Jay's cave. And there stood Ignatius, smiling, evidently well aware of what had happened. "O thou
of little faith, why didst thou doubt?" Those were his only
words of reproach, as he led the would-be deserter back to
the cave where Le Jay lay sound asleep. Knowing that
Rodriguez, having been so ill, would need a little extra
nourishment, he had fetched some wine and a few figs
from Vicenza. But how strange that he should have known
of the temptation, though a distance away!

"Master Francis' colour is very high," observed Lainez.
"Have you, too, been smitten with ague?"

Xavier shook his head. How his ready blood, always
coursing to his face in times of confusion, tended to betray
him! If Loyola had known of Rodriguez's temptation he
must also have had knowledge of the similar one that had
assailed him, Francis. But though their father had gone
quickly to the assistance of Rodriguez, he had allowed
Francis to wrestle with his, alone, unaided. It was strange
that he had not come; Ignatius would have remembered
that, in the early days of Francis' conversion, he had no
small trouble in weaning his neophyte from that great
yearning for the contemplative life that beset him then.
Suddenly, Francis, his flush having died down, found

himself shivering, his hands icy cold, his head heavy, his forehead clammy. Rodriguez, sitting next him, was also taken with a violent shivering. Le Jay, his companion in Bassano, noticed him first.

"The ague again," he cried; "two of them this time: Master Francis and Rodriguez."

Despite feeble protests, the two had to be transferred from the open-air monastery to the city's hardly more comfortable hospital. It would never do for Ignatius to come back with plans ready for the first Masses and find two laid low with a quartan, maybe a tertian ague.

They were a difficult pair of patients to mind; if their bouts of sweating, fever or shivering had coincided, it might have been easier to manage them. But when Rodriguez shivered and tried to burrow into the one blanket, Xavier, his blood burning at fever heat, tried to cool himself by throwing away the covering. The worst of it was when Xavier tried to practice charity for the sake of Rodriguez, while Rodriguez was exercising patience for Xavier's sake.

They were a gaunt and sorry-looking pair when, the fever having spent itself, they rose and prepared to go preach as Ignatius had ordered. It was a bit of an ordeal, Xavier admitted to himself. Standing on a stool in a little village square, waving with one's pilgrim hat—much the worse for the long journey from Paris and for being in continuous use since then—to call a crowd; it was a startling change from the days when, in the Beauvais College, a filled hall waited in silence for the master to enter and begin his discourse. Usually, a crowd of children would trail along for a start, laughing shrilly at the strange black gowns and stranger accents of these new preachers. Women, leaning out of windows or over tall balconies, would interrupt their conversations with their neighbours to look and listen; sometimes they would resume their conversations within a few minutes, sometimes they would listen to the end of the halting sermons and then laugh heartily at the preachers' bad Italian. Men, wondering if these were the new heretics everyone was talking about, came readily enough. They did not know if they were listening to true doctrine or rank heresy, and some of them did not care greatly which they heard; but it was good fun hearing these men of God make so many unintentional jokes: they said *cavalli* when they meant *cavoli*, *cane* for *carne*, and mixed many other words, so that one was sure of a few laughs, if nothing else, by standing listening to them. That tall athletic-looking one, the dark-haired man the others called Master Francis—why, rumour said that he had been a learned man in Paris, the seat of learning. If that was so why did he not betake himself to Bologna or Padua and speak in Latin to the students and the masters in the universities? Crazy fellows, he and his friends were, making fools of themselves in a little place where even the children and the village fool could mock at their mistakes and imitate their accents.

In October Ignatius came, having cleared himself and obtained an attestation which stated that he was in good faith, innocent of the charges brought against him, "of irreproachable doctrine, of excellent reputation and condition."

In a church in Vicenza, on a never-to-be-forgotten morning in October, 1537, Francis Xavier, for the first time, offered the Holy Sacrifice. As he immolated the Body and Blood of Christ for the living and the dead, he immolated himself, recalling the words of Him whose sacrifice His servant, all unworthy, was privileged to perpetuate: "Behold I come . . ." "I come to do Thy will . . ."

"This is my meat, to do the will of Him that sent me . . ."
"This is the will of God, your sanctification . . ."

Ignatius had brought news that the pilgrimage to the Holy Land would have to be abandoned. For the present it was evident that God did not intend them to fulfil that vow. The Turks blocked the Adriatic, and there was open war between Soliman and the Republic of Venice. It was decided that Ignatius, Favre and Lainez should go to Pope Paul III and ascertain his further pleasure regarding their Order, while the others went two by two to the university cities, Siena, Padua, Ferrara and Bologna.

Bobadilla and Xavier went to Bologna, where Francis' father had, in his youth, studied law. Bologna struck a familiar chord; meeting the students in their national groups on the streets that converged on St. Peter's, hearing them dispute a syllogism or argue hotly as to the merits of different professors, one might have thought oneself back again on the hill of Ste. Geneviève; it might be any November evening outside the Ste. Barbe or the Montaigu. But Francis did not join in the academical debates, though once or twice he felt a great wish to step into a circle of disputants and show how much of error or truth their arguments held.

On the third day he said Mass at the tomb of St. Dominic. Afterwards, a Canon of the Cathedral, uncle of a Spanish lady who had attended the Mass and recognized a *castellano* accent, insisted that Francis and Bobadilla should stay in his house while they remained in Bologna. It was in Bologna that Francis met the two Portuguese students who told him of their voyage to Goa. They had gone with the royal fleet on its last sailing, to visit their father, now a high official of Portuguese India. They were lucky to get back again with their lives, considering the storms and hardships they had met with sailing right

round Africa, on the way to Goa and back. It was a different world over there, they told Francis; a great world for
a young man. One could amass more wealth in a few years
there than during a lifetime in Portugal. People in Europe
had no idea of the riches of the East; it teemed with silks,
with gold, with jewels, with natives. They would have
liked to stay but their father had insisted that they return
and finish their education; then they might rejoin him in
Goa. It was a bit awkward, of course, that their father
should have a wife—Indian-fashion—and a family, all
coloured like their native mother, in Goa. But all the
Portuguese did likewise there. Probably when they too
went out they would have dancing girls and concubines,
just like all the nabobs. When in Goa one did as Goa did.

Francis was curious about the teeming natives. What
religion had they, if any? The students could not say.
There were so many outlandish creeds and cults in that
far place that it was small wonder that the Portuguese
there were not exactly exemplary Christians.

The very next Sunday Francis got an invitation from the
Canon, whose guest he was, to preach in the Cathedral.
He could preach at the students' Mass and in Latin, that
all might understand. A fine congregation turned up. Already an old Beauvais College man was teaching in
Bologna and had spread the news that the gaunt-looking
fellow in the black robe was, only a few years back, regent of a college in Paris; he was worth hearing on Aristotle; Master Francis Xavier had been wont to make an
impression in the Paris lecture halls.

But though Francis preached in Latin he disappointed
the students. Not a word on Aristotle, not a hint to show
that he knew a thing or two of philosophy. Nothing but a
sermon on the text: "Many shall come from the east and
the west and sit down with Abraham, Isaac and Jacob in

97

the Kingdom of heaven." The only interesting thing was his account of a galleon he had seen setting sail for the New World from Finisterre, some twenty years before. It was true what everyone was saying: the man, like his companions, was crazy; a Master of Beauvais running in and out of hospitals, doing the most menial tasks! If he wanted to serve God, why did he not use the talents given him? Any old woman could make beds, tend the sick. When Bologna gave him the chance to show the kind of master Paris turned out, he could do nothing better than mount the pulpit to exhort his listeners about their duty to the heathen. But, as the sermon progressed, they found that there was a strange force in the man's words. It was not what he said, but what he left unsaid, that impressed. No grandiose phrases, no rhetorical devices, nothing but the bare bones of argument, made so obvious that the dullest first-year man could take in what the preacher intended. It was such a surprise to the academic staff and students to hear a plain, blunt sermon on the four last things that, by the time the preacher descended from the pulpit—and he took but a third of the time others took to preach—the congregation, having recovered from its first disappointment, wished to hear him again.

They did. On all the Sundays of Advent and on the Sundays after Epiphany Master Francis preached his sermons, so different from other sermons. He preached the gospel, nothing more, nothing less. Salvation, the commandments, the sacraments, prayer, the Mass—somehow all these and similar things seemed easier after one had heard the Canon's guest preach on the Passion, on the Incarnation, on the love of God.

But at the coming of Lent, Francis Xavier slipped away from Bologna as quietly as he had come. He and Bobadilla left for Rome, where Ignatius had a small house on the

Ara Cœli, near the Tower of Marangolo. Bobadilla was worried, for his companion was a sick man. The fever that had smitten him the previous autumn now returned in a far more violent form. His stomach could keep down no food; bouts of fever, great weaknesses, sweats and shiverings succeeded one another, until poor Bobadilla wondered would Francis ever reach Rome. Already Hozes, one of the Company, had died in Ferrara. Ignatius would not thank Bobadilla should Xavier die on the road to Rome. And what an interminable road it seemed! From Florence they dragged on and on towards horizons where castles and towns, precariously perched between earth and heaven, seemed to hang from the skies. On through the broad plains to Siena and a longer stretch still to Viterbo. Finally, to Rome, where an exhausted Bobadilla knocked at the house in the Ara Coeli and dumbly pointed to the fever-stricken man he had half dragged, half carried all the way from Bologna.

Ignatius and the other Fathers were horrified at the sight of Xavier. Only thirty-two, he looked older than the oldest there. He certainly looked a man not long for this world. But it was a time for action, not delay. One was sent for a physician—the best to be found. Another to the friendly Roman who had lent them the house which they occupied—to beg his further assistance in the matter of blankets, bedding, medicines and nourishment for the sick man. They took turns at sitting up with him, Ignatius insisting on taking part of each night's vigil himself. He wondered that the sick man seemed to have a nightmare which recurred frequently. Lainez, Salmeron and the others had known about it before—they told Loyola how Francis often dreamt that he staggered along on an interminable journey, bearing on his back an Indian; from this dream he would wake, calling on Our Lord's Name and telling of how he felt crushed by the weight of the Indian, who seemed to grow heavier with each step. The next night, as Rodriguez and Ignatius watched the invalid, the nightmare returned. Rodriguez, a Portuguese and a rather accomplished scholar, noticed that Xavier seemed to speak, but not in words intelligible to Rodriguez's ears. In his delirium he muttered the same words over and over. Ignatius was listening, but seemed to have no difficulty in understanding.

"He speaks Basque," he explained to the other; "he says 'I must carry my brother to the Door of Glory.'"

"What a strange thing for him to say," observed Rodriguez. "The only door of glory I ever heard of is that of Compostela—*el Portico de la Gloria*—the great door by which the pilgrims enter the Cathedral. And he seldom speaks of his brothers now, though I understand they are noblemen of Navarre. If he dreams of carrying an Indian why does he mutter about his brother and the Door of Glory?"

"The Indian *is* his brother; all men are our brethren," said Ignatius, "and there is a *Portico de la Gloria* other than that of Compostela where, by God's grace, you and I, and Francis and his Indian, may one day enter."

.   .   .   .   .

It took several weeks before Xavier was able to be about again. By that time the others had their works and offices assigned to them. They preached in seven churches in the heart of the city; they looked after the sick and the imprisoned; they set about founding orphanages and Magdalen asylums. When Ignatius considered that Master Xavier was sufficiently recovered, he first of all gave him a severe scolding for neglecting his health to such an extent that he was of little use to either God or man, then

he gave him his new work. He was to be secretary to
Ignatius himself: correspondence was assuming alarming
proportions and Francis was well equipped to deal with
it, whereas Ignatius had always been far happier handling
the sword than the pen. There would be plenty to do, for
God's greater honour and glory, and if Master Francis
dared to get any more of his tertian or quartan agues, or
to have nightmares when, for God's greater honour and
glory, he should be taking his proper rest, he would be
drummed out of the Company just as smartly as that fellow, Michael the Navarrese.

But Michael the Navarrese, like a bad penny, had a
knack of turning up at the most unexpected times and
places. And he was seldom up to any good. At one time in
the old days in Ste. Barbe, he had lain in wait for Ignatius,
whose influence over his young master he resented jeal-
ously, and intended to stab him. At the last moment,
he found himself unable to carry out his intent, but confessed it afterwards to his roommates. In 1536 he had
followed the Company to Venice, begging to be allowed
to join their number; Ignatius did not think Michael
the Navarrese was sufficiently changed since the days
when he stole his roommates' funds and pocket money in
Ste. Barbe, and since the nights he spent roistering in
the Mule and the *Pomme de Pin,* to be a likely candidate
for a life such as the Company envisaged. He was refused admittance. And now his name was mentioned
again, and by no less a person than Monsignor Conversini,
Governor of Rome. Michael the Navarrese, evidently in
the pay of more powerful enemies of the Company, gave
the governor supposedly irrefutable evidence that this
Ignatius had been condemned for heresy and other
crimes, and had saved himself from the stake only by
flight, first from Spain, later from Paris. This challenge,

coming just as the Company was beginning to be solidly established, could not be ignored. Ignatius insisted that he and the Navarrese be brought face to face before the Governor—at which encounter Michael confessed his calumny and retracted all his accusations. But, to avert repetitions of such charges, Ignatius visited the Pope at his Frascati villa and obtained from him an official papal attestation rehabilitating the Father of the Company.

CHAPTER 6

THE Royal Portuguese fleet set sail for India every year on the feast of the Annunciation. On that day all Lisbon was usually *en fête;* the King, the court, the citizens—all who could walk or be carried—proceeded to the height near the Abbey of the Benedictine nuns at Belem, to wave farewell to those who sailed for King John's kingdom in the Orient.

But in 1541, owing to contrary winds, the sailing of the fleet had had to be postponed day after day for fully three weeks. It was not until the Thursday of Passion Week, April 7th, that five caravels, headed by the flagship *Sant Iago,* weighed anchor and sailed down the broad waters of the Tagus, past the cheering, waving crowds at the new tower and monastery of the Hieronymites, past the Abbey where the nuns, assembled in choir, sang the *Salve Regina,* past the harbour bar where seven fathoms was sounded, out into the open sea. The guns in the fortress behind and the guns of the countless ships in the river mouth fired farewell salvoes. The priests, confraternities and acolytes of the Church of Our Lady of Nazareth, who had formed a procession to escort the travellers to the ships, fell into line again, raised their banners, statues, and tapers that guttered in the sea-breeze, and returned to the church.

Old sailors, standing by the river banks, shook sage heads and told one another that it was time King John began to copy the Genoese and build some of the new three-masted schooners, that weighed anything from one to two thousand tons, had a ten-fathom draught, and could carry a thousand souls—not to mention an eight months' supply of provisions, and ammunition and a heavy cargo. Aye, such ships could carry fifty to eighty guns, which put them in a position to meet the pirates that watched all sailings to and from such wealthy countries as Portugal and Spain. These caravels just left, the *Sant Iago* and the others, while all very well for the waters around Europe, were no fit craft for the four-thousand mile voyage to India. Half of them foundered. Many men who left Lisbon on former sailings such as this had never reached Goa; some died of sickness; some went overboard in a cyclone or fog; some were taken by the corsairs or were shipwrecked going round that Cape, misnamed the Cape of Good Hope, or were driven on the coasts of Africa to become the slaves of some black-skinned, woolly-polled chief. The women, wan-faced and red-eyed, shivered as they remembered the winding sheets their menfolk had packed away in their belongings. And the Lisboteans returned, climbing slowly up the seven hills of their city, walking along the terraces lined with palm and dragon trees, talking in subdued tones of their dear ones gone to Goa, wondering if those same dear ones would be aboard when the fleet came home in sixteen or seventeen months' time.

Standing in the poop, waving back at Rodriguez until the latter became indistinguishable among the crowds on the shore, was Master Francis Xavier, priest of the Company of Jesus, Papal Nuncio and Ambassador of Portugal to the countries of the Indies, going at the command of

Ignatius and the Pope, as a missionary to the heathen in these far-off lands. Things had happened in such rapid succession during these past few years that Francis himself could hardly have told how it came about that he, with two companions—Micer Paul, an Italian secular priest who had joined the Company, and Mansilhas, the only recruit Xavier had enlisted during almost a year in Lisbon—should now be leaving Europe and Ignatius in the path of the past. The sails of their caravel, the *Sant Iago*, were reflected in the waters tinged with the flames of sunset. Francis was reminded of that time good old Don Miguel and himself had seen the galleon set sail from Finisterre. He was reminded, too, of what Ignatius had said to him at the moment of parting. "Go. Enkindle and inflame the whole world." There had been no need to wonder what texts of Scripture Ignatius had in mind when he said those last words. "I have come to cast fire on the earth, and what will I but that it be enkindled? I have a baptism wherewith I am to be baptised, and how I am straightened until it be accomplished." The parting commission, rapped out in the brusque military manner that characterised so many of Loyola's mandates, did not need either explanation or reply. Obedience, they of the Company had agreed, after some hesitation, was to be their distinguishing virtue. Obedience—willing, ready and exact—was what Xavier would render.

If anyone had told the young student of Ste. Barbe, marching to St. Denis' Abbey to receive his diploma in philosophy exactly ten years previously that, in 1541, he would sail for the Indies as Nuncio to the East, he would have laughed heartily. Truly, God ordered human affairs. First, there had been Bobadilla's illness, which prevented the latter's being sent to Portugal when King John sent his Ambassador to the Pope, requesting some "Company"

priests to evangelise his overseas dominions. Salmeron
was due to go to Ireland with Broet; Favre was gone to
Parma and was going on from that town with the Papal
Legate, Ortiz, to Worms in Germany; Lainez and Le Jay
and Codure were all assigned to or working on various
missions in Italy and Rome; poor Hozes was in Heaven.
There was no one left to accompany Rodriguez. It was
necessary to send at least two; the Ambassador had asked
for six, but the most that could be sent from so small a
number was two. Then with Bobadilla fallen so ill, there
were not even the two; and the Ambassador would not—
could not—wait. "Francis," Ignatius had said, "the work
is yours." And Francis, rising to the hour and the order,
had made answer, *"Pues, sus! heme aqui!* Very good. Let's
start. Here I am, ready." With a wry smile Ignatius had
said, "Hand me back the pen and parchment; and may
the Lord send me a new secretary soon! And you, Xavier,
you have twenty-four hours to put your affairs in order.
You will need to visit the Pope; you will also please mend
and pack your linen and, when you have the needle in
your hands, don't forget that rent in your cassock. It's
been getting longer every day for the past week. And
please write out and leave with me your vows as a member of the Company, your vote for whomsoever you wish
to have elected Superior, and your approbation—in advance—of the Constitutions, against the time they be
formulated and approved."

There was no time for farewells. No time to visit the
holy places of Rome. The last moments were spent waiting on the Holy Father, darning and laundering, writing
the documents for Ignatius. On March 16th, the Tuesday
of the Passion Week of 1540, the Master of Beauvais bade
a last farewell to the Pilgrim who had entered his life
sometime in the end of 1527—to the man who used to be

an odd-looking, middle-aged student, hopping in ungainly fashion along the dirty, narrow "Dogs' Lane" between the Montaigu and the Ste. Barbe, and who now was dearer to Xavier than any man on earth.

As was the custom when leaving the Torre del Melangolo, the house that the Company now called home, Xavier presented himself before Ignatius, to have himself and his belongings inspected, Fathers having been known to depart on long journeys with insufficient preparation or provisions. Ignatius noted, with a secret surprise, that, for the first time since Xavier's serious illness of a few winters past, he looked well and fit. Thin, of course—the champion ball-player of the Basque valleys would never run to flesh—but, although during the three years he had acted as secretary he had had but indifferent health, God, Our Lord, so it seemed to the Founder of the Company, had now given Francis back his health for the arduous work ahead. Well, the traveller had no provisions for the journey to Portugal; the Ambassador could be counted upon to see him safe on that score; but, for a man going to the ends of the earth, he seemed to have a light bundle. Ignatius undid it. Crucifix, breviary, and a book of excerpts from the Fathers of the Church, the remains of those underpants Ignatius had commanded him to wear in wintertime since his illness (rather raggedy-looking linen for a Papal Legate!), his vestments—such was Xavier's luggage for the Orient.

Ignatius, despite his iron will and deep spirituality, was a warm-hearted man. And, above all those whom God had sent him, he loved Xavier. Their temperaments, tastes, upbringing, even the differences between them, made them fit one another as the hand the glove. Where Francis was the dreamer, Ignatius was the man of action. Where Xavier was the man of intellect, Loyola was the

107

born organiser. Where the captain of Pamplona had fore-sight, determination, a soul all steel in the cause of God, the *hidalgo* of Xavier had enthusiasm, generosity and a heart wherein God had lit a flame of love that must yet, Ignatius thought, prove unquenchable. Taking Xavier by the shoulders, he felt the thinness of the soutane. The man would have ridden across the Alps in it, only that he, Ignatius, had noticed in time! But this was no time for scolding. Already the Ambassador and his entourage were in the Ara Cœli, their horses pawing the paving-stones. Hastily slipping off his own robe, the Father of the Company of Jesus divested himself of a flannel vest he was wearing and made Xavier get into it. It was as though he gave part of himself with this part of his vesture to his son going away. Looking rather more severe than usual, he buttoned Francis into the shabby soutane, grasping his shoulders again—a fine pair of shoulders they were, as good as ever came out of Navarre! And maybe Francis would yet need them to carry that Indian he had so often dreamt of. Xavier knelt for a blessing. *"Benedictio Dei omnipotentis, Patris et Filii et Spiritus Sancti descendat super te et maneat semper.* Go. Enkindle and inflame the whole world." And Francis was gone . . .

Although his companions had gone below, Francis re-mained on the top deck, looking back, remembering, marvelling how God had arranged all. At Bologna word had somehow got ahead of the cavalcade that the preacher everyone had heard in the Cathedral a few years before was passing through, on his way to the East, to convert the heathens. The Ambassador had business in Bologna that necessitated a delay of some days. The Church of Santa Lucia was crowded for Xavier's Masses, which his old friend and host, the Canon, insisted on serving; his confessional was besieged. Marching students

escorted him a mile on the road to Parma, finally standing
in two long files to give three cheers for the Master of
Paris University who thought it not a waste of time or
talent to leave all things to bring Christ to those who sat
in darkness and the shadow of death.

A great disappointment awaited him in Parma. There
he was to meet, he hoped, Favre—warm-hearted Favre,
his guardian angel in the early days of Ste. Barbe. Alas,
Favre had left Parma for Brescia only that morning, to
spend a fortnight preaching in that town. The Ambassador could not wait, so Xavier had to go without seeing
his old friend.

There had been many adventures in the three months'
journey to Lisbon. Once the Ambassador's secretary, suddenly disappearing from sight in an Alpine snowdrift, had
gone hurtling down the side of a ravine. No one had dared
clamber down the frozen slope to the point where, far below, the unfortunate man hung, his cloak caught on a tree
stump. Remembering how, in long-past winters, he and
other boys had played games that meant slithering over
similar glazed heights in the Sierra Leyre, near Xavier,
Francis had gone down, inching his way, until he gripped
the terrified secretary and slowly hauled him up to the
pathway.

"I was a secretary myself for the past few years," he
explained to all about; "I know what Fr. Ignatius would
say to me if I did not try to save the Ambassador from the
worry of letter writing."

Then there had been the case of Francisco de Lima, a
young and extremely wealthy Portuguese nobleman who
was returning in state from a tour of Europe. His entourage, which included a steward, pastry-cook, toast-
master, chamberlain, doctor, surgeon, secretaries, pages,
grooms, falconers, musicians and jugglers, far outclassed

that of the Ambassador in whose company he travelled. Despite all this ostentation, young de Lima had a bored and melancholy air. Yet Xavier was strangely drawn to him. Were they not both named for the Saint of Assisi, the Saint of brotherly love? It was not long until the two were riding side by side, the younger telling the tale of his wanderings in the cities of Europe, of how his senses sought excitement, his appetites satiation, while his soul starved. Especially he told of his experiences in Paris, a city well-known to his companion. It was strange, young de Lima thought, how this holy Father knew so much of places like the Mule, the *Pomme de Pin* and that disreputable resort known as the *Pet-au-Diable*. After his long talk with so understanding a man it seemed the most natural thing in the world to dismount at the next church they passed and spend a little time there. It would have been hard to tell which of the two was the happier when they emerged—the young nobleman, who had set his soul aright by a general confession, or Francis, who had been the instrument of his return to God.

There had been also, on that journey from Rome to Lisbon, the visit to Loyola, home of Ignatius. The castle of Loyola was unlike the home of his own childhood; it stood in a smiling, verdant valley in a well-populated province; but the serene, happy family life of Don Beltram and Doña Madalena reminded him of the life of Xavier.

Lisbon had been a surprise. It was a town of merchant princes, of nobles and statesmen. Everywhere there was colour, sunshine and the hum of business. Palace after palace, church after church, convent after convent, climbed the terraced hills that rose from the Tagus. Negro priests; Indian princes and ambassadors; fish-women with broad, saucer-shaped sardine baskets on their heads;

slaves; orange and lemon sellers; country folk marketing their olives, figs and mulberries, jostled one another in the streets. Swaggering adventurers who, a year or two before, had gone East working their passages as seamen, were now back home gorgeously attired, weighted with jewellery, fabulously rich, lording it up and down the quays, their Cingalese or Malayan slaves trotting beside them. Wealth strutted with power, vice elbowed misery on the wharves of Lisbon, a town grown too small for the magnificence it had so unexpectedly won. Rodriguez, who had got a sea passage to Portugal two months earlier, was overjoyed when Francis joined him there. They set to work as in Bologna and Rome. The prisoners in the jails, the sick in the hospital, the poor in the noisome alleys behind the quays, or in the lanes at the back of the palatial streets in the city centre, the victims of the Inquisition—these were the main objects of the two Fathers' solicitude during the nine months' stay in Lisbon. But there was another apostolate in that city; bidden to the court of the monarch at whose behest they were being sent to the East, they found scope for their zeal in a nobility whom wealth had made effete, among officials whom power had corrupted. And then, at the end, had come King John's decision to keep one of the Jesuits to found a College of their Company in Coimbra—Coimbra, where Francis Xavier's cousin, the famous Don Martin, professed Canon Law. Francis, much though he would have liked to live under the benign influence of Don Martin, hoped that God would permit him to fulfil, or, at least, to attempt to fulfil, Ignatius' command to set the world on fire with love of God. He had had letters from Don Martin, and had written him, hoping that they might arrange a meeting; Don Martin had been interested in the Company and

wished to know about the manner of their life. Francis
had written:

> With regard to your wish to know about my af-
> fairs, and especially my rule of life, it would be a
> great joy to me if we could meet . . . May God
> (among the many favours with which His Divine
> Majesty indulgently and mercifully loads me day by
> day) add also this very special grace to all the rest,
> that I may see you for once in this life and talk with
> you at leisure, before my companion and myself set
> sail for the Indies . . .

Later Don Martin had written, offering to join Francis
and the others of the Company, and go with them as a
missionary to the heathen. But Francis, faced with his first
major decision, a decision that could not, owing to lack
of time, be referred to Ignatius, had dissuaded his kinsman from accompanying him. The learned canonist—the
"Doctor of Navarre," of whom the Pope had said that he
carried more Canon Law in his head than all his fellows
did in their books and libraries—would be of greater
service to God and the Company in Portugal than in the
Indies; particularly now, when Rodriguez was about to
start for Coimbra, he being the one chosen to found the
College there.

.   .   .   .   .

The *Sant Iago* was veering south, hugging the coast for
fear of pirates. The night wind blew chill. Francis felt for
the letters he carried on his person, the papal briefs em-
powering him to act as Legate to the East, letters recommending the missionaries of the Company to the chiefs
and kings and overlords of all the islands in the eastern

seas, with a special letter to David, the King of Ethiopia. Having said the *Salve Regina,* he spent a few minutes reflecting on the fact that this was his thirty-fifth birthday; life was flying past more swiftly than the land-birds passing the *Sant Iago,* on their way to the shore, and he, Francis Xavier, had not as yet begun to serve God. He was an unprofitable servant, he told himself. Then, realising that it might be considered a breach of manners not to appear punctually at the Governor's table, where he and Micer Paul and Mansilhas were to dine during the voyage, he hurried below.

At the officers' table, the place of honour was reserved to Admiral Martin da Sousa, the new Governor of the Indies, going to Goa to take over from the son of da Gama, the man who had discovered the eastern empire of Portugal. Sousa's star was, at the moment, in the ascendant. The Admiral had seen twenty years' service with the fleet, having sailed not only up and down the eastern seas, but to Brazil in the wake of de Cabral. The captains sailing with him were a mixed lot, men who had seen life in many lands, on many seas, in Europe, in the east, and in the Americas. They had no intention of letting those priests of the new order, "the Company," interfere with their usual habits when aboard the flagship. Sousa, aware that the King of Portugal held these missionaries in more than ordinary respect, intended to be wary. One never knew who these fellows had been in the world; they might have the ear of someone powerful in court. He invited Xavier to sit next to him, though, indeed, he had no hope that the man would be pleasant company. No gentleman, Xavier, though he *did* have a papal brief appointing him Nuncio Apostolic. If he were of the nobility he would not have declined the offer of a servant to wash his linen and cook his *olla podrida* during the voyage. Scant respect the sight of a churchman doing his washing and stirring his stew would earn among the Orientals who attended on the Portuguese passengers. And when one of Sousa's officers had remonstrated with him, the fellow had calmly said, "This is how the Church *will* earn respect," and resumed his washing and pot-boiling.

The conversation was on current affairs. Wagers were being laid as to how long Catherine Howard would last as Queen of England. It was becoming hard to keep count of King Henry's wives; Catherine of Aragon, the repudiated, had died five years before in her bed; her usurper, Anne Boleyn, had been beheaded in that same year; Jane Seymour had died in childbirth the next year—1537; Anne of Cleves was the lucky possessor of uncomely features and an ungainly figure, which saved her life and gained her a pension when the King, after glancing at the unprepossessing German lady, ordered his Parliament to annul the marriage. Last year the fifty-year-old monarch had married a flighty eighteen-year-old girl, and the Howard family were being advanced as the Boleyns and the Seymours had been a few years before; and already there were rumours—rumours which might not have reached Henry's ears yet, but which were certainly common property not only in English court circles, but in every capital in Europe. The King had spent Shrove without taking any recreation; no chamber music—not a lute twanged, not a madrigal sung; and his usual jovial temper had soured. And the Queen, ignoring the danger signals, had gone on gaily keeping her various "secret" assignments, now with one of the King's gentlemen, a nobody named Culpeper, now with a young impoverished relative, whose only hope of getting on in the world was a chance to participate in plundering raids on the coasts of Ireland. Some of the officers wagered that Catherine

Howard would outwit and outlive the aging King; others put their money on the man who was so well served by his spies, spies certain to keep their royal master well posted as to the indiscretions of the wanton who, for the moment, might call herself Queen of England.

From England the talk moved to France; the French King had at last succeeded in getting Benvenuto Cellini to Paris, where the great artist was executing the most exquisite work in rare metals. François I was the worst kind of robber; not content with inveigling da Vinci and del Sarto to Paris twenty years earlier, he had now despoiled Italy of another genius. Cellini, however, was no diplomat; the King of France was so delighted with the golden saltcellar, the silver vase, the lunette, the bronze heads which this master craftsman turned out that he would have advanced him to the highest honours, showered him with wealth, but the fellow had incurred the anger and jealousy of the present favourite, Anne of Neuilly, and forgotten himself so far that the King now frowned on him. And with a new war brewing who knew what fate lay ahead of Cellini? Instead of indulging his aesthetic taste and living as a connoisseur of fine things, a patron of the arts, once François took the field and began to empty his coffers to pay for his wars, he would forget Cellini.

And, talking of art, another of the company wondered if Michaelangelo were going to go on for ever. Sousa suggested that the Company Fathers at the table should know that best, seeing that they had been in Rome for some years previous to 1540. Francis Xavier, who had, up till then, taken but little part in the conversation, assured them that the Italian genius was, at seventy-five, still pre-eminent in painting, sculpture and architecture. The officers laid a few more wagers as to who would live the longer, Michaelangelo, working for the Popes, or Titian, whom the Emperor—to be one better than the French King —had at the court of Madrid. Titian was, of course, five years younger than Michaelangelo, but both were, by any standards, old men. At which Francis Xavier begged leave to assure the company that, to all appearances, the great artist never grew older—only more inspired, more gifted, with each passing year. He had seen the *maestro* put the finishing touches to the great fresco of the Last Judgment for which he used all of the end wall of the Sistine Chapel. The whole painting was thirty feet wide and twice that in height, people said.

One of the officers had heard of it. Was not that the painting in which Michaelangelo took a neat revenge on one of the papal officials who had complained to the Pope of the nudes, both among the saved and the damned? Francis had not heard of that. He had been on his way from the Holy Father's apartments, where he had been sent on business connected with the Company, and the Papal Chamberlain who accompanied him had taken him to see the great artist completing his work. It was a compelling and awe-inspiring composition. If the officers were not bored he would tell them just how it went.

No one was bored. It was a pleasure to hear the resonant, cultured voice, to watch the expressive face.

"Well, here in the centre"—and Francis cleared a space on the table before him—"he has Our Saviour, with right arm raised, coming in judgment, stern and terrible. Beside Him sits His Mother, sad of countenance, no longer entreating Him for mercy for sinners. Above, two companies of angels attend the Saviour, bearing the instruments of the Passion. On the right the saved rise to heaven, escorted by angels; demons try to pull them back, but to no avail. On the left, one sees the damned falling into the abyss." While he spoke Francis had been indicating on the table-centre the positions of the various groups in the painting. "And here," and he pointed to the lower left-hand corner, "here is hell and Charon rowing his ferry across the Styx, with a single passenger—King Minos of Crete, I think Michaelangelo gives—a mythical passenger and a mythical boatman. That is how the picture goes. I was thinking, as I stood in the poop of this ship just now, of how many souls, now in health and vigour, on the *Sant Iago*, will have gone—solitary passengers—on that voyage Michaelangelo's ferry-boat of the Styx signified before we reach Goa."

"Come now, come now, Father Francis!" remonstrated the Admiral. "What a doleful note on which to begin a voyage! And you have hardly touched your food. Believe me, the only eatable meals to be expected on the journey to Goa are those one eats on the first day out. When we run into warm latitudes it will be nothing but smoked and salted pork or cod, with a little bread or rice for the rest of the way. You feel ill, perhaps? If you go to your cabin and rest for a little while, I will have the servants carry some food across later."

The officers were laying wagers on the numbers that would reach Goa alive, as Xavier and his companions left. Francis did not intend to dine with the Admiral and officers any other evening; he had accepted the invitation for the first evening, out of courtesy. Nor did he intend that Micer Paul, Mansilhas and himself should feast in the tiny cramped space called their cabin. Having fulfilled the obligations his office as Legate laid upon him, and his duties to the Admiral as representing the temporal power, he now considered himself free to see if there were any on board who needed his help.

The cabin allocated to the three missionaries was low

and stuffy, but they were glad of the little privacy it promised. Having prayed together, Micer Paul and Mansilhas listened while Francis gave directions for their work during the journey. It could well be that they might never reach Goa. It was a common thing for ships and passengers—all—to be lost on these long journeys. So it behoved them to travel as men preparing to meet their God, at any hour, in any place. Above all, they were obliged, by their calling and for the love of God, to practise charity. Francis proposed that they make a start right away. It might not be a bad idea to start feeding the hungry when the Admiral sent that food to the cabin.

A little later, when Sousa's lackeys arrived with their laden platters, they found a motley crowd waiting to devour the good food the Admiral had sent to the missionaries. The Fathers themselves served their guests a meal, when the servants refused to wait upon such riffraff.

That was the beginning of a journey the trials of which Xavier dismissed in a letter to Ignatius with the words "the sufferings were such that I should not, except for God's sake, dare to face them a single day for the whole world." Francis, never before on board a sea-going vessel, was horrified at the conditions which prevailed. In the ship's hold, packed like sardines, were a crowd of criminals, paupers, negroes, half-castes, vagrants, evildoers fleeing from justice, adventurers, seamen, gaolbirds—the dregs of Portugal and, indeed, of Europe.

For the first days the ship rolled and pitched; seasickness was the lot of all, and the miseries of the voyagers were made worse by the lack of space, the unbearable stench, the cries and groans of the hundreds cooped up in the suffocating, foul atmosphere of the steerage. Father Francis Xavier, man of inland mountains and valleys, was a bad sailor. He, like the others, was afflicted with con-

118

tinuous seasickness and fever; Sousa, Viceroy-elect of the Indies, had advised him keep to his cabin and lie down, but the Admiral did not yet know that as long as Xavier could drag himself about, he would not rest if another were in need. Day after day, night after night, he and his two companions descended the iron ladder into the holds. Between their own bouts of nausea they attended the unfortunates lying about in the half-light; they washed the patients and the filthy clothes of the sick; they divided among them the rations sent from the Viceroy's table for the sustenance of the Nuncio and his two friends; they scrubbed and cleaned the holds as best they could; they carried the dying up the ladder that swayed with every lurch of the boat, laying them on the beds in their own cabin, comforting them and preparing them for death. They wrapped the dead in clean shrouds, they read the burial prayers; they wrote to the wives, mothers, and families who waited on the return of those voyagers whose voyage had ended in the depths of the sea.

For fear of corsairs, the Indian Fleet as well as the Brazil Fleet sailed in close formation as far as the Azores, and several ships escorted the frigates as far as those islands. Then the Brazil squadron turned west, the escort ships sailed home and those for the east turned south towards the Equator. The ocean swell encountered southwest of the Azores intensified the lurching of the ship and the seasickness of the passengers, but the worst suffering lay ahead.

When past Sierra Leone, they ran into the doldrums, and lay becalmed for forty days off the coast of Guinea. There, under a brazen sky, they sweltered in the most intense heat. Most of the food went bad; even the well-salted cod and pork turned putrid; the bread, hard biscuits and flour became infested with maggots and weevils;

butter melted and ran like oil, as did the candles. The timbers creaked and finally cracked, the tar and pitch in their seams running in molten pools on the decks, in the holds, in the cabins. Occasionally, a bank of low-lying clouds would come up over the horizon and torrential rain fell, but it was a pestiferous rain that covered a man's body with boils and blains, that left his clothing crawling with lice. The water—which one had to drink through a cloth, with one's eyes closed and one's nostrils held—ran short. Murder was committed for a mouldy crust, for a spoon of the water which had turned to slime, for a foot of shade beneath the canvas awnings that hung above the decks—inadequate protection against the heat and the glare that sent men mad. Yellow fever broke out, and the disease known as the Dutch Illness, when a man's mouth blistered and his feet swelled, and his body began to turn black as a negro's; usually those smitten by this scourge speedily died. Although the Viceroy had a doctor and a surgeon in his entourage, their sole knowledge of medicine seemed confined to bleeding and purging, their main pre-occupation the health of the officers and the Viceroy, for whose sake they avoided contaminating themselves by going below decks to alleviate suffering. Both the physician and the surgeon warned Xavier to keep away from those stricken with fever and the Dutch Illness. Later on, seeing that their words took little effect, they advised him, for the sake of the work he hoped to do in India, to take precautions. The Father should wash his nose, mouth and temples with strong vinegar, especially when in likelihood of catching the contagion from the breath of the fever-smitten who were making their confessions or telling their last wishes into his ears—for Xavier was he whom every dying man on the *Sant Iago* wanted to have beside him in his last moments.

Don Francisco

For prudence' sake Francis took the precautions indicated, but he did not cease from his labours. He preached on Sundays, taught catechism every day, cleansed, nursed and fed—as best he could, with the assistance of his two companions—the sick and fever-stricken. He controlled his own spasms of fever as he sat with the seamen beneath the stars, listening to their seafaring yarns, joining in their sea chanties, delighted when, as was the custom on the Portuguese ships, they sang the Litany of Loreto before settling down for the night. He listened, interestedly, to the commercial talks of the merchants, glad to note that several put a donation into Our Lady's Alms Box, an offering to implore a blessing on their undertakings in the east. The outcasts and gaolbirds and ne'er-do-wells were glad when the Padre they called *el Santo* drew near; his presence silenced blasphemy, quelled quarrels, caused the ready oath to remain unsworn, the lewd song to stay unsung. He loved them all and they could not but know it— the seamen who manned the ropes and sails, the rabble in the hold, the officers in the coops called cabins, the good, the bad, the converted, the unregenerate. Remembering the hopes of his own earlier years he marvelled at the earthly hopes these men set their hearts upon, the sufferings they were prepared to endure to realise them, while so few were prepared to suffer even a little for everlasting life, so few set their hearts on a hope that could not fail.

And suddenly, one evening, as the sailors were singing the lovely Litany——

> *Sancta Maria,*
> *Ora pro nobis.*
> *Sancta Dei Genitrix,*
> *Ora pro nobis.*

121

> *Sancta Virgo Virginum,*
>   *Ora pro nobis.*
> *Mater Christi,*
>   *Ora pro nobis——*

the ship shuddered, stirred, and began to move slowly, heavily, timbers creaking. Sails, so long listless, slowly filled themselves with the welcome winds that—increasing rapidly—sent the *Sant Iago* and the rest of the India Fleet scudding southwards. A cheer went up from the seamen; all who could move clambered on deck, filling their poison-charged lungs with draughts of the heady air that now bore them onwards towards their destination. Even the poor fever-victims turned hope-filled eyes on Father Francis, Micer Paul and Mansilhas, as the trio moved about the holds, attending to the needs of the sick.

Finally, when a dying man was made as comfortable as possible in the bunk assigned to the Papal Nuncio, Xavier went on deck, to lie, wearied, his head on a coil of rope, his heart full of happiness. As he dropped off to sleep, the last sound he heard was the singing of the sailors, continuing their Litany.

> *Janua Cœli,*
>   *Ora pro nobis.*
> *Stella matutina,*
>   *Ora pro nobis.*
> *Salus infirmorum,*
>   *Ora pro nobis.*
> *Refugium peccatorum,*
>   *Ora pro nobis.*

·　　·　　·　　·　　·

Southward then, at Pentecost, with a following breeze, keeping a line that lay about four hundred leagues west of the African coast, stopping near the island called St. Helena just long enough for the rowboats to put into the bay of *Sant Iago* to cleanse and replenish the water casks and to fetch back some turtles and fruit—a welcome change from the uneatable scraps in the ship's stores.

Before they weighed anchor in the early morning, Father Francis offered the Holy Sacrifice on an altar that the mariners had erected on the freshly washed and sanded decks of the *Sant Iago*. It was the Ember Saturday of Whitsuntide. As the priest began the Introit, the worshippers suffered a great distraction: a flock of startled flamingoes, taking flight from their roosting grounds, flew between the galleon and the shore. The great birds made a magnificent spectacle as they wheeled inland in one immense, wedge-shaped cloud, their scarlet plumage contrasting vividly with the dark green of the mangrove swamps. But the celebrant of the Mass saw nothing of the flaming wings that soared above the sunlit seas. His mind was intent upon the Pentecostal liturgy—on this last Mass of the eight weeks of Paschaltide. He proceeded through the six successions of Collect, Lesson and Psalm, praying earnestly that grace might be given him to accomplish that which God, through Ignatius, had commanded him. "Go. Enkindle and inflame the whole earth," Ignatius had said. One could not enkindle others if oneself lacked fire. Of all the Masses of the Octave of Pentecost, this final one seemed to voice most eloquently, most urgently, the need of mankind, the need of Francis Xavier, for the Holy Spirit, the Living Fire, the Heavenly Dove.

. . . The charity of God is poured forth in our hearts, alleluia: by His spirit dwelling within us. Alleluia, alleluia . . .

. . . In Thy bounty, O Lord, we beseech Thee,

123

pour into our minds the Holy Ghost: by whose wisdom we were made, and by whose providence we are
guided . . .

. . . May the Holy Ghost, O Lord, enkindle in our
hearts that fire which Our Lord, Jesus Christ, from
the innermost depths of His own Divine Heart, sent
forth upon the earth and willed should fiercely
burn . . .

With fresh water aboard, the travellers took new heart.
Remaining at the same safe distance from a shore noted
for shoals and storms, the fleet took a good wide sweep
around that southernmost point of the dark Continent,
el Cabo de Buena Esperanza. There, frigid winds from the
Antarctic surprised the many who had come unprepared
for the change from extreme heat to extreme cold. Flemings and other Northern Europeans among passengers and
crew supported this change well enough and were glad
of a chance to make up for sleep lost in hotter regions, but
the Portuguese and Orientals suffered intensely—chilblains, frostbite, chills and chest complaints laying many
low. The men of the Company, though ill themselves,
were unceasing in their care of the sick, mixing medicines
and syrups, wrapping the scantily clad in the cloaks of
heavy cloth that had been specially made for themselves
against this part of the journey. Rounding the Cape meant
heavy work for the Admiral and his crew; many ships had
gone down at that point in former journeys to India, so
careful preparations were made and every precaution
taken. Working for days ahead, they brought the heaviest
guns below deck to give the ship greater ballast; the masts
were secured with hawsers; windows and hatches were
nailed up with heavy beams, while deck, steerage and
cabin passengers alike were all ordered into the holds.

Finally, when came a clear starry night, and the helmsman was able to take his bearings from the strange stars of those southern skies, the watch sang out that the danger point had been passed; they were safely clear of the Cape and might veer to the northwest and steer for the Straits of Mozambique, between Madagascar and the continent of Africa.

But there, again, a terrible storm swept suddenly upon them, hardly giving them time to reef the sails. Roaring winds buffeted the ship, mountainous waves rose fore and aft, torrential rains washed the decks, thunder reverberated across the vast wastes of inky black waters, while lightning gave the terrified passengers momentary glimpses of their peril as flash after flash showed the portholes covered with water, the ship gone down into such a trough between the waves that it seemed all but sucked under. In the hold the two lanterns that feebly flickered and had to be steadied each time a wave hit the frigate, showed Francis Xavier, held up by the mariners who knelt about him, exhorting all to have confidence, leading the Act of Contrition and the Confiteor, raising his hand in the general absolution, in the last blessing. Forcing himself to show a gaiety and courage he did not feel, he rallied the faint-hearted, comforted the sick, joked with the friends he had made, with the converts he had won during the voyage. The more seasoned sailors wondered, saying to one another, "He knows no fear." The despairing and terrified took heart again, and joined in the Rosary, or sang the Litany of Loreto, the *Salve*, and the hymns he had taught them during the voyage.

In the morning the storm cleared. The deck was like a street mart as those able to be on their feet hastened from the holds to dry their wet wrappings in the sun and wind. On open fires in crude braziers here and there along the deck, noisome meals of beans in oil, or rice in oil, simmered. Then at last, in September, Mozambique, the "smallest inhabited island in the known world," the "graveyard of the Portuguese," was reached. Fortune had been against them; it was now too late to venture the remainder of the journey—already the monsoons were beginning to blow. They would have to winter on this coral island, this garrison of Portugal on a strip of coastal swamp, this fever-ridden shore ringed by vast stretches of virgin forest peopled with who knew what blood-drinking cannibals.

AT CHRISTMAS, Francis Xavier fell victim to a fever as bad as that which had almost cost him his life in the winter of 1538 in Rome. Fearful lest the man who had effected such a change of life in his cutthroat passengers might die before they reached India, Sousa brusquely ordered him to bed, commanding the physician of the *Sant Iago* to see that he remained there and took the remedies prescribed for him. "No reaper wishes to lay down his sickle on the way to the harvest field," he told Francis.

On New Year's Day, 1542, a little eased of his fever, Xavier wrote to Ignatius and the Company in Rome:

> May the grace and love of Our Lord Jesus Christ always aid and favour us.
>
> On my departure from Lisbon I wrote you of all that had happened there. We left on the 7th April, 1541. I had the seasickness for all of two months, and suffered greatly for forty days off the coast of Guinea, on account of the great calms, where the weather is far from pleasant. At last, by the grace of God, we steered to an island where we still are.
>
> Certain that you will rejoice *in Domino*, I must tell you how God Our Lord has willed to employ us in the service of His servants. Scarcely had we disem-

127

barked than we occupied ourselves with the poor sick people off the frigates. I heard their confessions, communicated them, helped them to die well, used the plenary indulgences which His Holiness conceded me for these regions. Almost all die in peace and joy, thus assisted by a priest empowered to give a plenary absolution in their dying moments. Micer Paul and Micer Mansilhas attend to their temporal needs; our lodging is that of the poor afflicted ones. Thus we employ ourselves, according to our little means, trying to procure the temporal and spiritual good of all; and as to the fruit God knows, as it is He who works in us.

It is no small consolation to us to know that Señor el Governor and all the gentlemen of the fleet are well aware that our desires are very different from those of worldlings and tend, not to please men, but God alone. Such, indeed, was the nature of the pains and labours we embraced that, for the whole world, I would not dare face them for a single day . . . For the love of Our Lord, we ask you to remember us especially in your prayers and Masses, as you know well we are metal of base alloy . . .

At sea, as far as Mozambique, I preached every Sunday. Here, I do so as often as I can . . .

I wish I could write more; at the moment, my sickness prevents me. Today, I was bled for the seventh time; I feel a little better, God be praised. Please remember me affectionately to all our friends and acquaintances.

Francisco

·   ·   ·   ·   ·

Don Martin Alfonso da Sousa was in a rage. As was his custom on such occasions, he soundly cuffed his pages and swore at his secretaries; then, ordering a tall negro to hold his sunshade, he strode from the hospital towards the palm grove near the south shore. He had to be alone to decide what action he should take in a situation such as that which now presented itself. Reaching the grove, he leaned against a palm tree, and began to reread the letter in his hand. The negro, impassive, held the umbrella made in the vice-regal colours above his master's head, wondering at the strange ways of the pale chiefs who so engrossed themselves in those great handmade, handmarked leaves they forever carried with them.

It was considered as proper for an incoming Portuguese administrator to despise his predecessor as for the deposed official to bear a grudge against his successor. Hence Sousa, whose feats of arms as Admiral of the India Fleet had won him respect and fear from the Indian rajahs and princelings, considered himself in duty bound to despise and humiliate Stephen de Gama, the outgoing Viceroy. The latter would, the Admiral felt sure, never have reached his position as Viceroy of the Indies but for the fact that his father had been Vasco da Gama, the explorer who gave Portugal Mozambique and India. But— the letter that he had, fortunately, intercepted! That put a different complexion on matters. This fellow—this da Gama, who probably could not boast a drop of blue blood, this da Gama, who, without doubt, was descended from those infidel dogs, the Moors—had had the temerity to presume the fleet—and, of course, the new Viceroy—lost. Worse still, he had sent a ship to Mozambique to learn what had happened, hoping to ally himself with Alvaro, his brother, who was in command of the *San Pedro,* one of the four ships sailing with the *Sant Iago.* It was a conspiracy; a conspiracy, *a la mano de Dios!* But he, Sousa, had dealt with conspirators before and would do so again. Probably the plot had been for Alvaro and the commander of the *Coulam*, the ship sent from India, to poison him here in this God-forsaken swamp. Though the letter had not said so much openly, an able, wideawake administrator could read between the lines. Already he had taken the preliminary precautions of having Alvaro thrown into the dungeons on the island fortress, and the Captain of the *Coulam* put in chains and thrust into the secret hiding place on the *Sant Iago*.

Only that Father Francis would be sure to come pleading for mercy, as he did for other criminals, Sousa would have had the pair pinned to the ground with musket and cannon balls, and lashed to within an inch of their lives. No—he would have done more. He would have made an example of them and struck terror into others in India likely to be fellow conspirators. He would have had them keel-hauled a few times, as they sailed through the shark-infested waters up the African coast and, then, what the sharks had left would have been nailed to the mainmasts. Goa would then know that it was getting a new Governor who would stand for no disaffection. But, there was that Francis Xavier! The fellow would be running to offer his own lean body to the lashers, to give himself to the sharks, to let his own hands be nailed to the masts—Sousa knew him. And there would surely be a mutiny, for the crew would obey the man they called *el Santo* sooner than the Admiral.

Motioning the negro to shelter him with the sunshade, Sousa walked up and down by the palms, deep in thought. Before long he had come to his decision. Instead of sailing on the flagship, the *Sant Iago*, he would transfer to the *Coulam* and depart for Goa, at the first sign of favourable winds. Da Gama would be taken by surprise and Sousa would be master of the situation and in a position to deal effectively with any plots connived against him. He would

take Father Francis along, too; with *el Santo* aboard they
were sure of heavenly protection on the voyage; the other
ships could follow later, taking the other two missionaries.

In vain Francis begged that his companions might be
allowed to travel with him, or he to remain until they
sailed. But the Admiral was adamant; Francis must sail on
the *Coulam,* his fellow Jesuits wait until the other ships
were ready. So, at the end of February, Francis bade farewell to the dejected Micer Paul and the bewildered Mansilhas, and prepared to board the *Coulam,* as Sousa had
ordered.

The wind seemed set as they walked down to where
the *Coulam* waited; a slave market was in progress on the
beach and white-robed Hindu merchants—a red smear on
their foreheads, red shoes on their feet—haggled with
long-bearded Mohammedan traders for the terrified,
ebony-hued human merchandise being paraded by their
sellers, pummelled by their buyers, preparatory to being
sold.

"Business is good today, eh?" asked the Governor, pausing to let Father Francis see what was a strange sight for
a European.

No. Business was bad, he was told. Very bad. The
garrison and the men of the fleet were not buying this
time. Some western mullah, a Christian Brahmin, whom
His Honour would know, having brought him on his ship
from Lisbon, had made his countrymen promise to for-
swear the keeping of concubines, had told them that it
was forbidden by Allah, no less, to do so. And as for the
sale of good male slaves, sound in wind and limb, usually
bought up quickly by the lords of Mozambique, the
Portuguese, there was no sale for them either. This Christian Brahmin had ruined the first market of the year.
Well, it was to be hoped His Honour would see the mullah

away to Goa on his own ship. Then, poor merchants might do a bit of trade. Francis had walked ahead with one of the Admiral's secretaries.

"What language do they speak?" he asked, indicating a slave trader and a Hindu hotly debating the value of a well-built young native.

"Oh, an impossible lingo: Hindustani, Arabic, Portuguese, Cingalese—a mixture of several languages, just enough to serve the purposes of their trade."

"Can you speak it? Or understand it?"

"A little. If I listen I usually get the gist of what they jabber about."

"Try and find out what is the price of that slave."

Just then, the *Coulam* fired one gun to warn all to board at once. The Governor, taking Father Francis by the arm, moved towards the ship. As they passed the fortress, a voice from a hole at earth level, that let a little air into the dungeons, could be heard shouting and yelling.

"Sousa! da Sousa! I'll get even with you yet. Sail off to Goa, will you, and leave an honest man to rot in this hell-on-earth? May you never see land! And you, new priest, friend of Sousa's, you might as well put your trust in a tiger. Go back where you came from, priest. They have priests a-plenty in India. And believe me, when Alvaro Altaide is vindicated and returns to Goa, it won't be well for da Sousa—or for his friends. For all I know, maybe you, priest, were the one to put the new Viceroy up to this trick."

"Who on earth is that?" Francis had stopped to listen to the tirade.

"A poor fellow out of his wits," replied the Governor. "Just a touch of the sun. He'll be all right after a few days down there in the dark and damp. Hurry, Father Francis. They wait upon us." And he took Xavier's arm, linking him to the rowboat that was to take them out to where the *Coulam* strained at her moorings.

Soon the shore, where stood the Portuguese grandees, sheltered by the bright sunshades and fanned by the immense ostrich-feather fans of their attendant slaves, receded from sight. Francis stood alone on deck, blessing, through the ever-widening distance, the hospital, the fortress, the huts, Micer Paul and Mansilhas, the seamen and soldiers, the sick and the imprisoned—so many of whom he had reconciled to God, so many of whom he had attended —the poor victim of sunstroke, Alvaro, the captive in the dungeon.

"Father Francis," called da Sousa's secretary on his way to his duties in the Admiral's cabin. "Father Francis, I found out the price of that slave. Thirty pieces of silver." And he vanished inside the doorway of the Admiral's quarters.

"Thirty pieces of silver." Xavier repeated the words like a man in a daze. "For neither less nor more Judas sold God our Lord." And, turning towards the land again, his eyes sought in vain to focus the spot where stood a man who had fetched the same price as Christ. Although his eyes failed to find the native, his heart went out to the slave who, standing somewhere on that shore, embodied in himself all the misery of humanity. His hand rose to bless the man who, like Christ, had been betrayed by his brethren, betrayed and sold for thirty pieces of silver.

Later that evening, when the Admiral came to enquire how Father Francis felt, not having seen him about the ship since they weighed anchor, Xavier told him of his horror on hearing of the price of the slave. But da Sousa merely laughed.

"You will have worse sights to witness," he declared; "wait until we come to Goa. There they hold the slave market on the steps of the Cathedral. The slavers lead in the droves of Kaffirs they capture in raids on the African coast and hinterlands, all roped together, manacled and weighted. The top price there is always thirty pieces of silver. The Christians among the buyers count it a crime to pay any higher price than that paid for Our Redeemer."

"Christians!" echoed Francis.

"Yes, indeed. When giving their slaves the lash or the bastinado they count the blows on their rosary beads. But if I were you, I shouldn't take things so much to heart. You will need to save your energy and zeal for pagan India where millions wait, anxious to hear the Word of God," and the Admiral sauntered away. Francis felt uncomfortable. Those last words of da Sousa, "millions wait, anxious to hear the Word of God," seemed uttered with irony. What was the Viceroy hiding? Why was he suddenly sarcastic?

Malindi was a Mohammedan seaport where they put in for fresh water, fruit and poultry. There was a royal palace, with gardens and cocoanut groves, well-built stone houses, tapering minarets, Arab women who went about with veiled faces. Francis got permission to alight to bury a fellow voyager who had died aboard the *Coulam.* The Governor warned him not to make delay, as all would have to be on board for the state visit of the Sultan. The only sight-seeing he did was to hasten up the hill beside the cemetery, nearest of the heights along the shore where, years before, Vasco da Gama had erected beautiful stone crosses. There, in that little Christian oasis among Moslem surroundings, he stayed a while to pray.

He was hardly back when the Sultan of Malindi, a vassal of Portugal, came on board. Francis, who would have preferred to remain quietly in his cabin, was ordered

by the Viceroy to don his legatine robes and come on deck
with him to do the honours.

This petty potentate of Malindi had as gorgeous a
retinue as any European prince. He came in a royal barge,
the muscles of his Kaffir boatmen glistening as they plied
the oars. Trumpeters with horns and heralds with silken
banners preceded the Sultan. As magnificently attired as
any Medici or Borgia or Valois or Hapsburg, he was accompanied by several of his court, all equally splendid.
A learned dervish conversed with Xavier; he was interested in the priest, whom Sousa had introduced to all
as the *Mufti* whom the Pope of the Christians was sending to preach the Gospel of Christ—the prophet of the true
religion, come to enlighten the peoples of the East. The
conversation was conducted through the services of the
Admiral's secretary, who acted as interpreter. The dervish
wished to know how things were with the Christian
Mufti's religion in the West. Rumours had reached him
that all was not well there. Of course, it was the same
story everywhere; there in Malindi, they had seventeen
mosques; at one time all these places of worship would be
full; now, only three were in use, and in those three Allah
found but few to praise him. Could the Christian *Mufti*
explain such decay? The Christian *Mufti* was, however,
not surprised at the decay of practice and belief—in the
case of a religion such as Mohammedanism; what *did*
surprise him was the fact that it had lasted so long—at
which the dervish walked away, greatly insulted.

Afterwards the secretary took Xavier to task for having
spoken in such a fashion; it was unlike Father Francis to
speak so; and in the East it would never do. One needed
the greatest diplomacy in dealing with the natives, with
those in positions of authority. The secretary considered
it his duty to tell the Father such things. The Father hav-

135

ing humbly thanked his mentor and begged his pardon
for having shown such impatience, thereby disedifying
both the dervish and the secretary, the latter asked if
Francis had noted the Saracen with the peculiar garb and
headdress. Yes, Francis had noticed him; he appeared a
very dejected man. Yes, indeed. His garb showed that he
was a teacher of Moslem law; his talk proclaimed him an
eminent scholar. He told the secretary that if Mohammed
did not come on earth again within the next two years to
visit his followers, he—for one—would renounce his religion. Francis thought it extraordinary, the anxiety in
which so many unbelievers lived. It was probably God's
way of warning them of their state and leading them to
enquire after the truth.

The banquet for the Sultan and his party lasted far into
the night and, the following night, the Admiral and his
officers were invited to a reciprocal function in the palace.
Francis did not go. There were many on the *Coulam* who
would need a word from him, a service, a blessing, maybe
a sacrament. It was the Friday before Passion Sunday, and
he hoped for a little time for solitary meditation and
prayer. That Gospel in the Mass he had offered in the
morning—the raising of Lazarus—he wished to read it
again, as also St. Augustine's homily on the same miracle
of Our Lord. For the words of the Antiphon kept ringing
in his mind: "Lazarus our friend sleepeth; let us go, and
awake him out of sleep." It seemed to him that Lazarus
was all India, all the teeming East, and he one of the
disciples travelling—so slowly—to that sepulchre where
already corruption had set in.

The next day the *Coulam* moved north again, not mak-
ing much headway up the African coast. Passiontide,
Holy Week, Easter, had passed before they arrived at
Socotra, a barren island at the entrance to the Gulf of

Aden. There they anchored. De Sousa told Francis that there was a surprise in store for him on this isle; he would find that the inhabitants were Christians—of a sort. Socotra had been evangelised, tradition said, by no less a person than the Apostle Thomas himself, on his way to India; but, the Father would do well to be prepared for a peculiar mixture of many religions; the place had been much in vogue with Arab and Indian traders, for it had rich harvests of dates, and that red gum called Dragon's Blood, and the aromatic resins from which incense was made.

There were little churches, built probably by the Franciscans who had spent four years on the island half a century before, but now they were little different from the other mud hovels all about. At the doorways a revolting smell assailed the nostrils of those who entered.

"Butter—rancid butter," whispered the Viceroy, who had volunteered to show Francis the sights. "They smear it on the walls of the church each day; they rub the crucifixes with it; and they never wipe off the remains of such previous anointings. See, they keep incense burning and candles lit before all the crucifixes; yet I doubt if many of these so-called Christians are baptised. The form of religion or superstition, whichever one would call it, that they practise rules that they must attend here four times daily when the *caciz* chants hymns that neither he nor the congregation understand. Almost all the women are named Mary and all the men Thomas."

During their stay at Socotra, Francis found that the inhabitants were Christian only in name. All the prayers were said in Chaldean, a language not understood by either people or *caciz*. They often repeated a word that resembled the *Alleluia* of the Christian liturgy. They honoured the memory of St. Thomas, but knew nothing of the necessity of baptism. The *caciz* in each village

137

rattled his wooden clappers four times daily, and led the meaningless prayers, the endless repetitions and incensings. They held two Lents each year and fasted not only from meat and milk but also from fish.

With the help of an Ethiopian and an Arab trader, both of whom happened to be in Socotra at that time, and who were delighted with the novelty of seeing the Viceroy and his party, and of acting as interpreters for a Christian priest, Francis conversed with these shepherdless souls. He baptised a large number of children. When the wind changed and da Sousa announced that it was time to leave for India, the people begged that the successor St. Thomas had sent them be allowed to remain with them, and Francis himself, moved at the sight of this harvest—ready for the reaping—asked to be allowed to stay. He would stay until the remainder of the fleet caught up; then he would accompany Micer Paul and Mansilhas to India, having attended to the needs of these poor souls, so full of good will, so lost for want of a teacher. But da Sousa had replied, as previously in Mozambique, "Do not be so greedy to sit to the first feast, lest you lose one that is better."

"Do not forget us," the natives cried from the shore.

"I shall never forget you," Xavier called back to his first neophytes.

And so, sails were hoisted again, and a western wind drove them faster than they anticipated along the last lap of the long journey. On May 6th, the feast of St. John before the Latin Gate, a stretch of green shore hove in view, beyond it a tall range of mountains that thrust through undulating mists a confusion of table-like summits and jagged peaks into a clear sky. Forests and cocoanut groves became discernible as the *Coulam* approached nearer land. Late that night—as the sand-banks could be navigated safely only in daylight—anchor was cast half-way up the river mouth. They had arrived at journey's end—a year and a month after their departure from Lisbon.

Through the night boomed a cannonade, it being the custom for the fleet to salute Goa when entering the harbour. The gunners worked with a will; now that there was no further danger from pirates, it was just as well to dispose of the heavy ammunition. In the hold, the passengers, in the general rejoicing, smashed the crockery; when they returned they would be drinking from vessels of gold and silver, they told one another; cheap Lisbon platters and bowls and mugs were no tableware for nabobs, such as they hoped to be in a little while.

In his cabin, Don Martin Alfonzo da Sousa was penning a rather offensive document to tell Stephen da Gama that it was not the latter's brother, Alvaro, who had fired the salvo. No, nor was it the captain who sailed south for Mozambique that now steered the *Coulam* home. It was Don Martin Alfonzo da Sousa, Admiral of the Royal Portuguese Indies Fleet, ninth Governor of India and the Eastern Realms of Portugal. In his company came Father Francis Xavier, priest of the recently founded Company of Jesus, first Papal Nuncio to the East. Here da Sousa stopped writing and thought concentratedly for a while. Suppose that there had been no plot, that da Gama *had* sent ships south on a mercy mission and that the captain had told the truth; that he had been sent to see what had happened to the fleet, long overdue in Goa. What was it that Alvaro had shouted from the dungeon that day in Mozambique when da Sousa had had to dissemble a little, to pretend to Father Francis that Alvaro was a poor wretch of the garrison, suffering from a touch of the sun, down in a cellar for the dark and damp necessary for recovery? Alvaro had been inclined to think that the priest

139

had prompted the new Viceroy to the course of action he had taken.

Por Dios! That was an idea of Alvaro's: if there were no conspiracy Alvaro could be freed; if he wished to find anyone to vent his spleen on—there would be no one. Da Sousa would convey, subtly, that it was Father Francis who had read between the lines of the letters from da Gama to his brother. Alvaro, by that time, would know that the Nuncio was sacrosanct; to lay a finger on him would mean certain death to Alvaro himself—even the natives in the bazaars would have heard from their fellows who had been on the *Sant Iago* and the *Coulam* of the saintly man who had come to them. No one in Goa would harm Francis, not for a hundred threats of Alvaro.

Meanwhile, there was this letter to da Gama. A superseded Governor, be he a plotter or an innocent, needed taking down a peg or two. It would do no harm to inform His late Excellency that the Viceregal Palace should be vacated and at once. Also, he was to have all accounts and affairs ready for immediate and rigorous inspection by his successor. And every bell in Goa was to be rung at dawn, and the Bishop told to arrange for the Mass of Thanksgiving in the Cathedral. Adding a few similar sentences, da Sousa, with a few lordly flourishes, signed the letter. After rereading it, he affixed his seal, and called his secretary—to whom he had not entrusted the writing of a missive as important as this—bidding him go with the native boys in the longboat that waited nearby and deliver the letter to Stephen da Gama, even if the latter had retired.

In the early morning the air rang with so many bells that Francis could have imagined himself back in Paris or Rome or never-to-be-forgotten Compostela. The ship moved upstream, past embattlements, past shipyards, docks, arsenals; soon all could see a panorama where Los

Reyes—the Viceregal Palace—the fort of Our Lady of the Cape, the Franciscan Fathers' convent, the Diaz fort, the Cathedral and other landmarks were pointed out to the newcomers by those who had been in Goa before.

As they landed, a motley crowd of white, black and brown-skinned figures crowded to meet them. They were rowed ashore in longboats, and servants hastened to the Viceroy and his suite, with parasols to protect them from the already intense heat. Their first call was to the Cathedral, to assist at the Mass of Thanksgiving, the secretary told Francis, who had knelt down immediately upon landing and kissed the ground of the country to which God had sent him. After that, they would all repair to the Viceregal Palace where there would be tubs of warm water and aromatic herbs, with servants to wash down the travellers who, God knew, needed a good wash after that journey. Then there would be some Indian clothes set out and a barber to attend to one's beard and hair. And then a banquet. But first, to pray.

Trumpets blew a fanfare and cannon thundered up and down the river as the new Governor, in full regimentals, spurs and sword clanking, made his triumphant progress from the water's edge to the Cathedral. Behind, the gentlemen of his entourage smiled and nodded to old acquaintances or threatened to run through with rapiers the natives who did not stand back to let the conquerors pass. At the end of the procession a shabby priest toiled along. For him no brown-skinned boy held a parasol. No negro struggled with his trunks, for his luggage was light and he carried it himself. But he found the heat overpowering and now and then stopped to wipe his streaming brow. While the others strode to the front pews of the Cathedral, the Papal Nuncio, unnoticed, forgotten, knelt in the shadows near the door. After Mass, when da Sousa, eager to enter his new home, impatient to witness the discomfiture and the exit of his predecessor, hastened to Los Reyes, Francis waited to meet the Bishop.

John d'Albuquerque, Bishop of Goa, was a Franciscan. At one time he had been confessor to John III of Portugal. He was a holy and serene old man—a man who sought God. But the climate of India was hard to bear and, of late, he found it impossible to cope with the immense See that came under his jurisdiction. India and all the Portuguese settlements in the East were too much for one man, he told Francis. Even Goa was too much nowadays for a Bishop with few priests at his disposal. It was impossible to hold the Christians, let alone attempt to convert the infidels and pagans. He himself had come out with high hopes; but Francis would see for himself, in a few days, what a pass Christianity had come to in India. And he would see that it was not the natives who hindered the spread of the true religion; rather was it the Christians themselves who were followers of Christ in nothing but name. Instead of teaching, by example, the ideals of Christianity to the pagans, what had happened was that the Portuguese and other Europeans had learned the vices of the East and become more pagan than the pagans themselves. But Francis would see. Could he show his credentials? Now? Just a formality; a Bishop had his rules to keep, the same as the next. Francis would have letters from the Bishop of Lisbon, or from his own religious superiors. That good man, Stephen da Gama, had told the Bishop only that morning that a Nuncio had come. The great man had hardly disembarked yet; he had not been present at the Mass of Thanksgiving. The Bishop had had a throne prepared for him in the sanctuary, but he never turned up. He expected that when the Nuncio came it would be the same story with him and the Legate as with

da Gama and the new Governor—"Step down. Hand over
the reins." Had Francis met the Nuncio or could he say
when the Bishop might expect him? Or had the Bishop
better go down to the boat at once, now, before he went
round to the friary for a little breakfast, lest the Nuncio
think him disgruntled or discourteous?

"Forgive me," said Francis, going on his knees and
drawing out the papal briefs; "I am the Nuncio. But, may
it please Your Lordship to keep these documents. I will
use the powers conferred on me only when Your Excellency pleases."

Prepared for the arrival of a Church dignitary such as
those he himself had known during his term as Chaplain
to the King of Portugal, John d'Albuquerque could only
stare in amazement at the quiet-spoken, poorly dressed
man who, kneeling before him, handed him the Pope's
letters. Here was a man of God. Deeply moved, the aging
Bishop embraced the shabbiest Nuncio in the world.

"Your Latin has a *castellano* accent," he observed, for
they had conversed in Latin.

Yes, Francis had spoken *castellano* since his childhood;
he had been born Basque and Basque was his native
tongue, but they of Navarre were educated to speak
Basque and *castellano*. The Bishop was overjoyed, for he
himself was a native of Castile. Had Francis ever been in
Logrono, in Najera, in Burgos? Ah, yes, the road to Compostela! He himself had been on that same road exactly
fifty years before—in 1492, the year of the taking of
Granada, the year Columbus discovered the New World.
They would become good friends. Francis must first of all
accompany him to the friary to breakfast with himself and
the friars—no banquet, of course, nothing fit for a Prince
of the Church, just a little fruit and something to drink
and a good wash-down after his journey, if Francis wished

to avail himself of such poor hospitality as the sons of St. Francis—his patron—could offer. And the *fratres* would all be longing to hear of this new Company, news of which had reached even as far as Goa.

Walking with the Bishop to the convent of the Franciscans, Xavier suddenly realised the strangeness of his new surroundings. His companion drew his attention to the Persians and Turks in caftan and fez; to the Brahmins and other Hindus of high caste, wearing long gowns of yellow linen, their heads turbaned, their feet encased in painted wooden sandals. They never ate meat, never drank wine; the Brahmins avoided all intercourse with lower-caste Hindus; the Yogi, on the other hand, mixed with and tried to convert the pariahs. The Portuguese all lorded it over the natives. This fellow being carried past just now in a gilded palanquin was no *hidalgo*, as Francis might suppose—just an ordinary soldier of the garrison. The practice of the men stationed in Goa from May to October—during the time the monsoon lasted—was for a dozen or more soldiers to rent a house between them, as there were no living quarters in the fort. They put their funds together, bought a few fine suits and engaged some slaves to cook and wait on them. Each day two or three soldiers went out, dressed in the finery and attended by the slaves, aping the punctilious etiquette of their betters, while their comrades waited at home, scantily clad, whiling away the time strumming guitars or chewing betelnut, until their turn to promenade and strut about the city. Why, every Portuguese who came out, even gaolbirds, the moment they set foot in Goa were, according to themselves, men of illustrious birth and noble deeds!

Only the previous year a swineherd named Fernando had worked his way out on one of the ships, and, like all the others, on landing he called himself Don Fernando and proceeded to act the grandee. One day as he was borne through the streets in a litter, slaves, who could be hired for an *anna* a day, attending upon him, he met a compatriot, the son of the very man for whom he had herded swine not so long before.

"*Por Dios!* Fernando, as I live!" cried the gentleman.

For a long time Fernando brazened it out and pretended not to know his master's son. When, finally, he knew he could keep up the deception no longer, he alighted from his litter, saluted the other and begged him to keep his secret. "For, although I was a swineherd in Portugal, in Goa I am Don Fernando," he said.

Portuguese ladies were few and far between in Goa. Their menfolk neither wished them to incur the perils of the voyage to India, nor to come in contact with the sort of life led in the colony. But that lady whom they had just passed, dressed in gold brocade and silk gauze, she was the wife of one of the captains. Those going on foot behind were her slave-girls, negresses and girls from beyond the Ghats Mountains. Her footmen were Eurasian. Her progress to her curtained palanquin was necessarily slow because of the shoes she wore—pattens, with cork soles six inches thick. Ah, Goa was no place to bring a Portuguese wife! But Francis would learn for himself as the days went by.

.   .   .   .   .

It was the September of 1542. In England, the King, aging, obese, began to think of marrying again. It was seven months since he had had Catherine Howard executed for unchastity; she had fooled him, and he had had a hard year showing England and the world how he could rise above such a blow as had been dealt him by that slut still in her teens. Nature never meant him to remain

145

alone, bored for want of an appreciative companion; there
was another Katharine at the court, a widow who had
been twice married, each time to elderly men of substance
and high estate. Henry VIII thought she should again
venture matrimony, with another elderly man of great
wealth and of estate second to none in England. Now that
the Parliament in Dublin had acknowledged him King of
Ireland, and the Scots King, Jamie, and his army had been
well and truly trounced at Solway Moss, King Henry VIII
might well relax and think of love.

François, most Christian King of France, had, in that
same year of 1542, allied himself with no less a person
than the Magnificent Soliman. The *fleur-de-lis* and the
crescent had a sort of pirate's honeymoon up and down
the Mediterranean. And why not? Had they not beaten
the Emperor of Spain at Algiers, with his twelve thousand
and more to their five thousand? True, they had had a
witch on board who predicted that they should win, but,
to level matters, the Emperor had had the great Cortés,
home from Mexico, and Cortés' sons. Alas! Poor Cortés
was experiencing the same reward, the same gratitude
that Christopher Columbus before him had experienced.
More than any man in Spain he had a right to affection,
honour, rewards, gratitude from his country and his
sovereign. As soon as his greatness had exalted him high
above the men of his land and age, so soon did he become
the target for the spiteful, the jealous, the mean-minded.
He was not even consulted in Algiers, he who with a few
hundred men and a few horses had conquered a nation,
given Spain a vast and wealthy new empire—a country
where he, sinner though he was, had raised the cross on
the altars of Aztec gods.

In 1542 Titian was still painting in Madrid, Cellini

shaping beauty out of cold metal in Paris. A Master of
Paris University, Rabelais, was writing his uproarious
satires, of which no educated man could or would plead
ignorance. And yet another Master of Paris University
was on his knees in a corner of Goa hospital, writing to
his Father, Ignatius, and his brothers in the Company at
Rome.

September 20th, 1542

For the love of God, dearest brothers, I beg you to
tell me all the news about every one of the Company.
As I have no hope of ever seeing them again "face to
face" in this world; let me at least see them "in a
glass darkly," in your letters. Do not deny me—all
unworthy though I be—this boon . . . And please
send me diligent instructions as to how I should proceed in my dealings with the pagans and Mahome-
tans to whom I am sent, so that I may see, by God's
grace, and correct any blunders I am making in their
regard.

Here at Goa I lodge at the hospital, where I confess and communicate the sick. As well as that, so
great a number come asking me to hear their confessions that, could I be in ten places at the one time, I
still should not lack penitents.

My mornings go attending to the sick; then I hear
confessions; in the afternoons I used to go to the
prisons, where, after some instruction, the prisoners
made general confessions. Then, in the Church of
Our Lady, near the hospital, I began teaching the
children. As many as three hundred of them come. I
teach them their prayers, the Creed, the ten commandments. The Bishop of Goa asked me to do the
same in the other churches of the city, and results of

this work have been fruitful and a source of great
satisfaction to all.

On Sundays and feasts I preach to all the people.
The Church of Our Lady does not hold all the
natives who crowd in to hear . . . I say Mass for the
lepers every Sunday, hear their confessions and give
them Holy Communion. All of them have approached the sacraments now; since my first sermon
to them they have a great affection for me.

The Governor is now sending me to a land where
I hope to make many Christians. I am taking with me
three clerics from that region; two sub-deacons and
one in minor orders. They speak Portuguese well and
also the language of their own country, Cape Comorin, six hundred miles from Goa. As soon as Micer
Paul and Mansilhas arrive from Mozambique, the
Governor has promised to send them along to join
me.

I am glad to go. All the fatigues of the long sea-
voyage, the weight of others' sins loaded upon one
already weighed down beneath the burden of his
own, the sojourn among the pagans, the broiling sun
—all these, borne for God, afford great consolations,
are the fabric of celestial joys . . . What happiness
equals that of dying a little every day, breaking our
wills to seek and find not *what is ours but that which
is Christ's* . . .

By the merits and prayers of holy Church and all
her living members, you included, may Jesus Christ
Our Lord deign to make use of me, wicked servant
though I be, to cast the seed of His Gospel on this
infidel soil. Thus will men of great capacity be put
to shame while the pusillanimous will take courage,
seeing to what use God can put even dust and ashes
like me. Eye-witness of the lack of workers here,
with what joy would I not serve those who would

elect to come and labour in this vineyard of the Lord!

I conclude, praying God in His Infinite Mercy, to re-unite us one day in heaven and to grant us, in this present life, the grace and strength to conform ourselves in all things to His divine will.

Your useless brother in Jesus Christ,
Francisco

THE sea voyage down the six hundred miles of barren, sun-scorched coast that lay between Goa and Cape Comorin, the southernmost tip of India, was tedious—especially for travellers eager to reach the pearl fisheries. Once a year the Royal Fleet sailed south to collect the pearl tribute, the tax payable by the poor Paravas who peopled the Cape area, to the Portuguese, their rescuers from the Moslems. For long years the Portuguese had preyed upon the pearl fishers, exploiting their ignorance of the value of their catch to the western world, shamefully underpaying the divers, finally resorting to wholesale robbery with violence. The Portuguese, who had succeeded in wresting the pearl fisheries from Mahometan control at a time when the mild fisher-folk had suffered more than usual injustice and insult, took these low-caste Indians under the protection of the flag of Portugal. But soon the poor Paravas found that they had merely exchanged one set of rapacious oppressors for another. Whenever the Fleet called, their hard-won harvests were taken away—a fair levy, their new masters said, for the protection afforded them from the greedy Moslems.

The officials who made the yearly journey to collect and record the gleaming tribute, the mariners who

150

manned the ships, the soldiers and gunners who sailed to
fight any pirates who might attempt to capture the precious cargo on the homeward voyage—all went eagerly to
Cape Comorin. Any fellow with half his wits about him
could bring home sufficient pearls to ensure him a tidy
fortune; and the Paravas were easy game: a fool could
hoodwink them as a coward could frighten them. In the
September of 1542, the most eager of all who sailed for
the fisheries was Francis Xavier. He went seeking neither
pearls nor fortune; he sought only souls. Before the fleet
left Goa, da Sousa told Xavier that he himself had brought
some Franciscans to Cochin, one of the coastal towns, some
years previously, and no less than twenty thousand of the
Paravas had been baptised. But d'Albuquerque, Bishop of
Goa, himself a Franciscan, shook his head when Francis
questioned him about this. It was all very well, he said,
for those infants who had died still retaining their baptismal innocence. But the Franciscans had not understood
the various Tamil dialects of the fisher peoples, and the
latter had no idea of what the Fathers had meant by
baptism. He had no doubt but that the Paravas crowded
to the baptismal ceremonies; neither did he doubt but
that they at once proceeded from the font to their
temples, going through their usual prostrations before
Siva, Kali, the elephant-headed Ganesha, the ape, the lion
and the other gods. To those poor creatures Christianity
meant nothing more than a protection against the Moslems—though, indeed, from what the Bishop heard, the
invaders that swept in upon Cape Comorin flying the
crescent had been no worse than those who now went
flying the cross. In the Goa College there were several
students who spoke Tamil; Francis could count on getting
them as soon as they were ordained. At the moment, the
best the Bishop could do was to give him a sub-deacon

and two catechists from the seminary. When Micer Paul and Mansilhas arrived from Mozambique later on, the Governor had promised to find some way of sending them, too, to the pearl fisheries.

The Bishop hoped Father Francis would, at least, get a new *loba;* the one he was wearing might have been black in Lisbon, Rome or Paris, but the Indian sun had turned it green, a colour not at all suitable for a religious: and its seams were all coming apart. As for shoes, he had heard that there was a good shoemaker lost in Francis; that he was adept at sewing soles and uppers together. Such accomplishments might well come in useful at the fisheries, a barren, torrid region where the sun was, if one could imagine it possible, harder to bear than in Goa.

The Bishop was party to the stratagem by which Francis was sent to Cape Comorin in a new silk *loba.* The night before he sailed, a hospital servant was instructed to remove the ancient, disreputable-looking garment from its peg while the Father snatched a little sleep, lying on a rush mat beside the patients in greatest pain. In the morning, wakened, as usual, by the moans of the suffering, Francis flung on his *loba* and hurried to attend the sick. There was a very early Mass, as the fleet was going out with the morning tide, and afterwards only time for Father Francis to get a leathern umbrella, a necessary protection against the sun, some pieces of leather to patch his already much-mended shoes, the satchel with his breviary, Missal, vestments and sacred vessels; several friends accompanied him to the Bishop's house for a farewell blessing.

The Bishop smiled at the sight of his friend's new *loba.* He thanked Francis for having done him the honour of coming in such finery to bid him farewell. It was a welcome change from the discoloured black of yesterday.

152

Looking down at himself, Francis discovered that he wore a *loba* of good, rich silk. He must have taken the wrong robe when rising in the hospital—he would have to hurry back there and get his own and return this to the owner. Whereupon everyone laughed, and the Bishop told of the trick that had been played; it was no use going back to fetch the old cassock for it was no longer there. Francis wondered that a fine *loba* looking for a master in the dark could not have found its way to a more deserving wearer. Then, having knelt for the Bishop's blessing, he hurried to join the young Tamil-speaking students who were already on their way to where the ships waited. A crowd waited to see him off. Rich and poor, Portuguese and Indian, Moslem, Hindu and Christian, fire-dancers and sword-players, aged slaves and young nautch girls, soldiers of the garrison and children of the streets—all wanted the blessing of the *sadhu*, the holy man whose five months' work in Goa had made him known to all.

Picking his way through the crowds at the landing-place, he at last succeeded in boarding the vessel and soon the great port was left behind. As he walked up and down the decks, he tried to assort his impressions of Golden Goa. In the beginning he had thought it a fine city with many and beautiful churches, with a spacious hospital—the Royal Hospital—such as Lisbon or Rome could not show, and a separate Lazar-house; with pleasant gardens, buildings and squares; with many Catholics. But later he had seen that slave market which he had heard about before he came to India at all. One came upon it in the square where stood the Cathedral, the Senate and the Offices of the Inquisition. Almost every day there was a market, where the traders paraded their wares, male and female, drawing attention to their points of physique, listing their skill in the various arts and crafts. Francis had been taken aback the first morning he happened to cross the square while the market was in progress to find that the Portuguese gentlemen who had been at Mass in the Cathedral an hour before were the bidders, very few Brahmins and wealthy Indians being there. Later he was to learn more about the trade in human beings. Some of the girl slaves came from the Indian provinces, captured in a raid by neighbouring tribes, or by the more venturesome of the Moslem slave dealers. Most of them could do fine needle-work, weave tapestry, make lace, embroider; some could play on the stringed instruments that made music weird to Western ears; all could cook, dye, garden, make sweet-meats and preserves. They averaged about thirty shillings each. When they became the possession of a Portuguese they had to work to help to support their owners, to cultivate his gardens, and sell the produce in the bazaars; occasionally the better-favoured of those Indian girls became his concubines, but usually it was the negresses imported from Africa who were sold for this purpose—once in a while a chalk-faced Chinese girl, or a tiny Japanese, or a Burmese dancing girl. Hardly had Father Francis recovered from seeing his fellow Christians haggle over slave girls when he learned that some of the Portuguese had become wealthy through hiring out these slaves as prostitutes—indeed some found it so rewarding to organise a few slave-raids and sell in Goa market, that they were able to return to Portugal, rich men, a few months after they had landed in India. Of all the eastern customs the Portuguese had adopted, the one most detrimental to themselves was the keeping of slaves. They, the descendants of the intrepid navigators of the West, idled, luxuriated, became effeminate, decadent and vicious. For them Golden Goa had become the land of the lotus-eaters. Though many had hearkened when Francis

preached, there were some who were too sunken in the
sensuous ease of their new existence to heed this Ulysses
who would waken and urge onward their stupefied souls.
As he looked back towards Goa, now shimmering under
the sunlight, Francis sighed, remembering the ills of that
city. He had left enemies behind, like the Portuguese
merchant who, as the Bishop had told Francis, had written the following to the court at Lisbon:

> Many high folk think it was imprudent to send
> such a man as Xavier, whose manner of life causes
> scandal, to Goa. They say the white people will be
> despised by the natives because of him, for only if
> they see us as splendid and magnificent conquerors
> will we be able to impress upon them that we are a
> superior race.

Yes, he had caused no small scandal to the Portuguese
who lived easy while he, the Papal Legate, washed the
sores of lepers, tended the sick, went into the fetid dungeons of the Al Jabir and the Sala das Bragas prisons, to
pray with and comfort the galley slaves. He had vastly
annoyed those whose motto while in the East was "the
service of God and our own advantage," by telling them
that it was little use having a motto the beginning of
which was mocked while the remainder was adhered to
too closely. In the hospital, as in no other house in Goa,
he had been enabled to meet every class—to learn for himself something of the problems of that East the tassel of
whose many-coloured silk shawl Goa was. In the hospital
men were ready to talk about themselves, their lives, their
surroundings. And Francis had sat and listened. He listened to the soldiers unconsciously revealing their brutality, to the officials and adventurers revealing their
covetousness, to the idol worshippers deep in superstition,

to the merchants engrossed in their business deals, to the turban dyers and scimitar makers, to the poor slaves whose miseries needed no tongue, whose sufferings often were the silent accusers of the "Christian" masters.

Often Francis had found these unfortunates thrown out to die by the roadside, victims of brutality, viciousness, neglect; he himself had carried them on his back to the hospital; with his own hands he bound up their wounds—of body and spirit—pouring in oil and wine. As he sat on a raffia mat beside the sick in the hospital cots, all that India he had come to convert seemed to speak in the sighs of the slaves; in their sad eyes he read the unuttered reproach of the oppressed. But, by degrees, when they came to know him, he learned from them many things, both about India and about the Portuguese in Goa. He knew the grandees and soldiers who kept harems, the profiteers, the pimps who lived off the earnings of native women; he knew the cruel, the usurers, the gluttons.

It was a help when he visited the houses afterwards; knowing a man's interests, knowing how a man had appeared to his slave, decided one's avenue of approach. Ignatius had been wont to say, when talking of his dealings with men, "I go in at their door, but I see they come out at mine." Francis had done as his Father in God, so far away in Rome, had done. On the verandah of the merchant he discussed the state of business, the possibilities of making more money. He surprised the money lenders by his turn for mathematics, his calculations as rapid and accurate as their own. In the bazaars he spoke to the slaves who had served his meal the previous evening, complimenting them on their cooking, enquiring as to how they were treated. The mariners and sea captains were amazed at his knowledge of astronomy, his interest in matters connected with the sea. Soldiers found that he understood military problems. When, patiently and gently, he had become the friend of all, then, and not till then, he began to show them *his* door—the way he wished them to take on their departure from him. The merchant was made to see how little it profited a man to gain the whole world if, in the end, he lost his soul. The usurer and the slave trader were shown that there were less ignoble and equally remunerative livelihoods. The slaves were taught about the real Christ, whom their masters resembled so little. The sailors and the soldiers, surprised in their gaming and drinking by the visit of Father Francis, were told that while God did not expect men of their calling to live like religious, God expected Christians to live Christian lives. The Portuguese who lived with native women were either encouraged to legalise the union or to cut asunder the bonds—however alluring—that bound them.

Yes, that was Goa, the Goa he had known. Torturing him was the thought of the little he had been able to do for the Indians; he had come to the East to preach to them and already five precious months had gone by mostly in trying to bring back the lost sheep of the Christian fold. However, the little he had learned in Goa would help him on this new mission.

A spate of cursing and violent oaths roused him now from his pacing up and down the deck. It was a sailor, who, having staked all he had on the dice games being played astern, had lost his last coin, lost his dagger stolen from the idol in the temple outside Goa, and the gold earrings his Eurasian girl had given him. Now that he had nothing left to wager, his companions had put him out of the dicing ring. Flinging curses back at his erstwhile friends, he walked backwards round the masts and into Xavier's arms. A hotter curse than any died in his throat as he found himself face-to-face with *el Santo*, with "the heavenly Pilgrim," as the people in the Goa bazaars were calling Father Francis. He had to blurt out the tale of his misfortunes—money, dagger, earrings—all lost, irretrievably lost, since his fellows would not allow him that throw of the dice which might mean the turn of his luck.

Francis heard him through. He would go the gambler's road if the gambler would come back his way. He would loan the three *annas* and two Portuguese *reales* in his pocket, if the gambler would come back afterwards and tell how it went with him. He waited and prayed, hoping that the gambler would not be too long. He was anxious to get down to those poor Malabars sweating in the galleys, as he thought he recognised one or two he had known in the prisons of Goa. Before long, the sailor was back, his earrings in place again, his dagger stuck in his belt, his money rattling in his pockets—the money Francis lent him in his hand ready to return. "Keep it," the priest said, when he had heard the story of how the gambler's luck had turned. "Now, since you've told me so much about yourself—your swearing and cursing, your robbery of the temple dagger, your living with the Eurasian woman— what's to stop you from making your confession? You have made it to me. What about making it to God? Let me help you." And the sailor, his earrings glinting in the sunlight, made his peace with God. To prove his repentance he flung the dagger into the sea before his confessor had time to decide the problems in ethics involved. His penance? That was all right, Father Francis would do his penance for him, if he would tell the captain that the Father would like a little fruit and fetch it to where Francis would await him, down among the galley slaves. Yes, Father Francis would pray for him.

· · · · ·

Don Francisco

The pearl fishing season began in March and lasted for about two moons, the captain told Xavier. The *catamarans* —rafts made of three logs lashed together—were loaded with divers, with a rower to paddle the crazy craft through the surf. A whole fleet of them, sometimes fifty or seventy, set out for the oyster banks; they had to leave the coasts at midnight to reach the shoals by sunrise. When they reached the banks the diving commenced. The divers worked in pairs, one going down while the other worked the signal ropes. Usually the men worked the ropes while the boys dived. A "sink stone" was let down at the end of the rope, and when the diver was coming up, the man above pulled up the "sink stone" first, then the oyster crate, and finally the diver himself. Good divers could stay underneath for the space of three *Paters* and *Aves*. They worked naked, wearing only a sort of girdle, on which they supported their baskets while filling them with oysters. They got a grip with their toes on seagrass, and such plants and wreckage as were on the ocean floor. They carried ironwood spikes to beat off sharks, and a shark-charmer went out on every *catamaran* to lure the sharks away from the diving beds. Yes, it was a hard and exhausting life . . . The Paravas were short-lived men.

Occasionally Xavier's ship sailed close to the shore and sailors pointed out various sights: cattle, treading a ramp to raise well-water for the irrigation of the parched fields on the narrow strip of land between the base of the Western Ghats and the coasts; a jungle hermitage, where—if there were time to land—one could be sure of finding some *sadhu*, or holy man, squatting outside the little temple, eating a few berries now and then, swaying to and fro as he played hymns on his *sitar*, or murmured his invocations, calling mournfully upon Siva or Siva's consort, Kali—the "fish-eyed goddess." It was a pity Francis

159

could not have journeyed to Mysore the previous year, when the great pagan festival, held every fifteen years in Stravana Belgola, took place. One climbed a hill and then mounted a further five hundred steps hewn out of an immense boulder, and at the top stood the stone figure of Gomata, the saint the Jains worshipped. The statue was seventy feet high, and for weeks before the festival Jains from all over India came there on pilgrimage. A huge scaffolding was erected about the stone figure and a thousand priests climbed to anoint Gomata with the honey, sandalwood oil and butter brought by the pilgrims. Others made offerings of sugar, flowers, fruit and milk, which they laid reverently at the feet of this stone colossus.

One day the soldiers travelling with the fleet were wildly excited to see a long line of war elephants lumbering over a distant hillside, as some rajah went to do battle with a neighbouring prince. On the huge beasts' backs were the castles in which rode the captains and the standard bearers and many armed men. The trumpeting of these ferocious elephants was a fearsome sound to hear, the soldiers had been told. They were trained for war, wielding mighty swords with their trunks, tossing and mangling men before they trampled them underfoot; and after a victory their mahouts fed them a mash to which the remains of the slaughtered was added. *Por Dios!* What a benighted, uncivilised land—for all the magnificent cities and palaces and temples! One would not envy Father Francis, going to remain alone among these heathens, with the nearest Portuguese outpost several days' journey away.

At last they arrived in Cape Comorin, and made their way across the burning sand dunes, past the palm-roofed huts of the lean, dark-skinned fisher-people, to Tuticorin, the main town in that area. In Tuticorin Francis found a number of heathen temples, with coloured idols; on every street corner stood altars where stone snake-gods and ape-gods stared sightlessly at the chattering monkeys that swung in the fan palms overhead. In the evenings the Paravas, baptised and unbaptised alike, crowded the temples and street shrines, offering fishes to the fire-spirits that danced on the incoming waves.

On the first morning after his arrival, Francis offered Mass in a little reed hut on the shore. All those who had travelled in the fleet gathered around to form his congregation and the Paravas, curious and delighted, crowded close. The next three days were spent by the Portuguese in looking after the pearl tribute and in seeing how they might best enrich themselves. Francis, during these three days, made the dispiriting discovery that the young seminarians he had brought from Goa to act as his mouthpieces had been taken to Goa so young that they had almost forgotten their native Tamil except for the *Pater,* the *Ave,* and the *Credo,* and a few of the better-known Catholic prayers, and were of little use as interpreters. The former Master of Beauvais bent his whole mind, for those three days, to mastering and memorising prayers and some elementary Tamil phrases; he had the district searched for a few natives, more intelligent than the others, who had picked up a smattering of Portuguese; it was a poor and short preparation for the preaching of the gospel, but there was neither time nor opportunity for anything more.

On the third evening, as the fleet sailed away, Francis, standing upon this unknown shore, surrounded by a multitude speaking a strange language, suddenly felt an awful sense of isolation. For the first time in his life he felt utterly alone, a scholar among an illiterate people, a Christian among pagan tribes, a European in the East, almost as one deaf and dumb amid this babel of strange sounds. He was faced with an impossible task. What, he asked himself, could one man, with his poor human limitations, hope to achieve when hell and all the powers of darkness seemed arrayed against him? One man or a hundred men or a thousand—nothing. But one man, aided by God, a great deal.

Would he now, he asked himself, refuse to carry the Indian—that Indian he had so often borne in his dreams, the Indian whom God Himself had placed upon his shoulders? And his heart answered, "Never! I will bear him to the Gate of Heaven, to the *Portico de la Gloria,* to the very feet of God." He smiled as he remembered how Ignatius had chosen Bobadilla for this mission to the East; and—seemingly by accident—God had intervened and sent him, Xavier, instead. He was on this lonely shore by the will of God. He was at this fishery coast to do the will of God . . . "Whosoever shall do the will of My Father that is in heaven, he is My brother and sister and mother . . ."

Turning from the shore, he did not go to the little dwelling the sailors had made for himself and the seminarians; he returned to the palm-roofed Mass hut by the shore. He smiled as he remembered how, only that morning, the gambling sailor had come upon him, in the thorn thicket behind the hut, as Francis was flogging himself with his discipline. "This is the penance I should have got," the sailor cried, remembering his confession of the outward voyage; and, snatching the discipline, had rained blows on his own shoulders until Francis had had to beg him to desist. Before he had boarded his ship, he had told his story to the captain who took it upon himself to warn the Father that the Orientals would set little store by the penances practised by the Europeans: their own holy men practised mortifications and pains; there were *sadhus* and *fakirs* who could bear pains and sufferings intolerable to a Christian, and who could, strange to relate, work wonders to all seeming miraculous. The captain told Father Francis this so that he might not wear out his precious strength in fastings and mortifications; his flesh would get all the scourging it could bear from the sun by day and the mosquitoes by night; and in any case, his greatest macerations would not impress the pagans—who, not understanding that Christians undertook such penances for love of Our Lord, would see their own ascetics stoically enduring far greater suffering, for what reason the captain could not say. He just wished to tell Father Francis this before they left. They did not want to return next year and find him gone to heaven, the worn sickle of his body laid down forever beside his unreaped harvest.

At one minute it was daylight, the next, night. No long evenings, no slow sunsets as they had known in the West. Outside the Mass hut there was silence, broken only by the swish of the waves on the shingle, and afar off, somewhere in the hills, the thudding of the temple drums, the singsong of the Paravas gathered about their shrines. As in the cave in Parma on those other evenings when he was preparing himself in prayer and solitude for his ordination, the devil tempted him. "Alone," the tempter jeered. "Far from friends. Far from help. Unable even to make yourself understood. Alone—and oppressed with loneliness—and no help to be found on earth or in that mirage called heaven." From overwhelming melancholy he found himself plunged in terror, as the citadel of his faith, his trust in God, withstood these tremendous assaults. Steadying himself to meet the renewed onsets of a temptation that, because it was new and unexpected, made heavy demands on him, he asked himself how he would counsel another who asked him how one should act if faced with the urge to utter panic that such temptations against faith bring upon the soul. He would tell such a man to beseech God to console and help him, to deign to use him in His holy service. Kneeling, he prayed, long and vehemently, for help. Finally, he rose, and sang, just as they had been used to singing, in the Xavier *abadía*, each evening:

> Hail, Holy Queen, Mother of Mercy,
> Our life, our sweetness and our hope, Hail!
> To thee do we cry, poor banished children of Eve,
> To thee do we send up our sighs,
> Mourning and weeping in this vale of tears.
> Therefore, Most Gracious Advocate, O turn
> Thine eyes of mercy towards us;
> And after this, our exile,
> Show unto us the blessed fruit of thy womb,
> Jesus.
> O clement,
> O loving,
> O sweet Virgin Mary.

Then he lay down on the sand, hoping to sleep. But it was only too true what the captain had said about the mosquitoes. Here was a western skin, easily stabbed, unlike the tough, leather-like skins of the fisher-people! Each time he drooped his head in sleep, several of the vigilant insects zoomed through the darkness and gorged themselves with European blood. In vain he beat them off, smarting as he felt the blains caused by their bites rising on his face, neck and shoulders. At last, too weary to fight any longer, he lay down and slept. And the Paravas, creeping silently at midnight to their little rafts with the swallow-tailed sails, peeped in at this stranger, this holy man from a

164

faraway land who, the Portuguese had told them, had come to bring them strange tidings of good news.

. . . . .

In January, 1544, Francis Xavier, still at the pearl fisheries, began to write a letter:

> To the Reverend Father Ignatius, General of the Society, at Rome.
>
> May the grace and charity of Our Lord always help and favour us, Amen. I set out with three native students of Goa seminary, and, on arrival here, we visited some villages the inhabitants of which, eight years ago, received baptism. As no Portuguese reside in this region, which is very sterile and poor, the faithful, without priests, know nothing more than that they were baptised. Since we came, I have been busy baptising all infants born since then; some of these are so young as not to know left hand from right; others, the older ones, give me no peace begging me to teach them some prayer. They give me no time to say my office, nor yet to eat; such importunity has made me realise the meaning of the words "of such is the kingdom of God." Besides the Sign of the Cross I have taught them the *Credo, Pater* and *Ave.* They are quite intelligent and if they had anyone to instruct them would make good Christians.

. . . . .

No need to tell the brethren of that first long year, alone, at the pearl fisheries. No need to mention the difficulties he had encountered, the monotonous messes of rice, flavoured with pepper, the broiling sun, the mosquito-ridden nights, the snakes and bats and monkeys, the dreadful labour of mastering a language where the slightest inflection of voice or change in the stressing of a syllable gave words a meaning far different from that intended. He would, and did, tell them of how God had come mightily to his aid, the night the woman in the unfriendly king's territory had lain dying in childbirth. When spells and incantations and sacrifices to Kali had failed, when the woman had been pronounced beyond aid by the spell-casters and midwives, when even the mourning rites had begun, a short instruction, baptism and the blessing of the Church had resulted in the woman's safe delivery; and all that household and neighbourhood, hearing of the miracle, had asked for instruction in the Christian faith and had since been baptised.

But he would tell Ignatius and the Company that now he was no longer alone. He could continue telling of his work since Mansilhas had arrived.

> Micer Paul was kept in Goa by the Bishop to take charge of the Holy Faith College there. Mansilhas is here with me. We go among the natives, but they do not understand me well, nor I them—their language being Tamil, mine Basque. With the help of the more intelligent natives I succeeded in translating the prayers into Tamil, also the commandments. When I knew them by heart myself, my practice was to go through the place with a little bell in my hand, gathering all I could, both children and adults; twice daily I got them together thus and taught them prayers. The children taught their parents and all at home, and also their neighbours . . .

As Ignatius would doubtless be sending the Fathers in Rome to this and other missionary regions, he penned several pages telling of the simple, direct method he had evolved for catechising.

I have received only one letter from you, dated February 1542. God alone knows the joy it gave me. It arrived here only two months ago, some twenty months after you had penned it! The vessel bearing the post had, like ours in 1541, to winter in Mozambique.

Such numbers become Christians that often my hands are numb at the end of a day from the fatigue of baptising. And sometimes I lose my voice from the constant repetition of the *Credo* and other prayers and instruction . . .

Again, thinking that an explanation of methods he had found useful would be of use to future missionaries, he spent a long while writing of how he utilised the enthusiastic young people and children in the instruction of the sick.

How many, in these countries, fail to become Christians, simply for the lack of a teacher of the Christian faith! Often I think of running throughout the universities of Europe, and principally Paris and the Sorbonne, there to shout at the top of my voice, like one who had lost his senses—to tell those men whose learning is greater than their wish to put their knowledge to good use, how many souls, through their negligence, must lose Heaven and end up in hell. If all who, with so much labour, study letters, would pause to consider the account they must one day render God concerning the talents entrusted to them, I am sure that they would come to say: "Here I am, Lord. Send me where Thou pleasest, even to India." How much happier and safer they would be, eventually, when facing that dreadful hour from which no man can escape. Then, with the faithful servant of the Gospel they could say: "Lord, five

talents Thou gavest me; behold five others I have
gained . . ."

I will write to our good Doctor Picard and also to
our Maître, Cornet, to show them how many millions
and millions of Gentiles could be converted if we had
workers, hoping that they too will look for and direct
here men who are not seekers of themselves but of
Christ.

There are five hundred students in the College at
Goa where Micer Paul is . . .

It took another closely written page to tell Ignatius all
about Goa College—the nursery, he hoped, of a future
native priesthood.

He was not able to finish that letter until four months
later. In the interval he had visited some Brahmins in one
of their monasteries, which adjoined a pagoda near a
Christian village. He had had one Brahmin convert, a
young Nicodemus-like man, who came to Francis secretly
by night. And he had had hopes when he found himself
in the grave assembly of white-robed priests; they had
spoken suavely and he had answered their questions on
his religion. Taking pen and paper again, he wrote at
length the various questions of these men—questions
which would show Ignatius, Favre, Salmeron and the
others how, in the East, men reasoned in a different way
from in the West; minds approached problems from angles
unthought of in Paris or other universities of Europe . . .

How glad I was to hear that the Vicar of Christ
approved of our Rule and way of life, that Rule
which God manifested to Ignatius, His servant and
our Father.

Pray that God who has separated us for the good
of Christianity will one day reunite us in Heaven.

For this intention invoke the prayers of those babes whom I baptised with my own hands in this land and whom God saw fit to call to His eternal mansions before they lost the robe of innocence with which I was privileged to clothe their souls. There must be, as I reckon, at least a thousand of them now; I often pray to these little saints to ask God that we, while exiled in this life, may know His will and accomplish it completely and in the manner that He desires.

At Cochin, January 1544.

Your most affectionate brother in Jesus Christ,

Francisco

CHAPTER 9

MANSILHAS needed almost as much care as the Christians and the catechumens. Francis, who had journeyed to Goa at the end of 1543 to fetch the young man from there to the mission fields at Cape Comorin, could not keep count of all the letters he had had to write to him. Micer Paul had said that there was little use keeping Mansilhas in the College; he was so slow and dull-witted that it was doubtful if he could ever be ordained; he seemed to make no headway in Latin, though, strange to relate, he had picked up a little Tamil from the Malabar students in Holy Faith College. A little Tamil would go a long way at the fisheries, Francis had replied; and he immediately arranged to take Mansilhas back there with him. Micer Paul, with pardonable pride, showed his superior through the College. It never seemed to dawn on him that Father Francis, a Master of Paris University, was the ideal person to have charge of the youths of the seminary, all of whom were fairly well grounded in Latin by this time. It never occurred to the Papal Legate that he was, as some of the Franciscans in Goa said, wasting his intellect and learning in the mission to the benighted fishers of Cape Comorin. Mansilhas could cope with the work there, people said. Francis had not quite understood what they meant by that remark—not at the time; but after Mansilhas had been several months at the fisheries he understood quite well.

He found himself unable to spare time to write any letters save those to his simple, good, but exceedingly stupid, helper. The last letter he had sent to anyone other than Mansilhas was the one he had written to the Queen of Portugal, Catalina of Castile, granddaughter of the great Isabel *la Católica*. Having heard that, of the revenues accruing to Portugal from the pearl fisheries, four hundred crowns a year went to the Queen as her Slipper allowance, he wrote to her, asking her to make over this money to a fund with which he hoped to pay catechists in the mission field. He assured her that such an act of charity would provide her with slippers far more ornamental and valuable than any she could buy—the prayers offered for her by the converts among the pearl fishers, the souls saved, would make fine slippers for climbing the stairway to Heaven's banquet hall.

For the remainder of 1544 he wrote Mansilhas almost thirty letters—an average of three a month. It was necessary to look to the young man's own spiritual state before anything else; he was one of the Company—not yet ordained, not yet fully formed—and Francis felt himself responsible for this son of Ignatius, writing him regularly regarding his soul as he felt Ignatius himself would have written.

> Make up your mind that among the Paravas you are suffering your Purgatory, that God is allowing you, here and now, to pay the penalty of your faults. It is a great grace to be able, while still in this life to expiate one's sins and at the same time gain merit for Heaven . . .
>
> Above all, practise patience and charity, making yourself known by your labours on behalf of the

171

people, because, if they come to love you, you will
be able to do much for them. Learn to bear patiently
with their weaknesses . . .

Alas! Patience was not Mansilhas' strong point!

Recollect, that if they are not as good as you wish
they were, they will become so, one day. Be content,
as I am, with what you can do . . .

. . . When you feel it beyond you to fulfil all your
duties, do the best you can and rest consoled, thank-
ing God who has placed you in circumstances where,
even if you wanted leisure, you could never have it,
owing to your duties in His service . . .

. . . It is better that you should have no fixed
home but always be on the move, in one direction or
another. That was my practice when I was in that
area where you are now, and that is how I manage
here, except at the moment, when I find myself without an interpreter . . . Be to these Paravas like a
good father with naughty children. Do not let the evil
you see on all sides discourage you. Do not yield to
despair—you are doing more than you think . . .

Once or twice, when discouragement and disillusionment had been almost too much for Francis himself, he
had been glad to have Mansilhas within writing distance,
and wrote of his troubles to the younger man.

How disturbed I have been to hear that the Portuguese have seized and carried away a servant of the
Rajah of Travancore. If this is true, I must abandon
my plan of going to visit this Rajah, with whom I had
hoped to treat on matters concerning the kingdom of
God . . . When I hear how our Christians are perse-
cuted and oppressed by both the heathen and the

Portuguese, my heart is wounded to the core. It racks me with pain when each succeeding day brings news of fresh outrages committed against these babes in the faith by those who—their elder brothers in the same faith—should indulgently cherish and protect them. This grief is a pain forever gnawing at my heart. Only three days ago I got word of the seizure and ravishing of several native slave girls by the Portuguese stationed at Punical . . . I have written to Church and State authorities, urging that immediate action be taken against these miscreants and that their prey be rescued from them. I am strongly minded to embark on a *dhow* or even a *catamaran* and go to Ethiopia, Prester John's country, where there are no Europeans to oppose one and to pull down as fast as one builds up . . .

. . . I have not been so well. For four or five days I was laid low with fever, being bled twice . . .

. . . For eight days I have been on the sea—and you know what it is to be on a *dhow* or a rowboat in the surf in monsoon weather . . . Only God our Lord knows what I have suffered on this voyage . . . May we get more rest in Heaven than we do at the pearl fisheries! . . .

When I see so many evils that I am powerless to remedy, it makes me wish that I could die a martyr for the faith, sooner than have to live a witness to such things . . .

Then there were situations with which Mansilhas could not cope, when he would send a swift runner with orders to wait for the answer of Father Francis. Such an occasion was when word was sent that the women of Punical had gone on a drinking spree—rendering themselves incapable through overindulgence in *arrack,* a fermented palm-juice. Francis had sent back a beadle with the runner to

enforce law and order. Chastity was a problem at any
time for the women of these regions; *arrack* drinking
could not be allowed to add to their difficulties. At another time Mansilhas had to be warned not to put too
much confidence in the Paravas.

> Do not be too confident that they will do as you
> tell them without supervision. Only too well I know
> their apathy and hopeless stupidity. As there are
> rumours that the Badagas are about to raid these
> coasts you must make yourself responsible for your
> people's safety, since they cannot be relied upon to
> take measures for their own protection . . .

It was on the Saturday of the octave of Corpus Christi
in 1544 that disaster struck at the little Christian communities dotted all along the pearl fishing coast. The
Badagas, troops of the Emperor Sadâ Siva, ruler of
Vijayanagar, descended upon the Paravas, plundering
each village as they came to it, slaughtering such inhabitants as had not fled to inaccessible rocky caves and to
islets off the coast. A messenger despatched at speed to
Father Francis met him travelling on foot to a village
where he hoped to offer Sunday Mass. Would he come
to the aid of his converts? Although exhausted after his
day's journey, he set off again for the south, his guide
pointing out to him as they hurried along the flames
shooting into the skies now in one region, now in another,
as the palm-roofed huts of native villages were set on fire.

For the next six weeks Francis Xavier had to bear the
trial of seeing the work to which he had devoted such
time, thought and labour, practically wiped out. He wrote
to Mansilhas on August 1st:

> . . . I walked down-coast to the Cape—after fail-

ing to make any headway by sea, where the monsoons blew in our teeth for a full week—and I visited
the unhappy Christian survivors of the invasion by
the Badagas. Such misery I have never witnessed.
The fields are littered with the dying and the mutilated corpses of many of our converts. On all sides
the wounded cry for attention and relief; aged men,
spent with hunger, crawl along, searching in vain
for food and shelter; mothers give birth to their children on the public roads . . . If you saw the sights
I daily witness, your heart would be wrung. I have
taken all I can to Manaper . . .

The Portuguese commandant in charge of one of the
major garrisons at Cape Comorin welcomed the invasion
as an occasion for profit making and did a brisk business
selling horses to the Badagas. Thinking that these invaders from the hill country were as simple as the Paravas,
he tried a little double-dealing on them, and discovered,
too late, that they were as wily as himself. In their fury at
his attempt to trick them, they burned his house and ship
and he was reported to be starving on the island where
he had taken refuge. Although this man had been a violent enemy of Francis, who had more than once up-
braided him for his cruelty to the Christians, Xavier could
not allow him to remain in misery. As he knew that he
himself would be unacceptable to the commandant—who
had written him abusive letters accusing him of having
instigated the Badagas to mistreat him as they had done—
Mansilhas was ordered to proceed at once to the aid of
the marooned man. "Go, before it is too late, for his plight
calls upon us to show mercy and charity." Even this kindness did not decrease the enmity felt by the commandant
for Xavier. No sooner had he recovered from his experiences at the hands of the Badagas than he resumed

his former treatment of the Christians, hindering the work of the missionaries in every way possible.

Writing to Rodriguez, in faraway Coimbra, during the January of 1545, Francis said:

> Do not permit anyone dear to you to come to India to take charge of administrative or financial affairs for His Majesty. All who come here in such capacity end up by earning the words of Holy Writ: "Let them be blotted out of the book of life and let not their names be inscribed among the just." So customary has ill-doing become here, among the Portuguese, that all go by the road *I-grab, you-rob, he-snatches.* I marvel at the endless variations of that verb, *rapio;* each newcomer adds a new mood, tense or participle to it; the lingo and vocabulary of avarice is enriched daily as the Europeans enrich themselves by robbery disguised under many pretexts—robbery done with impunity, with no hesitation and in full and unashamed view of all.

The year 1545 proved as disappointing as 1544. Although he had written at length to the King of Portugal, protesting against the greed and rapine of the officials in the East, begging that something be done to end such corruption, nothing happened. He had written a second letter, fearing that his first one had not been stern enough.

> . . . Fear, lest some day God, the Sovereign Judge, should wrathfully address your Majesty with these words: "Why did you not chastise your servants who, under cover of your name and that of religion, harmed the Christian converts of India by their violence and cruelty?" To Heaven ascends the voice of India, complaining of how your Majesty allows the avaricious to treat her, complaining that while you

draw vast treasure from her empire you allow but a
bare and meagre pittance for the relief of her
grievous spiritual needs.

The King, crushed with the burdens of empire, was
moved to do what he could.

Among all these trials and disappointments, there had
been some consolations. There had been the conversion
of the entire population of an island that lay between the
mainland and Ceylon, and the possibility that the Cingalese might yet turn from Buddha and become worshippers
of the true God. And there had been helpers coming; each
year native priests were being ordained in Goa and a few
were already doing wonderful work in South India and
the island between India and Ceylon. And there had been
all the good news from Europe—even though letters had
been few and far between—the Constitutions of the Company approved by the Pope, Rodriguez' College in Coimbra almost ready to send out apostles to the Indies, the
good work beginning at the Council of Trent, and news
of the brethren. Xavier had written advising Ignatius that
such members of the Society as might be thought in-
competent for preaching or hearing confessions in Europe,
would be very welcome as catechists in the East, provided
they were men of virtue and not altogether illiterate. Before three years were out he was to know better. Bodily
strength and ability to bear fatigue were indispensable
qualities for men coming to a trying, wearying land such
as that Francis worked in. The heat was excessive, water
scanty, and food unpalatable and monotonous—rice, fish
and milk, year in and year out, if one were fortunate
enough to get such a diet; often one had to make do for
days on end with an occasional handful of dry millet and
a draught of bitter-tasting water. From Rodriguez who

had written that he would soon be sending Fathers of the Company, trained in Coimbra, to India, Francis had begged men "on fire with zeal." He hoped that, when the fleet came this year, his burden would be lightened; and, remembering his dream of former years, he smiled wryly as he admitted to himself how heavy a load the Indian was for one man's back.

His joy in the New Christian community of the island off Ceylon was turned to grief when news came that a local Rajah, considering their conversion as tantamount to siding with the Portuguese, had given the islanders the choice of apostasy or death; when young and old alike declared that they would stand staunch in the new faith, the Rajah had ordered the massacre of the entire population, and six hundred souls had perished. It was a dire blow: although Xavier reminded himself over and over that the blood of the Christians was the seed of the Church, and although he knew that God who permitted evil could draw good therefrom, he was depressed and sad at heart. The brother of the Rajah who ordered the massacre fled to Francis; his own life was in danger from his brother, who was, he said, a usurper. If Father Francis would ask the Portuguese to help him regain his rights, he would throw open to the Christian missionaries the dominion unlawfully taken from him by his brother. It seemed a providential opening to an extensive area hitherto barred to Francis. Perhaps the blood of the murdered Christians was pleading for the conversion of those who had, cruelly but surely, sent them to Paradise. He interrupted his labours and set out, on foot, for the north, there to tell the tale to Martin da Sousa.

The Governor seemed most anxious to intervene on behalf of the dispossessed prince. He assured Francis that a punitive expedition would at once sail for the island, de-

throne the Rajah, set up his brother in his stead, and
leave the road clear for the missionaries to preach there.
Francis returned again to his labours, confident that
justice would be done and further harvest fields made
available to the reapers of God. It was good to have met
a Christian governor like Martin da Sousa; the man had
seethed with righteous anger when Francis had told him
of the massacre—in fact Francis had had to soothe him.
He could not know how Martin da Sousa had heaved a
sigh of relief the moment Francis was outside his door.
"Whew!" he gasped to his secretary, wiping the sweat
from his forehead. "*El Santo* can be a trial to sinners like
us. He imagines that His Majesty's fleet can be sent here,
there, anywhere—just for the sake of his particular work!
In this case, it suits us nicely; there may be good pickings
in this Rajah's domains; and once we get the Indians of
that province involved in civil war, the rest will be easy.
When they have fought to exhaustion, we will step in and
take over. Give orders for all available ships to proceed at
once to the south."

The ships set sail, manned with soldiers ready for war.
But they struck not a blow against the usurper. Before
they came to his coasts a Portuguese ship, laden with
pepper, spices and jewels, ran into a storm and was driven
ashore in the false Rajah's dominions. He promptly seized
the ship, cargo and crew, and held all to ransom. Word
was brought to da Sousa, who hastily countermanded the
orders given the fleet. One did not wage war against a
prince who held such a wealthy cargo bound for Portugal;
one sent embassies, bearing rich gifts; one wooed the
Rajah into returning the seized goods.

Again Francis experienced not only grievous disappointment but disillusionment. Martin da Sousa had seemed
so anxious to help spread the gospel. Yet a few bushels of

peppers and spices, a handful of baubles, had won the day; these trifles counted more with the Christians than the saving of immortal souls.

The Rajah, delighted to find that the Christians were, after all, no better than others, congratulated himself on his masterly handling of the situation. In future he would know how to treat with the Portuguese; despite all the rumours about their *sadhu,* Francis Xavier had not succeeded in converting his own people—and he would presume to convert the Rajah's subjects from the religion of their ancestors! The Rajah sent orders that a thorough search was to be made throughout his dominions for any Christians who might have escaped the island massacre; all such, when found, were to be kept and used for bait when next the Rajah went shark fishing.

.   .   .   .   .

Francis was in Mylapore, a town on the eastern coast of India, some days' journey from Cape Comorin. Conscious of having reached a stage in his work where it was imperative to stop, pray and reflect before deciding on future plans, he went to the shrine of St. Thomas the Apostle at Mylapore, there to spend some time in prayer and recollection.

It was quiet in Mylapore. About a hundred Portuguese families were settled there and, though the vices which infected Goa also flourished in this much smaller town, the people, both the Portuguese and the natives, were docile and a little labour among them yielded great spiritual fruit, leaving Francis time to rest and recuperate, to pray and contemplate. There he remained to recover from an accumulation of fatigue and from the heart-wounds he had received through the destruction of the Christian communities—won with God knew what toil—and from the Portuguese, who, he had thought, were supporting him but were of late becoming worst enemies of Christianity in these climes.

The shrine where, according to local tradition, the remains of the Apostle rested, was his favourite resort. There one was shown the body of St. Thomas, the javelin that martyred him, a phial of blood, the pilgrim staff enshrined in a reliquary as precious as any in Compostela. Francis asked himself several times why he had not come there before. Surely, before going anywhere in India, he should have visited the shrine sacred to the memory of Thomas, the onetime doubter, who had gone forth, after the first Pentecost, preaching his Master to the Parthians, Medes, Persians, Hyrcanians and Bactrians, finally coming to India, where he worked his greatest miracles and where he met martyrdom at the hands of a Rajah who had ordered him to be pierced with many javelins.

Beset by perplexities, doubts and despair, what more fitting patron could Francis have found than the disciple "who, doubting, had touched, and, touching, had believed"? Surely the virtue that had gone forth from the pierced hands and side of the Risen Christ to heal His follower's faith, continued to be transmitted by Thomas to those who, down the ages, invoked his aid. "Because thou hast seen Me, thou has believed," the Saviour said; for Thomas, seeing a man, had believed and confessed the invisible God, crying out "My Lord and my God!" Francis Xavier found an extraordinary delight in repeating the responsories from the Office of St. Thomas, as he sat in the dim church, strange bronze sunbeams streaming through the mother-of-pearl windows.

I saw men standing together, clad in shining garments; and the Angel of the Lord spoke to me, saying: These holy men became the friends of God. I saw a mighty Angel of God, flying through the midst of heaven, crying out with a loud voice and saying: These holy men became the friends of God . . .

These are they who, living in the flesh, planted the Church in their blood: they drank the chalice of the Lord, and became the friends of God. Their sound hath gone forth unto all the earth, and their words unto the end of the world . . . They drank the chalice of the Lord, and became the friends of God . . .

These are holy men, whom the Lord hath chosen in charity unfeigned, and hath given them everlasting glory: whose teaching enlightens the Church, as the moon by the sun. By faith the saints conquered kingdoms, and wrought justice. Whose teaching enlightens the Church, as the moon by the sun . . .

Soon he was able to write to Micer Paul and Father Diego at Goa:

I have come to the city named for St. Thomas, and am availing myself of the opportunity, while here in this holy place, to pray that God may enlighten my soul and let me know His holy will as to what I should undertake, and to give me the means of accomplishing that same blessed will; for "He who gives the will, can also give the performance." Moreover, here God has remembered me according to His customary mercy; He has infinitely consoled my soul and made me know that it is His will that I go to Malacca and from thence to other islands of that region. Mansilhas, now Father Francis Mansilhas, with some native priests, remains at Cape Comorin; and where they are, there is no need for me . . . So, if this year I find no Portuguese craft sailing for

Malacca, I shall not fear to embark with Mussulmen or heathens. Indeed, such is my trust in God, that, did nothing but a raft set out for Malacca, on that would I venture. I hope to set out by the end of August. Please send me a small Roman breviary as soon as you can. My dearest brothers, do not cease to commend me, a poor sinner, to God, in your daily Masses and prayers.

Francisco, the least of your brethren

May 8th, 1545

At Mylapore, there was plenty to be done for the people of the Portuguese settlement; there were many old soldiers who had quitted soldiering for commerce and who were, only too often, leading disordered lives. For them, Francis kept the mornings and forenoons; in the afternoons and evenings he preached to the natives and put himself at their service. As in Goa, there were scandals to be removed—by painful means, if necessary. Had not Our Saviour said: "If thy right eye scandalise thee pluck it out and cast it from thee; and if thy hand or thy foot scandalise thee cut it off and cast it from thee; it were better for thee to enter into life blind or maimed or lame than, having two eyes or hands or feet, to be cast into everlasting fire"? There were liaisons to be regularised, usuries and cruelties to be abolished, libertines to be converted and their slaves released and re-established in freedom of body and spirit.

He lodged with old Father Coelho, the chaplain of the shrine, sharing his bedroom. Before retiring, host and guest would sit, looking out through the palms and bamboos across the Bay of Bengal where, in a still more distant east lay Malacca and, beyond Malacca, other islands and great empires, such as China and Japan, almost as far east of India as India was east of Europe. Father Coelho chattered and gossiped to his heart's content; it was seldom he had anyone to whom he could talk—and never, since he had come to Mylapore, had he had a priest visitor. He told Francis the hundred legends connected with the shrine. Francis had several years before read that Marco Polo, Odoric and other medieval voyagers had been to this coast and found no remains of St. Thomas at the end of the ancient pilgrim road in Mylapore; they reported having found nothing but an empty fosse. And for centuries Europe had claimed Ortone, a town near Edesse in the Abruzzi, as the tomb of St. Thomas. But he did not disturb Father Coelho's happiness by casting any doubt on the authenticity of the relics in Mylapore. What mattered it to Europe or Asia where the Apostle's mortal remains lay? Certain it was that Thomas had passed through Mylapore; most probably he had met his martyrdom there; it was evident, from tradition and from the ease with which grace worked in the souls of inhabitants of this region that a holy influence permeated the place. But Francis kept these thoughts to himself.

One evening Father Coelho took his visitor to task.

"Father Francis," he began, apologetically; "you thought that you slipped out unobserved, but I know that you have been going most nights, when you thought me asleep, to that corner of the sacristy where we keep the Lady Altar tapers." He coughed and fidgeted for a moment before continuing; he did not want to refer to the vigils and flagellations which, he had good reason to believe, were the occasion of these nightly excursions. "I only ask you not to go there alone any more. That place has a reputation, not for good. The devils are strong in India, and they have been known to attack certain persons . . . just in that corner where we keep nothing now but the tapers I mentioned . . . To please me, in future, when you wish to go there, bring my Malabar servant and bid him remain within sight or, at least, within call." Francis flushed hotly, laughed in embarrassment, but promised to bring the Malabar in future.

That night and every following night, the servant, carrying his raffia mat, followed Father Francis to the door of the little room where the Father wished to pray, alone. The Malabar, delighted at being allowed to sleep, curled himself on his mat and slept. One night he awoke to hear a babel of sounds coming from where the priest was; at one moment it seemed as though a hundred horses were galloping and champing there, at another it seemed as though many cudgels were belabouring someone. Petrified with fear, the Malabar thought of running to fetch Father Coelho, but just then, from the interior of the room, he could hear the voice of Father Francis. "Holy Mother, will you not come to my aid? Holy Mother, will you not come to my aid?" And after this cry had been repeated several times there was silence. Soon Father Francis stepped out, serene as ever, careful to step gently over the Malabar, who feigned sleep.

In the morning, Father Coelho noted, with no little surprise, that Father Francis did not rise for Matins as was his wont. When the old priest had finished saying that portion of the Divine Office, he returned to the bedroom.

"Your Reverence is ill?" he enquired.

"I don't feel so well, Father," replied Francis, who seemed extremely ashamed to have to admit to indisposition. The Malabar, who had been present during this interview, followed his master out and told the story of what had happened the previous night. Returning to the room where Francis lay, Father Coelho spoke reprovingly, "Did I not tell you that you should not go to the shrine by night!"

Xavier only smiled. For the next two days he was ill, his old enemy, fever, having attacked him. On the third day, he insisted on getting up and dined with Father Coelho; at least, he sat to table, but seemed unable to eat and still looked far from well. The older man was disturbed; never had he seen Father Francis other than in the gayest humour; this evening he had not laughed once. Father Coelho would have to think of something to make his companion smile. He would repeat the words the Malabar had heard Francis cry out the other night; if the Holy Mother could not help her son to recover his good spirits and pull himself over that border line that lay between sickness and health, no one could. They rose, said grace, and then Father Coelho began to repeat, "Holy Mother, will you not come to my aid? Holy Mother, will you not come to my aid?" Although so embarrassed that the ready blood rose to his face, Francis smiled. But he told nothing of what had transpired in the taper room.

During the night of August 14th, vigil of the feast of the Assumption, Francis, who had resumed his nightly vigils at the shrine, returned to the priest's dwelling, rather hurriedly, in the small hours. Father Coelho, always a light sleeper, noted that his friend seemed disturbed.

"What is it?" he asked.

"I was keeping the vigil of the feast," said the other. "It is the vow-day of the first members of our Company, you know. As sleep was overpowering me, I walked to and fro. And I heard Matins being sung in the choir—solemn Matins; I could distinguish both words and music—the Invitatory, Psalms, Hymns, all—" he broke off, as though he regretted having told Father Coelho anything.

"But, why did you hasten back?" asked the latter. "This time it was not the demon attacking you, yet you hastened back. The night the devil beat you into a fever you came home calmly."

"I tried the side door, but it was locked—the key on the outside. And the other doors—I found them all closed and was unable to open them. A great fear came upon me; somehow I got out by the vestry."

"She saved you from something worse than the last time," said Father Coelho, rising and going on his knees. "In these climes, dear son, the Evil One assumes many shapes; I can well believe that the singing you heard, though taken from the hymns and psalms, was a lure set for your destruction. Let us say the rosary to the Holy Mother, who surely came to your aid."

On Saturday, the feast of the Assumption, Francis renewed his vows. Eleven years before, he, Ignatius, Favre and the others had pronounced those vows for the first time, at Montmartre. He would have liked to sit down and recall every detail of that morning; the intervening eleven years, when looked at from one viewpoint, seemed eleven centuries, when looked at from another angle, seemed eleven days. And Paris, though half a world away in one sense, in another was just behind the nearest hill. But Francis could not delay to enjoy his memories. Juan de Eyro, a young Portuguese merchant, was waiting to see him.

Juan had heard Francis preach in Mylapore, and had been so moved that he came to the priest and made a full and sorrowful confession of his life. In the fervour of his conversion he offered himself as a candidate for membership of the Company. At first, Francis tried to put him off; he had had experience of men who had volunteered under stress of sudden emotion and who had decamped as speedily as their fervour evaporated. But Juan de Eyro had been most insistent in his entreaties and, hoping to

induce Francis to change his mind, proceeded to demonstrate the genuine nature of his vocation by settling his
affairs, selling his goods and distributing the price among
the poor. At last Francis gave in and Juan's good resolu-
tions immediately began to wilt. Sadly surveying his depleted possessions, he decided that the best thing to be
done, before *El Santo* dragged him away to the islands of
the head-hunters or some equally dangerous and unprofitable place, was to gather up the remains of his
worldly goods; with the proceeds he bought a small boat
to sail away from Mylapore.

Just as he was boarding the ship, a messenger came
telling him that Father Francis wanted him immediately.
Although he denied being Juan de Eyro, the messenger
was adamant. *El Santo* had described him carefully, and
he fitted the description. Shrugging his shoulders, he returned with the messenger. It was no use trying to hide
anything from *el Santo*. He went in to a stern Father
Francis who reproached him, confessed him, and received
him back into his friendship. For fear that the devil should
again tempt him, de Eyro sold the boat and made ready
to sail east with Francis. On the feast of the Assumption,
as Xavier came to where de Eyro awaited him, he noted
that the man had letters. One was from Goa, from Micer
Paul. Enclosed was a letter from da Sousa recommending
Francis to the Governor of Malacca. Micer Paul told the
news that da Sousa would be Governor no longer. A new
Governor was coming out on the fleet, expected by the
end of August. Da Sousa had made himself very un-
popular in that he lowered the pay of the soldiers and
tried to prevent them from becoming traders. He was
also severe and hot-tempered. Francis more than anyone,
perhaps, had reason to be glad of the eclipse of a man
whose care for a cargo of pepper, spice and jewels had

lost him the chance of entering and possibly evangelising a vast territory; but it was not in his nature to rejoice at any man's misfortune. He only remembered that Sousa had given him an introduction to Malacca. He had spent a long while in Mylapore. He had rested body and soul. Who knew but that the labours ahead would be more arduous than those already endured? Life was short—the years were flying by; only eleven years since Montmartre, and he had as yet done nothing for God. He was an unprofitable servant. Calling Juan de Eyro, he bade him enquire at once when the next boat sailed to Malacca.

10

IT WAS the year of Our Lord, 1547. At the end of January the King of England died. This Tudor who had seized life with greedy hands, who for thirty-eight years had dominated England, manœuvring himself into an unparalleled position as spiritual and temporal ruler of that kingdom, resisted with all the strength of his crumbling body, with all the old stubbornness of his tenacious spirit, the implacable enemy whose besieging force came closer, ever closer. Cranmer knelt by the King's bedside, his voice faint in Henry's ears: "Do you believe in the faith of Christ?" he asked. But already Death, the besieger, had begun to make breaches in the five walls of the senses, and human words, mingled with the noise of battering-ram and cannonade, lost themselves and their meaning. Norfolk was to die at dawn; but the King had been unable to hold the pen to sign the death warrant, as now he was unable to lift any weapon to defend himself against the foe already within his fortress walls.

In one anteroom his daughter, Mary Tudor, wept; in another Katherine Parr's ladies condoled with her, the last of his six queens. In the corridors of Whitehall Palace, Hertford, Paget, Gardiner and others supported and disputed the claims of the various heirs. An hour after midnight the King died. Before the end he pressed Cranmer's

190

hand. Who could say whether the pressure had been an answer to Cranmer's question or merely a death spasm? Cranmer held that it meant His Majesty had indeed died in the faith of Christ. But many there were who wondered which faith His dying Majesty had meant by the "faith of Christ."

The news of Henry's death was regarded by the King of France, François I, as a bad omen for himself. He became more restive and uneasy, continually shifting from one château to another. He sent to Navarre for his sister, Queen Marguerite. But alas! Marguerite was also an invalid, and all she could do was to embroider him a new doublet. François had now little time left for finery, little need for any clothing but a nightshirt. Hot baths, poultices, the best surgeons in Europe could not heal his diseased body. The beauty created for him by da Vinci and Cellini, the drawings of Clouet, the copy of the Pieta Michaelangelo was doing for him had now little appeal for François, the aesthete. No longer did his mind linger on the writings of Erasmus and Rabelais, no longer did he compose verses for his ladies. He sent for his last surviving son, the melancholy Henri, and could not but note the anticipatory glint in the Dauphin's eye. Suddenly, he saw himself—not the brave leader, but the foolhardy, swaggering braggart; not the gallant, but the debauchee; not the magnificent benefactor, but the extravagant wastrel of that treasure entrusted to him by his people. But François, as on occasion during his rascally life, rose to greatness at the end. Seeing himself as he really was, he deplored the misspent years. He sent for his confessor and concentrated on the business of preparing to meet his God. In the next room, one of his mistresses sobbed and wept loudly. What would become of her, she asked, noting how Diana de Poitiers had arrived to stand by the side of the Dauphin.

The Duke of Guise called from the sick room, "Le vieux galant s'en va!—The old sport is going!" All knelt and said the prayers for the dying. Far away, in Pau, Marguerite, the Queen of Navarre, dreamt that a pale, well-known face looked into hers and a hollow voice said, "Sister! My sister!" It was March 31st, the eve of Palm Sunday, 1547. The King of France was dead.

A fortnight after the death of the King of France, the proceedings of the Council of Trent had to be suspended owing to an outbreak of spotted fever which removed from all earthly council tables the General of the Friars Minor and an Italian bishop. The Pope, Paul III, was rather annoyed at the suspension of the Council, which seemed to promise so much in the line of reform. Two Fathers of the Company, Lainez and Salmeron, the new Order's greatest theologians, had been at the Council. Held up for some time because of Salmeron's having caught the fever, they eventually returned to Rome. Ignatius had several letters of interest to show. Some from Rodriguez, giving glowing accounts of the wonderful strides the Company was making in Portugal, and forwarding the latest letters received there from their old friend, Xavier, who seemed to be moving about the islands of the distant eastern archipelagoes like a whirlwind—now in Malacca, again in Banda or Amboina or the lands of the head-hunters. Bobadilla was chaplain with the Emperor's army in Germany, attending to the sick and wounded. Ignatius was just a little uneasy about Bobadilla but he did not mention his fears to the others. Later that year he had cause for further uneasiness. Prudence had never been Bobadilla's virtue and the news of how, in public sermons, he was censuring the Emperor as a lukewarm Catholic was perturbing. Ignatius thought it most rash of Bobadilla to denounce openly a monarch whose favour the newly established Spanish province of the Company would need. It was really most annoying, after all the labours of poor Peter Favre, who had literally killed himself travelling through Spain to make foundations in Valencia and Salamanca, and to start colleges at Valladolid and Gandia; Favre had barely dragged himself back to Rome to die, and now Bobadilla's hasty and ill-timed invectives, which he delivered in every other cathedral and university from Louvain to Rome, bade fair to damage the wonderful work of Favre in Spain. So angry was Ignatius that, when Bobadilla arrived in Rome, he refused to receive him; intolerant zealots such as Bobadilla had no place in a Company named for a gentle Saviour. The fiery sermons that were the talk of Europe might befit a Luther or a Zwingli; they could do nothing but harm to the cause for which Peter Favre had worn himself out. Would to God Bobadilla had some of the virtue of that holy man, now, happily, in heaven. Why, when ordered to return to Rome from Spain the previous year, Favre had risen from a sickbed to obey, saying to those about him: "Obedience is necessary, life is not." It was useless for Bobadilla to expostulate, saying that, after all, the Emperor—who had most reason to take offence—had not seemed half as angry as Ignatius; Charles had, it was true, forbidden him the Imperial court and any part of the Empire, but he had kindly given him money to journey to Rome. Ignatius said nothing but closed the door. He knew Bobadilla would be there waiting when he opened it next morning.

Meantime, the Father of the Company of Jesus had much correspondence to see to. There was a long letter from Francis Borgia, the thirty-seven-year-old Duke of Gandia, who, a widower for some years past, had been brought in touch with Ignatius through Peter Favre. This grandee, for long major-domo to the Emperor's heir, was posing a problem. He wished to settle his affairs and arrange for his children's future; then he proposed journeying to Rome to join the Company as a novice. It was something that needed much thought and prayer on the part of the Duke himself and on the part of Ignatius. The Duke of Gandia, Spanish nobleman, owner of great wealth and estates, arbiter of the destinies of innumerable vassals, would need his Emperor's permission to embark on so weighty a step as that proposed. It was exasperating that Bobadilla should antagonise the Emperor at the wrong time by his show of zeal . . .

There were letters from Xavier—Xavier the dearest of all, Xavier the furthest away, sailing lonely Eastern seas, labouring where none of the brethren could encourage him with a cheering word. His letters had become far fewer since he had left India; he seemed far busier. Letters had been forwarded from Lisbon, from Rodriguez, to whom he had written urgently begging that more priests be sent from Portugal to the various settlements abroad. In the autumn of 1545 he had been in Malacca, finding time, amidst countless other labours to get a smattering of the language of the Malays and to translate the prayers and catechism into that tongue, before going on to the next island where the Malay language was spoken. In the January of 1546 he was off to Banda and other islands almost beyond the reach of communications with India or Europe. He sailed no longer on the ships of the fleet but entrusted himself to the company of Lascars and other heathens. Everywhere he touched he spoke of the baptism of infants, the instructions of the adults, the tending on the sick and the dying, the sermons and confessions. In one letter to the Fathers in Goa which had been forwarded to Ignatius, Father Francis had asked for copper chalices and sacred vessels. "They will be safer," the letter ran, "*a gente non sancta.*" Nothing was sacred to the unholy. Ignatius could read between the lines. What sacrilegious robbery had been left untold in that letter? Knowing Xavier, he could guess that such a deed had not gone un-atoned—and it was not the heathen who would have made reparation for the desecration of the holy altar-plate. Ignatius' heart went out to his old companion of Ste. Barbe, as he pictured him keeping vigils before the altars of the rude, palm-roofed huts that served him for churches. The generous-hearted Xavier probably had scourged himself to the blood, in his anguish at the irreverence done to the things of God. He might celebrate the Holy Sacrifice with a copper chalice, but the cel-ebrant's soul was of a rarer metal than the souls of many priests who held aloft the Blood of Christ in priceless cups of gold, richly chased and studded with precious gems.

Far into the night Ignatius sat at his desk in Rome, reading the letters of Xavier and his other sons, replying to each at length and with care. It was cold in Rome, but it would not be cold in the faraway climes where Francis was. Laying aside his quill, the Father General of the Society of Jesus prayed for a while, thinking of the can-non ball that had lamed him at Pamplona, taking from him the commission he held in the army of an earthly sovereign to raise him to high command in another sphere. Yes, Ignatius had learned much from *el Gran Capitan* that stood him in good stead since. Now he, too, had to dispose men to the best advantage of the faith—to the greater honour and glory of God. And he served a Master who was not ungrateful, as Córdoba's had been. Ignatius was glad that Granada, the city that had given a tomb to Isabella, gave a grave also to *el Capitan*. Peter Favre, when in Spain, mindful of the old stories of soldiering days that the Pilgrim had related to Xavier and himself in the little room in Ste. Barbe, had gone to Granada and found the tomb of Ignatius' beloved Captain, where no less than seven hundred captured banners hung their heavy folds over the greatest soldier Spain had known since the Cid.

As he sat at his desk remembering these things, Ignatius shook his head; it was sad to see how men who had given their fellows the most sterling and unselfish service met with so little thanks in the end. He had heard that it was the same with Cortés, the most magnificent and fearless of the Conquistadores. He wondered if he were alive or dead. He bowed his head and prayed for those country-men of his, the Conquistadores, whom God had made so noble and for such great things and who had suffered so much from little-minded, mean-souled men. Then, taking up his pen again, he began to write to Xavier. There was God's Christopher Columbus, venturing into unknown places, discovering new fields for the gospel; *el Gran Capitan* of the Church, gaining victories in bloodless en-counters, turning the untutored heathen into strong and perfect Christians, teaching them to use the armour of the spirit, raising the standard of Christ on territory long in possession of the ancient enemy of mankind. Xavier was Cortés, making forced marches in the East as Cortés had done in the West, exploring, conquering, consolidating an overseas empire for a King who would not forget, whose rewards and honours were not of this world.

And, even as Ignatius wrote to Xavier, calling him a Cortés in his own mind, the real Hernán Cortés was dying in a little castle on a hill near Seville. A few months back he had made his will, assigning his estate to his son, Don Martin, providing for his children, legitimate and illegiti-mate; he had left funds for the building and maintenance of a hospital, monasteries, churches, a convent and a university college in that land where, his conscience told him, Spaniards—himself included—had not dealt justly with the natives. He gave instructions that his heirs were to find out if his lands in Mexico had been taken by force from *peons,* or if any natives had been enslaved in his name; such lands were to be restored to the rightful owners and such slaves freed.

Having confessed his sins, which were neither few nor light, he turned himself to God. He was not sorry to die; for ten years he, who should have been the first Spaniard, in that he had achieved more than any other of his generation, was forced to idle about courts "eating by weight, drinking by measure, sleeping without rest, living with so much leisure that each moment of time had to be ticked off by a dot on the clock; and with all this measuring of time, life was so empty that one could mistake death for life." The Emperor, though polite, was frigid, aloof, casual, often insulting—as on that day when he told Cortés that the conquest of Mexico was not his; Velasquez should, by right, have conquered that land "if Cortés had not stepped in as a usurper."

He did not wish to remain any longer a hanger-on at court—he and his three sons and a lot of lawyers who cost much but achieved little. He wrote the King: "I am not of an age to hang about in inns, but rather to retire and settle my account with God, for it is a long bill I owe Him and I have little life left to put my case before Him. And it is better to lose one's wealth than one's soul."

The foolhardiness of one of his captains, his own impatience with another, his failure to become a courtier skilled in the niceties of court etiquette, in the intrigues of politics, his natural honour—which forbade him to insinuate himself into the graces of the Emperor—all these had conspired to make him throw away a conquest as great as any in human history. As he lay down to die, Cortés, always a man of courage and earnestness, put the past behind him and, ever the leader, bade that last lone follower, his immortal soul, to make ready for a journey to a City more magnificent than Mexico, to parley with a King infinitely greater and more powerful than Charles, Emperor of the Kingdoms of Spain, or Montezuma, Emperor of the Aztecs. When friends were arranging his body for burial they found, in his rigid clasp, the little gold medal of Our Lady with the Child—and on the obverse side, St. John the Baptist—which he had always worn on a chain about his neck.

. . . . .

In the same year of our Lord, 1547, while the deaths of these makers of history provided the news which the letter-couriers of Europe carried from town to town and from country to country, Francis Xavier had been moving swiftly from island to island of the archipelago six hundred leagues east of India. Malacca was his first and last port of call in this world of islands and islets. It was a vast city, the chief emporium of spices in the East. In its suburbs lived Chinese, Japanese, Indians, Siamese and, of course, the conquering Portuguese. It was built on an excellent harbour, "where one monsoon commences and where another gathers, and where people from all the East congregate." Daily, boats put in from neighbouring islands—Ternate, Banda, Amboina, Bali and the Moluccas, with fragrant čargoes of cloves, mace, nutmegs, ginger, cinnamon, spices, pepper, precious gums, resins, and aromatic drugs.

Of all the maritime discoveries of the age the discovery of these eastern islands had been an achievement that made Portugal envied above any country in Europe. The Emperor Charles tried in vain to induce John III to exchange Sumatra and the Spice Islands for Brazil. Charles, through Magellan, had originally claimed the Moluccas, but at a time when his coffers were low he had mortgaged them to his Portuguese brother-in-law. Finally, to raise further loans and to save himself from the importunities of merchants who wished to farm the spice and pepper trade themselves, Charles sold his right to the Moluccas to John III. Likewise, the King of France—whose Dieppe poet-sailors, Jean and Raoul Parmentier, had staked France's claims to Sumatra, Java and other islands—finding himself heavily in debt to John III, offered his rights in the East against the remission of his debt. So Portugal was, at the time Francis Xavier sailed to the islands, the only European power trading in and drawing rich revenues from these regions of perpetual sunshine.

On a morning of the very week when Hernán Cortés lay dying in Spain, Father Francis Xavier was celebrating a marriage in the Church of Our Lady of the Mount. He loved this little church, the sight of which had cheered him more than two years previously when the ship bearing him from India had come into the road and he could see the Portuguese houses rising on the hill, the Malay quarter with its noisy, gay bazaars and—crowning Malacca —Our Lady of the Mount. When the wedding party had betaken themselves downhill to the festivities which Father Francis had promised to attend later, word was brought him that two men waited to speak with him. Though he would have liked to remain a little longer in prayer, so much did he consider himself the servant of all that he hastened to receive his callers. One was a Portuguese ship captain known to him, the other a small middle-aged Oriental, of what race Francis could not quite say—certainly not one of the savage, untutored Malays, not a Siamese or Burmese, nor yet a Chinese. The

199

captain introduced him. The man was one Anjiro, a gentleman from Japan—a new country much further east, which some Portuguese blown out of their course from Siam to China had discovered about five years previously. Xavier had been so occupied with his work on Cape Comorin at that time that he knew nothing of this. Would the captain, George Alvares, tell him about this land? Meanwhile, if they stepped into his house—he indicated the palm-leaf hut near the hospital—he could offer them a little refreshment.

Anjiro sat, his eyes riveted on the holy bronze he had travelled so far to see, and listened while the captain told what he knew of Nippon. Alvares had been only nine miles inland, having visited a port named Yamagawa. The land he had seen was cultivated and hilly, but he had been told that there was fine rolling country further inland. There were splendid woods of cedar, laurel, pine, chestnut and oak. It was a country of flowers and fruit and vegetables, and the people of the land were an industrious lot—none of the lolling in the sun that one saw in India or Siam or Burma or these islands, but steady, intensive tilling of the soil. He had asked about the crops; they sowed wheat, barley, turnips, radishes and beets in November; peas, lentils, millet, beans, cucumbers and melons in March; rice, yams and onions in July. Nothing of the shiftlessness or savagery of the islanders about the Japanese; they had substantial holdings, not unlike those in the richer regions of Spain or Portugal, with orchards and kitchen gardens, not much livestock or poultry, but small, hardy horses. The waters on their coasts teemed with many kinds of fish and molluscs. He had seen some hot springs and the natives, a very cleanly people, were given to bathing and washing in these warm springs and rivers. The people were excessively well-mannered; a thousand rules governed ordinary social intercourse. The women were very domesticated and house-proud, and exceedingly adept at spinning and embroidery. There were occasional earthquakes and frequent windstorms in those islands, and dangerous typhoons made navigation very hazardous. The nobles went fowling and hawking as in Europe— there was abundance of deer, pheasants, pigeons, hares and rabbits. The men were proud and warlike. From their childhood they carried swords and handled a bow not unlike the English longbow. They were a generous and hospitable people, neither bigoted nor narrow-minded and very anxious to know about the Europeans. Their own virtues they expected to find in others. They ate frugally, mostly rice and vegetables, seldom touched meat and drank but sparingly of *sake*, their rice wine. They never drank cold water, but barley water in summer and an infusion of some herb in winter. They had no prisons or courts, each man doing justice on those of his own household. Theft was held in great abhorrence, and a whole village would organise a thief-hunt, if it were rumoured that a thief was about; when caught, the miscreant was killed like a marauding fox. Slaves were few and, as a rule, Japanese men kept but one wife. They loved music but detested gambling; they had theatres and comedies. They seemed to George Alvares to be worshippers of Buddha, for they had many pleasantly situated temples and had prayer wheels and prayer beads. They were men of iron discipline and self-control, and despised the Portuguese for so easily betraying inner emotion. The women enjoyed great freedom, being allowed to journey abroad unescorted and unchaperoned. Many castles and fortified towns were on the summits of their hills—indeed, words failed Alvares to explain to Father Francis what a wonderful race resided in that kingdom the Chinese called *Chipangu*, the Land of the Rising Sun.

Xavier listened, entranced. Up to the present his lot had been cast among savage, half-savage or half-civilised peoples; in most cases he had had to divide himself, giving half his energies to the evangelisation of these pagans, seldom little more than barbarians, the other half to the reforming of Portuguese colonists the bad example of whose lives tended to make the watching neophytes lapse back into that darkness from which they had been drawn with such patience and effort. And now, at last, here—at the Finisterre of the East—was a noble and civilised people. A splendid vista opened up before him; hitherto he had been sowing the good seed of the Gospel by the wayside, on stony ground, among thorns. Was *Chipangu* the good ground that would bring forth fruit—thirty, sixty, a hundredfold?

George Alvares indicated Anjiro, the Japanese, who had listened impassively to the long account of his country, understanding a little here and there, gathering the general gist of the sea captain's account from the latter's many and expressive gestures. Anjiro was a fugitive; he had committed a murder—killed a man on a point of honour—in Japan, and the relatives of the man he had slain pursued him to take, Anjiro expected, a life for a life. He had hidden in a monastery of bonzes, and hoped to find there protection from his pursuers and peace of soul, for the deed he had done caused him great remorse. But the bonzes could neither give him back his peace of mind nor guarantee his safety in the event of the avenging party visiting the monastery; so, in desperation, he had fled to the Portuguese ships, where he was welcomed by the captain and some traders, they having frequently done business with him in the course of their stay in those parts.

He told them his story and they said that only one man could restore tranquillity to a self-tortured mind like that of Anjiro's—the great bonze of the Christians, Father Francis Xavier. So, Alvares concluded, rather lamely, here was Anjiro; and here was Father Francis. The captain's part in the business was ended. Before many days had passed Anjiro and Xavier were fast friends.

Anjiro spoke pidgin Portuguese and had some idea of the Malay tongues; when spoken to slowly and in words carefully confined to the vocabulary he used, he could converse with the Christian bonze. Xavier marvelled at his intelligence and at his thirst to learn; when attending catechism lessons he carefully transcribed, in quaint characters that went up and down, the articles of the Creed. He memorised without much apparent difficulty; he asked searching questions. He was pleased when Father Francis asked him many questions regarding his own country and his own people. No, he did not think that the Japanese would become Christians immediately: they would ask the Christian bonze many questions first; they would carefully watch his conduct to see how it accorded with his teaching. But, if he gave reasoned answers to their questions and if his life gave no cause for complaint or criticism, then the King, the nobility and others would certainly become followers of Christ. It was a dangerous journey from Malacca to Japan; there were stormy seas and Chinese pirates to be braved. Anjiro would be glad to go to India and to study and prepare himself for baptism; he would also teach the Father his language and help him translate the Catechism and the Gospels into Japanese.

Asked why the Japanese wrote from the top to the bottom of a page instead of from left to right, Anjiro replied, "Why rather do you not write like us? The head of a man is at the top, his feet below. Is not the head the seat of reason, man's most important member?" Father Francis made time to jot down all the information Anjiro gave him regarding his country and all the answers the Japanese made to his questions. He intended to send both to Ignatius and to his old Masters in Paris University. The latter would be intensely interested in noting the subtle reasoning of the East. How Francis would have enjoyed hearing a debate between the scholars of the Montaigu and those of the Ste. Barbe or the violet-gowned men of the Beauvais, on the different workings of the Oriental and Occidental mind!

．　　．　　．　　．　　．

Although Xavier wished to go, with all haste, onwards towards Japan, he curbed his natural impetuosity, reminding himself that Japan was worth extra preparation. It would be a pity to risk failure by precipitate, unplanned action. Besides, he needed to call on Mansilhas and the pearl fishery communities; he needed to see how things were in Goa, to attend to the affairs of the College and of the Company there. Perhaps he would get the chance—missed before—of preaching the gospel in Ceylon. Anjiro and two Japanese who had joined him in Malacca were to attend the College in Goa. If they studied for two years or even longer, while Francis attended to all that called for his attention, and prepared in the Japanese language not only catechisms but books on doctrines of faith and morals, then he could the better proceed to the evangelising of Anjiro's people.

He left Malacca a week later for India. What a lifetime of work and adventure had been compressed into the two years and a few months since he had sailed east from Mylapore! As usual, on arrival at Malacca, he had found that the Portuguese officials needed spiritual aid no less than did the natives of that island. Frequently he had to spend entire days in the confessional, without time for food or drink. He slept in the little hut near the hospital, later in the hospital itself. It was embarrassing to find that, in the nights, when one hoped for a little privacy for prayer, the curious came prying; whispers outside the curtain of bamboo canes meant that intruders were there where he had hoped to be alone with God. Once or twice on such occasions he had ventured out of Malacca searching for solitude; but beyond the city, between the river and the impenetrable jungle, there were mangrove swamps where swarms of mosquitoes—heavenly disciplines—fiercer even than those he had known in India, stung and tormented him. Even there he had been followed, this time by people anxious for his safety; it was dangerous to walk in the dark by the river bank, where alligators waited to devour, where hooded cobras and giant pythons slept "ear on ground" that they might hear approaching footsteps in the dead of night. Vampire bats might suck his blood and orang-outangs carry him away— the Father had better return to the city. He had gone round with his little bell and gathered the children to prayers and catechism. He had tended the sick. He had visited the people, rich and poor, in their homes. It was Goa and Mylapore all over again, save that here there was an even greater intermingling of races and one had to fight against the enervating clove-reeking climate which sapped one's own energy even as it sapped the morale he was perpetually trying to stiffen in the natives he won from heathenism and the Portuguese he converted from evil ways.

New Year's Day, 1546, saw him away again on a trading-ship that moved warily through the dangerous reefs and shoals of the Straits, on past Sumatra, between

Java and Borneo and on by Celebes until, seven hundred leagues away from Malacca, they came to lonely Amboina, with its white shingly beaches, its bay, floored with a forest of coral, its volcanoes that smoked by day and reddened by night, its cocoanut palms, where red-crested cockatoos screeched and birds of paradise gleamed. The natives lived in compounds a good distance apart from one another. He had gone about to the seven nominally Christian villages, luring the shy inhabitants from the huts to which they fled at his approach by singing hymns in the Malay dialect they spoke in Amboina. On this island he had the happy experience of meeting many Spaniards, captured by the Portuguese in the northern islands. What a relief to speak *castellano* again! What a happiness to find some Biscayans who spoke his native Basque! Not only did he find them most amenable to his exhortations, but one, a priest from Valencia, was so taken with Xavier and his way of life that he offered himself as a candidate for the Company.

On again to the Spice Islands, to Ceram, to Ternate, whence he set off, against all advice and warnings, for Morotai, the Islands of the Moros, whose natives were poisoners and cannibals, not a bit averse to celebrating feasts where a murdered father or brother was served up as the main dish. He had been all alone among these benighted savages; no Portuguese would venture there, and such was the unenviable reputation of the islanders that Francis had thought it wiser not to risk a catechist's life— it was sufficient to risk his own. In these remote islets he had spent the happiest three months of his life. Here, at least, no renegade Christians ruined his preaching by their bad example. The Portuguese had wanted him to take antidotes to various poisons with him when coming. Had not these islanders killed, and probably devoured, the only priest who ever ventured near them before? But Francis refused. To do so would have implied a lack of confidence in God, and he did not want to add to his other burdens the burden of fear.

The natives transported him from one island to another in their canoes. When he finally left them in January, 1547, they wept, gathering in crowds on the shore to watch him set off to return to Ternate. Writing to Europe he said: "These islands should not be called the Islands of the Moros but the Islands of Hope in God." There, where his loneliness had been greatest, God had visited him oftenest.

In Ternate was another Portuguese settlement where the general depravity had reached so low a level that an Eastern proverb said, "As Malacca is Goa gone bad, so is Ternate Malacca gone bad." The native Sultan, a Mohammedan, kept a hundred wives and as many concubines; the Portuguese, numbering a garrison of fifty and about as many traders, thought it incumbent on them to follow the Sultan's example. Of all the islands of the archipelago, Francis had found none so utterly given to immorality and vice as Ternate had been when he first came there in 1546. Half a year later, when he visited the island for the second time, all was changed: there was peace and goodness; in the evenings the Malay fishermen set out into the magnificent island sunsets singing, not only the traditional love songs of the island, but also the Litany of Our Blessed Lady. The Sultan's mother, the regent, long an ardent follower of Islam, became a Christian, taking the name of Isabella.

On his way back to India he was held up at Malacca for the last five months of 1547, owing to the monsoons. In October the Sultan of Achin made a long-dreaded raid on that city. This native ruler of the northern end of

Sumatra was one of the strongest and most warlike of several island princes whom the Moslems—hopeful of driving out the Portuguese from their profitable possessions in the Far East—had steadily reinforced with men, arms and ships. His galleys sailed under a flag bearing the device "Achin, drinker of the troublesome blood of Kaffirs." At two in the morning, on a dark, rainy night, fifty Achinese galleys, manned by five thousand fighting men, announced their arrival in Malacca by setting fire to ships anchored in that port. The sleeping garrison awoke to war cries, flames and utter confusion. At dawn the attackers were found lying close to the shore and the garrison trained all available artillery on them. They retreated out of range of the cannon, and finding some poor fishermen further out in the bay, cut off their ears and noses and sent them home with an insulting letter to the captain of the Malacca garrison. The mutilated men, covered with blood, were being carried into the hospital when Father Francis came downhill on his way from saying Mass. When he had attended to the wounded, the captain of the garrison showed him the letter announcing the Sultan's intention of cruising and pirating as much as he liked in the Straits, concluding with a challenge to the Portuguese to stop him—if they could.

"How should I reply to such a challenge?" asked the captain.

"By an attack," replied Father Francis, rather to the surprise of the bystanders, who had never before heard *el Santo* recommend the use of force.

"But," demurred the captain, "we have only seven galleys to their fifty; and the seven we have are far from seaworthy."

"Let me see them," said Xavier. And he and the captain went down to look at the galleys. They were in poor shape. The shipwrights were sent for, but reported that nails were scarce and it was hard to say where in Malacca could be found the amount of pitch needed to recaulk the ships. Rigging—all—would have to be overhauled before the galleys, beached several months before, could be refloated. Clearly, the shipwrights were in no way anxious to make the ships ready to sail; the captain, too, now that the first scare was over and that the pirates were known to have taken nothing more valuable than a few stray geese in their night raid, was inclined to treat the matter lightly. And the indolent Malays seemed little inclined for action. But Francis, knowing the prestige and power of Portugal throughout the East, did not wish to see the military reputation of the Westerns impaired: the religion he preached had been the religion practised—very imperfectly indeed—by the Portuguese; if they suffered, Catholicity suffered. They were bad props for the gospel, but, if they were destroyed, on what could the infant church in these lands lean? He spoke to the crowd assembled by the galleys. He appealed to the wealthy merchants, who would not have to risk the seas or the encounters with the Achinese, to get the rotten galleys put into a fit state for the brave men who would man them. He reminded the Portuguese of the intrepid mariners who had first sailed these unknown seas to give new lands to Portugal. He urged the soldiers to go fight that Sultan who tyrannised over every Eastern seaport, that infidel who hated Christianity and had despoiled many Christian churches and shrines, and massacred or enslaved any Christians he captured. Despite the fact that he used the most impassioned and eloquent words, only one hundred and eighty volunteered to go chase the pirates. But the merchants, highly apprehensive lest the Achinese return and seize their spice cargoes in the harbour, paid handsomely those who worked on the ships. In five days the galleys were ready. On the morning of Tuesday, October 24th, they made ready to sail and Father Francis gave them his blessing before he went to Our Lady of the Mount to say the Mass of the feast—the Mass of St. Raphael, patron of travellers —for the success of the venture. A great congregation assisted at the Mass.

Just after the priest had said the words *"Domine, non sum dignus,"* and had bowed over the altar to communicate, a man rushed into the church, ran up the aisle and into the sanctuary. Seeing the priest about to take the chalice, he fell on his knees beside him, his great distress evident to all the people. As Father Francis finished communicating the man attempted to interrupt, but *el Santo* made him a little gesture to wait; the priest finished the Mass and then the messenger blurted out the awful news that the flagship, the first of seven, had sunk when crossing the harbour bar. Moreover, the men on the other ships, taking this as a bad omen, were about to mutiny, saying that they were being sacrificed in an attempt to do the impossible. The captain was in a panic and had asked would Father Francis come quickly. As soon as Xavier had prayed he went to the mutineers, who were stubbornly muttering that the sinking of the galley was a heaven-sent warning that they were not to go to certain destruction. *El Santo* smiled and his smile calmed and reassured them.

"Is that all the trust you have in God?" he asked. "You lost a leaking galley. Be ready to sail and God will send you two good galleys, and that before the day ends."

With this he returned to the hospital and tended the sick, bathing the sores of the patients as was his custom. In the evening an excited sailor ran up-hill with news that two galleys were sighted but that they did not seem to be

putting in to Malacca. Father Francis asked for a fast boat
and good oarsmen to row him out to intercept the galleys.
He was rowed out at once. When he boarded the galleys
he found none other in charge than one mercenary captain, de Mello, a cutthroat fleeing from Burma, where men
waited to repay his dreadful deed of the previous year
when he had attempted to seize the bride at a Hindu
wedding. The buccaneer welcomed Xavier and did him
all honour. Did not the whole East call this man "the
heavenly Pilgrim"? Did not all the Europeans in India call
him *el Santo?*

"How can I serve Your Reverence?" he enquired.

"I ask you, by the five wounds of Our Lord, to join
forces with us against the infidels of Achin," answered
Xavier.

"I was going to sail past Malacca to avoid paying customs," said de Mello, "but, since Your Reverence asks me
to help so holy a cause, I cannot refuse you—provided
that you procure for me in return exemption from the
harbour taxes."

Francis hurried back to Malacca, where the necessary
certificates were made out by officials, some of whom remarked that de Mello, as ever, took advantage of saint
and sinner alike. One eye on heaven, no doubt, while talking to Father Francis; the other on business! Next morning, the certificates having been sent out to the waiting
galleys, de Mello made a magnificent entry into Malacca,
all his guns firing, all his banners flying as he swept into
the road where the other six galleys were at anchor. They
set off at once, Dom de Sa as Admiral, de Mello second in
command. As the Portuguese knelt for Xavier's blessing,
el Santo said, "Always have Christ crucified in the depths
of your hearts, and show in your bearing content and
happiness, with true courage, so that even the most

cowardly of the galley slaves may take courage from your example."

For a whole moon they sailed up the Malay coast watching for the Achins, Dom de Sa, sword in hand, resplendent in his waistcoat of mail made of iron leaves, his red satin coat studded with gilt nails. Every now and again he changed from one ship to another, that he might reanimate the soldiers and remind them that, back in Malacca, they had a saint interceding for them.

The Achinese, as was their habit, had their galleys lying in ambush, in a river mouth half-way up the straits. Hearing that eight Portuguese war galleys were sailing up towards where they hid, the pirates decided to attack. They came—a fearsome sight—down the river on the ebb-tide, their drums beating a tattoo in time with the oars, their fighters yelling war cries, the arquebuses and cannon on their prows discharging volley after volley. Dom de Sa, guessing that the swiftness of the current at the river mouth would prevent the enemy fleet from forming up in effective fighting array, waited close to the shore in a little backwater, out of the pull of the current, a headland protecting him on one flank. As the Achinese galleys were swirled about in disarray at the river mouth, he raked them again and again with a grapeshot of hard pebbles. Some of his men boarded the nearest pirate ships, throwing fireballs on to those and adjacent ships as they went, while his arquebusiers, with accurate and deadly aim, picked off those who appeared to be in charge of operations on the enemy galleys. The pirates, finding some of their vessels sinking, others on fire, turned about and made, with all possible speed, for their Sumatra home. They left twenty-five galleys behind of which the Portuguese gladly took possession. The engagement lasted less than half an hour.

The day on which this glorious victory took place was

December 4th, the second Sunday of the Advent of 1547. The fleet had been by this time almost six weeks gone and no news had come, save messengers from Sumatra, whom none knew whether to believe or disbelieve, saying that the Achinese had defeated the few Portuguese galleys and were making ready to besiege Malacca. Every Friday, since the departure of the ships, Xavier had preached at the Misericordiae Church; on Sundays he preached at Our Lady of the Mount. Several times in those weeks he had to rebuke some of his flock for consulting sorcerers, trying to find out the issue of the encounter with the Achinese. As he passed through the streets he heard women murmuring that he had sent their menfolk to death. After Mass each day, he would ask all to join him in saying a *Pater* and an *Ave* for the success of the expedition and the safe return of the Malacca men, but, as day succeeded day and week followed week, the responses to these prayers grew weaker and weaker; some even got up and left the church.

On Sunday, December 4th, he celebrated Mass in Our Lady's Church, as usual. The Lesson was from the Epistle to the Romans: ". . . *the gentiles are to glorify God for His mercy, as it is written: Therefore will I confess to Thee, O Lord, among the gentiles and will sing to Thy name. And again he saith: Rejoice, ye gentiles and magnify Him, all ye people . . . in Him the gentiles shall hope.*" Father Francis chose those lines for his text. Suddenly, in the middle of his sermon, he broke off and, to the amazement of all, began to describe a great battle as though the action were taking place before his eyes; then, turning to the carved, eagle-wood crucifix beside the pulpit, he clasped the feet of the Christ, crying: "Love of my soul, do not abandon those whom Thou hast redeemed by Thy Precious Blood. Jesus, my God, by the bitter agony

213

of Thy last hours on earth, do not desert those Thou hast saved." Tears streamed down his worn face, and for a few moments he knelt, his arms on the pulpit rail, his head bowed upon them. The congregation stared, aghast. When all Malacca had worried, he alone had smiled; when even the most sanguine had given way to forebodings, he had held on, strong in hope. Was their whole world crashing about them? Was even *el Santo* giving way to despair?

When he lifted his head, his face was alight with joy. "People of Malacca," he said—and his voice was vibrant— "Good news! Be glad and rejoice and grieve no more. Our fleet has overthrown the enemy, sunk many Achinese ships and taken others from the pirates; our side lost but three men, and the fleet is setting out for home, laden with captives and spoils." On Tuesday, the Feast of St. Nicholas, a fast boat arrived, with news that the victors were towing home the twenty-five galleys captured and would be in Malacca for the feast of Our Lady's Immaculate Conception. When the fleet came home, it was found that all had happened exactly as the Father had said.

During those last five months of 1547, he profited of his enforced delay at Malacca to turn himself more and more to God. As in Mylapore two years previously, his body rested a little from the interminable journeyings, the ceaseless labours; but his spirit, ardent and indefatigable, sped eagerly onwards in quest of God. He spent many evenings sitting on a height above the harbour, allowing his spiritual energies to gather and renew themselves. Noting the sun burnishing the sails of the spice-ships coming from the distant islands to Malacca, he frequently recalled the saying of St. Augustine that had never failed to enthral him: "We come to God by love and not by sail." How long ago it seemed now, that night in the Ste. Barbe, when he had made, through Ignatius, his capitulation to

214

God; that night when he had resolved to give all to God. Giving all had meant that he had, incessantly, to give more; and, as he gave, so much the more he became conscious of the penury of the human heart: man was a pauper, with nothing worthy of God, nothing with which to return that immense outpouring of love and grace lavished upon him by the divine Lover. Xavier's yearning to love God was a consuming fire; like Daniel, he was a man of desires, a man athirst for God. But, like all lovers, he could only lament his inability to love more, to give more, to do more . . . His only distraction during this time of prayer at Malacca was the thought of the Japanese *samurai*. Behind Anjiro's diminutive figure, Francis saw the teeming millions of Japan; he hoped to enkindle and inflame each one of Anjiro's race with the love of God; he would bring God to them; they would bring him to God.

He left Malacca at the end of 1547. As his caravel pulled out from the shore, the bells of Our Lady on the Mount pealed a farewell chime. Xavier sighed. He had accomplished so little there. In Malacca and in the islands, as in Goa, the Europeans had both helped and hindered him. They had built churches, given him transport, lodging, and, in general, hearkened to his appeals to amend their lives. But they had also given the natives the bad example of their greed and cruelty and evil living; they had disgracefully abused power, And in those countries that, for the present, he had neither time nor an official mandate to visit—such as Siam and Burma—their conduct had been notorious. So far, no Portuguese garrison had gained a footing in either Siam or Burma, but bands of Portuguese mercenaries had hired themselves to the highest bidders in the internecine rebellions in these countries and in the wars that raged between the two realms for several years past for possession of the Sacred White Elephant. Stories of the perfidy, dishonour and wickedness of the captains of these bands of mercenaries were widespread throughout the East; even Father Francis had heard many tales. The same de Mello who had helped in the expedition against the Achins was guilty of attempting to abduct a Hindu bride; he had killed her bridegroom and the friends who had rushed to her protection, but the girl strangled herself with her wedding veil sooner than allow herself to be taken captive.

When Father Francis left Malacca for Goa, de Mello also took advantage of the easterly monsoon to return to Pegu. The pirate was sailing to his death and *el Santo* knew it. Vengeance cruel—and not undeserved—awaited him in Burma. Villain though he was, he had obliged a saint; sinner though he was, he recognised sanctity and knelt for Xavier's blessing before leaving Malacca. He was to need that benediction sorely not many moons later when a Hindu mob stoned him and tore him to pieces while yet alive. But he died as became a Christian—begging pardon for his many and grievous sins, offering his sufferings in union with those of the dying Saviour. "If Thou, O Lord, wilt mark iniquities, Lord, who shall endure it?" was his cry as his enemies closed in upon him; and as the jagged stones hurtled upon him from all sides and clawing hands fastened themselves on his members, he uttered the name of Jesus to the end.

As de Mello sailed north to Burma and death, Xavier sailed west, reflecting, sadly, how the crimes of Christians poisoned so many minds against Christ. Before they had even heard of God Our Lord, the Siamese and the Burmese hated Him—because of His followers. It would not be so in Japan, he had every reason to hope. Looking back, he sent his blessing to Malacca and, beyond Malacca, to the faraway islands that lay under turquoise skies on those coral-floored seas several hundred leagues towards sunrise.

CHAPTER 11

SOME of those on the caravel on which Francis was returning to India had been on the expedition that defeated the Achinese. Over and over again they were asked to tell the epic tale of how eight galleys defeated fifty, of how, when they saw the Achins' ships dashing into and ramming one another in the current, they began to call aloud on the holy name of Jesus, as Father Francis had told them to, and found themselves suddenly imbued with a super-human strength and courage and skill in combat.

As the Malayan coast receded from view, the sailors watched Francis pace the decks, barefooted, his *loba*—the same one that had been given him leaving Goa in 1543—discoloured from sun and tropical rains, and patched in a hundred places; and they agreed that never had such a priest come to the East before. From Goa to Cape Comorin and Malacca and the Morotai, all were telling of the miracles that had been wrought everywhere he went. At Cape Comorin and on the Coromandel coast and at Malacca and again in the Spice Islands, it was rumoured that large congregations of different peoples and races, speaking not only different tongues but different dialects of those different languages, all heard him speak in their own tongue. On the fishery coast he had

217

done wondrous things and cured countless sick; later when he found that people spoke of these wonders and were inclined to venerate him on that account, he worked similar wonders through the little children who attended his catechism classes, sending them to make the Sign of the Cross on a sick person, to touch with his crucifix someone possessed by demons. There had been marvellous things done in Travancore and Mylapore.

One of the sailors had a friend who had been on a ship taken by pirates and who had escaped by swimming ashore at night. Almost naked and entirely destitute, he went to Father Francis for alms. The priest opened his purse and found it empty; he handed it to the sailor telling him not to despair, that he would pray for him; and behold! as *el Santo* prayed, the sailor felt the purse grow suddenly heavy and when he looked inside there were thirty gold *fanans*. Another had a friend, a trader who knelt and asked the Father's blessing before leaving on a distant voyage. Father Francis gave the man his own rosary, bidding him to say it daily and to have confidence in Our Lady when the hour of need came. The ship was wrecked and all souls aboard lost, except the merchant, who, with the Father's beads about his neck, managed to cling to a plank; he kept calling on Our Lady, and a great wave coming cast him safely onto the coast not far from a Portuguese settlement. His miraculous vision of the fight in which the Achin fleet was defeated was but one of hundreds of wonderful things related of *el Santo* in Malacca and on the islands of the faraway seas. The sailors retailed them to one another as the ship sailed across the Bay of Bengal. Father Francis did not like anyone to speak of such miracles; when anyone mentioned them to him, he flushed and got embarrassed and said that it was not a sinner like himself who worked these marvels, but God who had been pleased to heal the sick and the infirm; God drove out devils when His afflicted ones had faith in Him and when Francis had prayed for and with them. All very well, the sailors said, but why were Francis' prayers heard, and not those of the other priests in all the places where the Portuguese had churches? It was because he was holy and had utterly surrendered his will and all his desires to the the will and good pleasure of God that God so often deigned to do for Xavier what He would not for another. They were no theologians but they knew. And they agreed on one point: of all the miracles, the greatest was Father Francis himself. The man was a living miracle. Hard on himself, easy on others; working himself to the bone, not for his own aggrandisement, but for the greater honour and glory of God; living in this world while his heart was in heaven; loving God so much that love and happiness and grace welled up in his soul and spilled out on to the souls of all he met. No wonder the Indians and the Malays and the islanders had called him "the heavenly Pilgrim"!

.   .   .   .   .

As they came into the Strait of Ceylon a tropical storm hit the ship; the top-heavy craft lurched and plunged and was in imminent danger of foundering. After struggling for a long time against the elements, the captain announced that he could not hope to save both cargo and passengers—the ship's load must be lightened if ever they were to make port alive. So, into the ocean went the cinnamon and ginger, the spices, the gold dust, the bird-of-paradise plumes, the tortoise-shell and ivory and coral ornaments, the jewels and damasks. But still the storm raged and for three days and three nights the ship was thrown hither and thither while the terrified passengers wept and prayed and made vows never again to go to sea, never again to engage in any other business save that of saving their souls. Juan de Eyro, the volunteer for the Company who had journeyed from Mylapore to Malacca with Father Francis and who was now accompanying him back to Goa College, told the captain that *el Santo* had predicted this tempest before leaving for India. The captain and the officers asked where *el Santo* was; they had not seen him since the storm started. God grant that he had not been swept overboard! No, the Father had been in the holds hearing confessions, encouraging and comforting all; de Eyro had seen him praying in his cabin a few moments before. Just then, the lookout shouted that they were drifting onto the Ceylon sandbanks; all was up. The captain could not hope to save many; he could not hope to save even himself; but he would do his best to save Xavier. Going to *el Santo's* cabin to call him, he hesitated, seeing him so lost in prayer before his crucifix. Finally, feeling the ship lurch heavily to starboard, he shouted to Father Francis, who followed him out on deck. The pilot had left his wheel, the officers were in a group watching and waiting for the fatal moment when a fresh squall should send them keeling over into the deep. Xavier asked for the sounding-line, threw it over the side and let it down into the waves, saying "Great God, Father, Son and Holy Ghost, have mercy upon us," and immediately the ship ceased from listing, righted herself and weathered the fast-subsiding storm. Writing a day or two later to the brethren in Rome, Xavier told of the tempest and of how he had invoked God and the Holy Mother, Queen of Heaven, the angels and the saints, and especially those saints who on earth had belonged to the Society of Jesus, and how, among those latter, he had particularly called upon "the blessed soul of Peter Favre," his old companion of Ste. Barbe.

They landed in Cochin in mid-January. Here, all the abuses of the Portuguese colony seemed to have multiplied in the three years he had been away. He began again to visit his Indian missions, going from Cochin to the pearl fisheries, back north then to Goa and up and down from Goa to one of the missions and back again, resuming his life of incessant labours and journeyings, noting with heavy heart that the greedy Portuguese officials were now, more than ever, the stumbling block to the conversion of the natives. He wrote to King John in blunt language, advocating that strong measures be taken against corrupt officials. He wrote Rodriguez asking for more workers—workers of a calibre that would be capable of withstanding the temptations of the sensuous East. He wrote Ignatius asking to have some holy and virtuous Father sent out, "someone whose vigour and zeal may stir me from the apathy into which I am sunk."

The Bishop of Goa, despite his age and infirmity, was visiting and confirming at Cochin. He was overjoyed to meet Father Francis again; John d'Albuquerque had his own troubles and was glad to receive one friend to whom he could unburden himself without fear of having his confidence betrayed.

In response to the various complaints sent by the Bishop and by Francis himself to King John, concerning the unchristian and scandalous conduct of certain Portuguese in Goa and elsewhere in India, a churchman, Miguel Vaz, had been sent out as head of the Inquisition to deal with the manifold abuses so prevalent among Catholics in India. Xavier nodded as the Bishop told his tale, remembering the half-caste and Indian wives of so many Portuguese, who became nominally Christian and, shortly after baptism, relapsed into pagan superstition, worshipping Kali and Siva and sometimes using their influence on their

221

husbands to make the latter join them in their unholy
rites. Miguel Vaz had come out, a good man and full of
zeal, Albuquerque's right hand. But, alas, he had little
understanding of the problems of India and proceeded to
act on European lines, hunting down sorcerers and converted Jews; he had sent some wealthy native Christians
in chains to Portugal, accusing them of crimes against the
faith which they could not have been guilty of, seeing that
they had been but poorly instructed and were ignorant of
the truths they were accused of denying. Hearing of the
scandalous behaviour of certain Portuguese in a coastal
fortress, he had proceeded there in the January of 1547,
intending to visit the full power of the Inquisition on the
culprits. While there, he had been poisoned. "By whom?"
Father Francis might well ask. Vaz might have been
murdered by anyone—Moslems, Jews, natives, Portuguese
—but the wicked had hastened to spread the report that
he had been poisoned at the instigation of the Bishop of
Goa, whose authority he had been usurping. Francis
would soon hear for himself the tales that were going
round. The worst of it, the Bishop said, was the frightful
scandal being given the natives who, always watching the
Europeans, always listening, could not fail to draw their
own conclusions regarding the death of Miguel Vaz. The
incident had not helped the cause of religion. Indeed, it
might well prove a setback from which the Church in
India would take several years to recover.

After visiting the Bishop, Francis went to the pearl
fisheries, to see how his first native converts in India were
doing. Six members of the Society were labouring there,
their superior a young Italian Father of a most lovable
disposition. Francis had much to ask him about Rome. He
asked the Father how he had come to join the Society and
found that he had been a student in Parma University—

one of that guard of honour which escorted Francis Xavier a mile beyond Parma on his road to Lisbon and the East in 1540. His professor in Parma had been none other than Father Peter Favre, onetime fellow student of Father Francis in Paris. Father Favre had often spoken of his friend, Xavier. Later on, in Rome, Ignatius too had chatted to the young Parma novice about Father Francis and the student days in Ste. Barbe. And again in Coimbra, Rodriguez, another student-friend of Father Francis, had never tired of telling stories of his old friend, "the ball-playing Basque."

The young Father was only twenty-eight; his long years under the gentle, holy Favre had left their mark on him more surely than the comparatively short periods he had spent with Ignatius or with Rodriguez. Of all the men sent out from Europe this young Italian was the only one of the spiritual calibre that, again and again, Francis had begged Rodriguez to send him. The Rector in Coimbra seemed to be rather of the opinion that, if a man did not come up to the requirements of the Portuguese or other European provinces of the Society, he would do very well for the East. True, Francis had stated, in the beginning, that anyone who could baptise and catechise and had good health would be invaluable. But through his own experiences with Juan de Eyro, another who had left him since returning to India, and Mansilhas, whom he had to dismiss for disobedience, he had come to realise that inferior material was inferior anywhere—in Asia or Europe. Only recently he had written again to Rodriguez, asking that a worthy Rector be sent out for that project dearer than any other—Goa College. He hoped for great things from Holy Faith College. Since the Society in Europe could supply but a tiny fraction of the missionaries needed, he arranged that the College of Goa was to be

223

set apart for native priests who could be trained there for the apostolate to their own people. None but Asiatics were to be accepted. In the College they would be isolated not only from the heathen influences but also from the Christian life of Goa—both of which tended to have a bad effect on youths destined to be priests, lay brothers or catechists.

Micer Paul was a man of little learning and a hopeless preacher. But he was humble, simple and mortified, devoted to the sick and poor, and undoubtedly a man of holiness and prayer. He was just the one to have charge of the bodily and spiritual welfare of the young native seminarians. He lacked the gifts of organisation and government which were needful for the Rector of what Francis hoped would become a great college—one that would eventually provide India and all the East with a sufficiency of zealous and holy native priests to enlighten their various peoples and set the whole East on fire with the love of God Our Lord. There were two suitable men who had come out from Europe, one Netherlander, one Italian; Father Gaspar Berze would have been a good man to put in charge of the College but the Portuguese would not agree to a Dutch Rector. The same objection against nationality held, though possibly less strongly, against the young Italian Father, now Superior at the fishery coast. Besides, he was needed at Cape Comorin and Travancore, that mission area being, in its own way, as important as the College.

While Francis was anxiously considering and praying about this matter of the rectorship of Goa he received word that Rodriguez had himself taken the rather high-handed step of making the appointment from Coimbra. He had sent out to Goa the previous year a Father Gomes, a man whose appointment the Governor rather favoured.

Don Francisco

Rodriguez wrote extolling the newcomer's good qualities
—not at all bothering to apologise for making the appointment without first consulting Xavier. The latter was
troubled; he had himself considered appointing Gomes,
who was a popular preacher, but one who trusted more to
his own eloquence, resonant voice and appropriate gestures than to the Holy Ghost, whose mouthpiece he should
be. He was a man of faulty judgment, with little tact, inclined to be pompous and self-opinionated. Already Francis had heard him airing his views as to how Goa College
needed reorganising on the model of the European colleges in which he himself had studied. He had spent one
of his first evenings in Goa explaining to that shabbily
dressed Father Xavier—whom he privately thought most
unfittingly attired for a man in his position as papal representative in the East—how Ignatius' idea was to make
their colleges the nerve-centre of the entire Society.
Xavier had said nothing; he could have told the newcomer
that no one in the whole Society knew the mind of Ignatius as he did, though so long and so far away from the
Father General. He listened, quietly, deferentially, so
much so that the following day Gomes wrote to Rodriguez
telling him of the impression he had made upon Xavier,
and of how his idea of making another Coimbra—nay,
another Paris—out of Goa College "fully satisfied Father
Francis."

Although he could have done so, Xavier did not coun-
termand the appointment made by Rodriguez. But when
he heard the new Rector hold forth on the excellence of
the methods of Coimbra and remembered the Tamils,
Indians, Malayans, Moluccans, Cingalese, negroes,
Chinese and Japanese and others in Goa College, when
he thought of the dozen different languages spoken there
and of the three students who once had been Buddhist

priests, he was filled with forebodings. The native youths over sixteen who were received there were only too often familiar with vices unknown to European boys of the same age; already they had a big problem in weaning these youths from evil habits, in keeping the younger boys, who had lived in the College from childhood, from becoming contaminated by the influence of the others. Furthermore, if one admitted but children, they forgot their native tongue and, by the time they were ordained, were unable to preach to their people.

A Father was to be sent to Ormuz—a town on the Persian Gulf notorious as the Babylon of the age, a veritable cesspool of iniquity—to found a mission there. As the conversion of such an infamous city would win any man glory both here and hereafter, Francis proposed that Gomes be sent there, hoping that when he left Goa, the question of the college rectorship could be more easily settled. But Father Gomes had no intention of wasting his sweetness on the desert air of Ormuz, which was reputed to be one of the hottest spots outside hell, both as regards climate and morals. Letters began to circulate in Goa telling how the Portuguese had missed bullfights and *fiestas* sooner than miss hearing Father Gomes preach. The Bishop was induced to appoint the new Rector preacher-in-ordinary of Goa Cathedral. When the rumour got about that the popular Father Gomes was being sent to Ormuz, a regular furore broke out at the bare idea of this eloquent man being wasted on heathens and evil-doers. High and low signed a petition demanding that the Rector be allowed to remain in Goa. Sadly and reluctantly, Francis gave in. The Dutch Father asked to be allowed to go to Ormuz. Just about this time the fleet arrived, with many letters from the brethren in Europe. There were letters from Ignatius for all but Xavier. The

Rector, reading portions of his letter aloud to the other Fathers, assured those who listened that there was nothing Ignatius liked better than discipline. He himself had learned that, if nothing else, from his time in Rome with the Father General. And Rodriguez had often commended him in Coimbra for being so excellent a disciplinarian. Humbly, Xavier acknowledged to himself that he had probably misjudged the Rector. Ignatius had deeper intuition and probably Rodriguez had decided that discipline would be a good thing for Goa College, with its strange assortment of students. God had permitted that Gomes should be made Rector, and who was Xavier to question the will of God? Besides, a popular preacher would do much good in Goa. God had also permitted that Ignatius, "the father of his soul," should be silent to him, when his heart had counted the days until the fleet came with the letters. That was something far harder to bear than the anxiety about the College and the Rector. It was, for Xavier, one of those times in his life when much had been asked of him—like that time when his flourishing communities of Paravas had been wiped out; like the time da Sousa and the Portuguese had preferred a cargo of condiments to the evangelisation of a whole province; like the time the Malaccans had murmured against him and left Our Lady of the Mount for the soothsayers in the bazaars. But, though he loved Ignatius above anyone on earth and was wounded to the heart at having been forgotten when so many others were remembered, he had so accustomed himself to living in the spirit of the words "Yea, Father, for so it hath seemed good in Thy sight," that his friend's apparent coolness and neglect, since it had seemed good in the Heavenly Father's sight, was only one more manifestation of that blessed will to which he answered gladly, "Yea, Father. Amen."

For the rest of his time in Goa he set himself out to be particularly kind to Father Gomes. At the same time there was much to be seen to; he wrote what was probably the longest letter of his life, a document over one hundred and twenty thousand words in length, giving the Dutch Father going to Ormuz the most minute instructions for his missionary work there—how to deal with different penitents; how and on what to preach; the obligation of rendering strict obedience to the local ecclesiastical authorities; avoidance of the meshes of political or commercial disputes; instructions for catechising the heathen; the necessity of becoming acquainted with the customs, opinions, law, government, and vices of a locality or a people; the knowledge of human character, so needful to a pastor of souls, a knowledge to be gleaned from those living books, souls. Of these and a hundred kindred matters Xavier wrote the Dutch Father, imploring him to remember above all that he must look first to the saving of his own soul; then he might venture to help others save theirs.

He also wrote to the King and to Rodriguez and to Ignatius. He told the latter of the arrangements being made for India and of his hopes for Japan. Anjiro, the *samurai*, had been baptised and named Paul of the Holy Faith; the Japanese and his compatriots at Goa College had made wonderful strides in their studies, being already well able to read and write Latin. The plans for Japan were totally different from those adopted heretofore in dealing with pagan nations, inasmuch as the Japanese were a highly civilised, educated people, who judged all things in the light of reason. Francis was preparing himself for this, the greatest of his apostolic ventures, by studying the Japanese language and customs, by enquiring concerning the religion practised in that country, by making translations of the prayers, the commandments, the Creed, and the Catechism. He would be grateful if Ignatius would send learned men when sending Fathers to the East; they would be needed there to argue with the Brahmins and the bonzes. He wondered if he had not been mistaken in his decision to preach to the outcast classes in India: the Brahmins steadfastly refused to listen to one who preached to pariahs. In Japan he would begin at the other end of the social strata; it remained to be seen whether this experiment would prove successful; but Paul of the Holy Faith had assured him that if the rulers and priests became Christians, all other classes would soon follow suit. He concluded with these words:

> I am leaving, at Easter, for Japan. There, at least, there are neither Jews nor Moslems nor Christians of evil life, only heathens, a people eager-minded, greedy of new things, curious to know about God and nature. I ask that some priest of our Society may offer Mass for me once a month in St. Pietro in Montorio, the chapel on the reputed site of St. Peter's martyrdom . . .
>
> And now, father of my soul, to whom I write on my knees, still kneeling I pray you to intercede for me with God in all your Masses and prayers that, as long as I live, He may enable me to know clearly and accomplish to the full His most holy will.
>
> Your useless son,
Francisco

He wrote another letter to Rodriguez, telling him that he was about to leave, having arranged that, in his absence, Father Gomes was to act as Rector of the College but not as Superior of the Fathers in India. Micer Paul, having been longer in India, had been entrusted with the spiritual and temporal care of the students in Goa and was to be responsible for the government of the Society in India while Francis was away.

He also wrote King John III, asking him to appoint a certain priest chaplain at the court in Lisbon, not for the priest's own sake so much as for that of his three sisters who had been left penniless orphans. If the priest got on well at court, his sisters would get the opportunity of being introduced to many eligible young men and of making marriages suitable to girls of good, though impoverished family, such as they were. The degradation of womankind in the East had never failed to distress Xavier. In Goa and Cochin, as in Mylapore, Malacca and the islands of the Indies, the absence of even the ordinary, natural consideration for woman as the bearer and nourisher of human life, amazed and horrified him. Only in Japan, he had been told, would he find a race the daughters of which had a womanly dignity that won them the respect denied their sisters elsewhere in the East. Such a report only increased his desire to visit that land. "A nation," wrote an old Jewish scribe, "is as great as its women." Remembering his mother, Doña Maria, his sister Ana, his aunt Violante, he was struck anew by the tremendous contrast between the Christian West and the East where so many people still sat in darkness and the shadow of death. In nothing was that contrast so marked as in the status of women. Francis hoped and prayed that the women of Japan and, indeed, of all the East, might yet achieve the high destiny of handing on, aflame with an ardent and resplendent faith, the torch of life—Christian life.

It was useless remonstrating with the pagans and infidels regarding their treatment of women. To them he could only repeat the words of Our Lord: "I have yet many things to say to you, but you cannot bear them

now." In their eyes, woman was a chattel, to be bought
and sold, acquired or discarded at will. The Mahommedans found the Christian practice of allowing women
in churches and religious assemblies incomprehensible:
one did not allow one's camel or one's dog into the
Mosque. Allah was worshipped only by rational beings;
all the world knew that a woman could no more think or
pray than a dog or a camel. Their father, Mahomet, had
not taught the repugnant doctrine that women possessed
souls.

But if the heathens and Mahommedans could not
abide such teaching, the Christians could. So, from the
pulpits of the various garrison towns, Francis had frequently taken the Portuguese to task for their evil lives.
They had come East, he told them, and, throwing restraint
to the winds, had outdone the unbelievers in vicious
living, bringing shame and obloquy on their holy religion.
How, he asked, could they so far have forgotten their
birth and baptism, their homes and upbringing, as to
adopt the infidel attitude towards women? Had he to remind them—Portuguese—of the first Christian woman, the
Virgin Mother whom God's Son had set forever upon a
pedestal, sinless, immaculate, holy? Was it possible that
the subjects of King John, bemused with the riches and
pleasures of the sensuous East, had lost sight of that Ivory
Tower standing beyond the moon, beyond the stars, far,
far beyond the sun?

Leaning from his pulpit he would begin listing the
shrines of Our Lady that studded Portugal, the land
known as "the Garden of Europe planted by the sea." He
would call upon Our Lady of Calm, Our Lady of Pity,
Our Lady of Exile, Our Lady of a Good Voyage, Our
Lady of a Good Death, Our Lady of Healing, Our Lady
of Help, Our Lady of Guidance, Our Lady of Anguish,

Our Lady of the Poor. Or, awakening a wave of nostalgia in his listeners, he would describe the pilgrimages of Portugal: Our Lady of the Pass of Grace, of the Snowy Nevadas, of Loule, Rocha, Saude, Atalia, Mercianna, Arrabida, and a dozen other shrines well known in name, if not in fact, to his congregations. He rejoiced, he told them, that Europeans had as yet no possessions in Japan. There he could hope to preach Christ crucified, the Son of the Virgin, without being hampered by the bad example of Christians—Christians in name but not in deed.

From Cochin, where he was to board a ship for Japan, he wrote at length to Micer Paul, hoping that the letter would eventually find its way into the hands of all the Fathers in Goa—particularly Father Gomes. Micer Paul had wisdom and would know that several portions of that letter had been written, not for him, but for the new Rector.

Enjoining mutual charity, obedience, brotherly concord, prudence and patience upon all the brethren in Goa and throughout India, Francis Xavier, then just forty-three years of age, left Cochin on April 21st, 1549. It was Easter Sunday, and his ship was bound for Japan.

CHAPTER 12

ON THE eve of the feast of the Assumption, 1549, a junk, captained by a Chinese pirate, approached a harbour on Kyushu, one of Japan's main islands. The passengers included a murderer returning to the scene of his crime and a saint bent on extending the kingdom of God. Major items of cargo were gifts for the Emperor, the Great Voo, and a joss, or idol, to appease whom many chickens had been sacrificed and many incense-sticks burned on the seven-week journey from Malacca.

The saint, Francis Xavier, had long since relinquished all earthly honours. Who now remembered that the royal blood of Navarre flowed in the veins of the erstwhile nobleman of the Basque country? Who, in these out-landish parts, had ever as much as heard of that Mecca of sixteenth-century scholars—Paris University—or its promising professor of Aristotelian philosophy?

His interminable journeyings and rigorous asceticism were already, after seven years in the tropics, making inroads on his once magnificent constitution. The lithe limbs of the runner, the agile form of the *pelota* player were spare as ever; but now the shoulders sagged a bit, the man tended to walk with head forward, arms hanging; the dark hair was streaked with grey; but the fine eyes held fires that smouldered as ardently as ever, and the winning

233

smile was not less ready than of yore; the countenance, always pleasing, now had an indefinable attraction, in some way it indicated those inexhaustible twin-springs of love for God and compassion for men, whose bright waters played—unfailing fountains—in the heart.

Standing on the deck of the junk, Xavier looked out towards Japan. He had come a long way to this Land of the Rising Sun—from Navarre to Paris, from Paris to Rome, from Rome to Lisbon, from Lisbon right round Africa and across the Arabian Sea to Goa. Then he had delayed, going thirteen times up and down the west coast of India between Goa and the pearl fisheries; he had delayed again, going to Malacca and over and thither among the islands; he had gone back to India and Goa and started out then on the longest journey of all, the six thousand mile voyage to Japan.

Leaving Cochin on Easter Sunday, they arrived in Malacca on the morrow after Ascension Day. It was the first time Francis had been on the sea without being seasick, and he was in the highest spirits. The Governor and all Malacca, remembering the victory over the Achinese and the wonderful things *el Santo* had done when last in their midst, gave him a rousing ovation. When the Governor, son of the great Vasco da Gama, heard that Francis was bound for Japan, he found a Chinaman who was leaving in his junk for that country and prevailed upon him to take Francis and his companions. As the Chinaman was nicknamed "the Robber," da Gama thought it advisable to make him leave his wife and all his money and belongings in Malacca as a guarantee that he would sail to Kagoshima and land his passengers there. Da Gama also helped Xavier to the extent of presenting him with five tons of the hottest Malaccan pepper, the sale of which was to finance the expedition. He also pressed on his acceptance several costly presents to soften the hearts of the rulers of Japan. "If we were da Gama's brothers," wrote Francis to King John III, "he could not have done more for us." But the pepper needed more room than could be spared in a junk, so most of it was sold on the Malacca mart, and the price realised set aside against the expenses anticipated in the Japanese enterprise.

Between Corpus Christi, June 20th, and the Feast of St. John the Baptist, Midsummer's Day, he wrote ten letters—several to the Fathers in Goa, two to King John, and others to the Fathers in charge of the various missions throughout the East. It caused surprise in Goa that Father Francis should have ordered a Father to proceed at once to Cape Comorin to take over the area where the young, saintly Italian Father was in charge. How could Xavier, so far away, have known, even before they did, that the Superior at the pearl fisheries had been murdered by the Badagas, who were again leaving a trail of destruction and slaughter in their wake as they raided the southern mission fields?

On the very eve of sailing he wrote in haste to Micer Paul and Father Gomes. There was a matter he had omitted from his previous letters and it was imperative that it be attended to at once. Whom had he run across in Malacca but his good old friend—companion of many an eastern voyage—the wealthy bachelor, Christopher Carvalho! This *gran amigo* of Xavier's had allowed himself to be talked round into giving up his roving and settling down. And Father Francis had bethought him of the very girl for Carvalho—the Fathers would know her, the orphan daughter of poor Diego Ferreira. The Fathers would know her better as the daughter of "Mother" Ferreira. Not without reason did the community in Goa call that good woman "Mother"; when they had been badly off and she better off than now, she had certainly mothered the Society in Goa. This was their opportunity to repay her. Francis had done his part, having brought Carvalho to the point of agreeing to settle down—for the greater glory of God, for his own spiritual good and for temporal reasons too. Not only that, Francis had so praised the widow's daughter to this crusty bachelor that he had given his word to marry her the moment he got back to India; and as he was a man of honour, he would not break his word. But the Fathers had to do their bit. They had to speak of Christopher to the girl in just such a way as Francis had spoken of her to his friend, so as to ensure that, before she met her suitor at all, she might be well disposed towards him. And "Mother" was to be let into the secret, and the patent she held concerning the office which her dead husband had bought from the Crown was to be sold; it would be a good thing if Father Gomes hinted to his many friends in the Treasury that they would do a good and charitable deed by buying back this patent for more than its worth. The proceeds could be given to "Mother," who would then be able to give her daughter a dowry and to accept the home Carvalho would offer his bride's mother, with her head in the air, so to speak—a little independent of her son-in-law, since she would have means of her own. The Fathers would find no difficulty with Christopher, of that Father Francis was certain. And, anyway, the rover had tired of roving and now "his heart yearns for the port and fixed anchorage of matrimony."

Carvalho had been waiting for *el Santo's* letter. When the junk left Malacca for the East, the friend of Xavier began searching at once for a vessel sailing to India, there to meet "Mother" and the unknown maiden to whom he had plighted his troth.

Francis had several times looked back at the Indian

coast. His blessing went out to the pearl-fishers, to the little missions studding the coast of Travancore. From afar he saluted St. Thomas at Mylapore. Sadly he noted the gilded temple domes that succeeded one another on every hilltop and mountain on the receding horizon of India. As many pagodas as ever reared their haughty, multi-winged roofs to heaven; the gross, obscene images of Kali and Siva, of Ganesha and Buddha, still stared, stony-eyed, from the altars where they squatted. About these altars vast multitudes of souls created by God the All-Holy—souls redeemed by Jesus, the loving Saviour—prostrated themselves before idols of gold and clay, of brass and stone, practised their foul, degrading rites. How little Xavier had been able to do for India! What had it availed, all his preaching of the gospel "in season and out of season"? Truly he was an unprofitable servant, he told himself over and over again.

Gazing at Paul of the Holy Faith and his companions, who were profiting by the time aboard ship to continue their studies, his heart became hopeful again, his ready smile returned. What a happiness to travel to a land where dwelt a race such as the Japanese, where the people were honourable, industrious, intellectually minded; where law and order had a meaning for high and low. No indolence, as among the Indians and Malays; no back-sliders, like the Goans and pearl-fishers; no primitive customs and low level of intelligence, such as one found among the Papuans and other island savages; no rapacity, no cruelty, no dishonour and wickedness, like that of the Portuguese of the colonies.

His heart, buoyant as ever, rose in him at the thought of the new mission field ahead. A mere nothing now seemed the thousands of miles he had tramped under equatorial suns; forgotten were the monsoons, the endless

237

voyages and seasickness; no more he remembered the jungles and swamps with the clouds of mosquitoes by night, with the asps and basilisks and other noonday devils.

.   .   .   .   .

Here he was, on the eve of the Assumption of Our Lady, at the gates of Japan! Taking out his breviary, he read the Vespers of the morrow's feast. At the words of Psalm 112: "From the rising of the sun to the going down thereof, the name of the Lord is worthy of praise," he lifted his eyes to the coastline he had so longed to see. Between verses of the Vesper hymn, *Ave Maris Stella,* he wondered, with a holy impatience, when this slowest of slow-moving ocean craft would make port . . .

> But twilight on the waters
> Was quiet and grey,
> And she glided steady, steady and pensive,
> Over the open bay.

The straw sails hung motionless from the bamboo yardarms. Up in the poop the pigtailed Chinamen poured libations of cocks' blood before the joss; the smell of the incense and rich spices being burned before the idol wafted to where Francis knelt, reciting his Office; a singsong chanting, led by the Robber, the Chinaman who owned the junk, made it hard for Xavier to concentrate on the Vesper hymns. Having finished drawing lots to discover the will of the idol as to whether they should land before dark or wait until the following morning, the Chinaman announced that the joss wished them to wait until the morrow. Xavier suddenly remembered that the feast would be the fifteenth anniversary of the day he and the others had made their first vow in Montmartre. Igna-

tius and Rodriguez and the others would be this very evening praying for him—wherever they were. Peter Favre
would be his advocate in heaven tomorrow when he set
foot on this wonderful land. He walked up and down,
trying to discern something of the land from where they
lay-to in the bay. On an island in the bay a volcano
smoked steadily. A city showed in the shadow of a long
line of hills on the mainland. From habit, his eyes turned
to the heavens where star after star shone forth—the gold-
armoured sentinels that stood at the entrances to God's
gates, at the portals of His doors. Well for Favre, already
in his eternal home, already united to God, Xavier sighed.
An intense desire for God that was at once a delight and
a torment welled up within him. To ease his longing he
began to hum an old Basque song:

> Waves, waves of Vigo sea,
> My beloved, where is he?
> God! Let me see him soon!

> Waves, waves dashing high,
> Saw you him for whom I sigh?
> God! Let me see him soon!

> Have you seen him on the sea,
> My true lover pledged to me?
> God! Let me see him soon!

> Should you see him on the deep,
> Say his love doth wait and weep.
> God! Let me see him soon!

The Chinaman eyed him askance. Only that his wife
and other valuables were being held in Malacca, to be
redeemed if and when he landed Xavier in Japan, he

239

would, long since, have knived the Christian dog and
thrown him and his companions to the sharks. The joss
had indicated that the Christians were responsible for the
Robber's misfortunes on the voyage; and what misfortunes they had been! The gods of the sea wanted a life,
and when Xavier's Chinese servant fell headlong into the
hold during the storm—which was nothing but the gods
shouting their demands—the Christian *bonze,* by what
magic the Robber knew not, had saved and healed the in-
jured man. And then the sea gods, thwarted, angry and
hungry, had reached with their watery arms right on to
the boat and dragged the skipper's daughter overboard,
where they devoured her. Then there was the danger they
had run into at Chang Chow, where the Robber meant to
winter. No Portuguese or other foreign devils there, as in
Sancian, where they had threatened to send him in chains
to Malacca if he did not proceed at once to Japan with
the *bonze*—the one they called *el Santo.* But at Chang
Chow he had heard of a fleet waiting in the harbour—
whether a fleet of pirates or the Chinese fleet he could not
say, and he had not delayed to find out. The pirates would
rob, maybe murder him; the Chinese would murder, certainly torture him, for he was committing the unpardon-
able crime of bringing foreign devils into the Dragon
Kingdom. He had just set sail, intending to land at Canton and let his passengers fend for themselves from there,
when the southwest monsoon, which was thought to have
blown itself out the night the girl went overboard, blew
up again, and there was nothing to be done but run before it. For a whole fortnight it blew them steadily up the
Straits of Formosa and up the East China Sea, and here
they were—at Japan. Yes, only for his fear of the Governor of Malacca, the Robber would have slit the throats
of those Christians with as little compunction as he felt

when slitting the chickens' throats before sacrificing to the joss. A queer religion they had, anyway; no joss for kowtowing, no killing of cocks, no burning of joss-sticks, no casting of lots to know the correct answers to the questions one asked one's idol . . . The Robber would be well rid of his passengers. He was sorry he had ever agreed to bring them.

On the morning of the Assumption Francis Xavier entered the strange land where mourners wore white, where mulberry and black were the colours of joy, where the written word went up and down. Dwarfed trees stood stiffly against clear skies; fields of irises waved their bright flags in the morning sun and lotus-blossoms spread their pale petals on the dark, satiny surfaces of innumerable carp-ponds. It was not yet chrysanthemum time; but there were giant magnolia blooms and the leaves of the maples were already mottled with scarlet. All the colour, all the loveliness of the enchanting south island of Japan was lost on Francis as he walked up from the landing place. He saw only souls to be saved. Groups of Japanese women stood to stare at the Christians, uttering little bird-like cries of amazement; pedlars, carrying their wares on long bamboo poles slung over their shoulders, and coolies—their thin cotton tunics stained with sweat— whispered to one another as they passed Francis by. He remembered that Paul of Holy Faith had told him that the Japanese despised the Westerners for their loud speech and display of emotion. He stepped aside to avoid being knocked down by the *samurai* who rode past, two swords crossed in his belt, his scorn of the shabbily clad Europeans more evident in his indifference than in any glance of disdain. Bands of almond-eyed children followed Xavier and his companions, exclaiming in chorus: *"Ijin! Ijin!* Foreign devil! Foreign devil!"

241

They were at the most southerly point of Japan, in a town named Kagoshima, the native town of Paul of the Holy Faith, who had fled from there not so long before, with a murder on his conscience. When the first surprise of the people at seeing Europeans subsided, attention turned to Paul and word was sent to his wife and family that their Anjiro was back, safe and sound. It was a new experience for Francis to witness the reunion of Paul and his relations: prostrations, compliments, self-deprecatory speeches on both sides, but not the slightest indication of joy, relief, or any other emotion; even the children made their bows and recited their greetings in the same polite but almost inhumanly cold manner. His family and friends asked Anjiro many questions. Where had he been all this time? Why did the foreigners call him Paul? When they heard that he had changed his religion they were more interested still, not quite believing that there were other religions than the two known in Japan—that of Buddha and the worship of ancestors, Shintoism.

The next day, Anjiro went, not without some trepidation, to the castle of his feudal chief, the local *daimyo*. Francis gave him a painting of the Virgin and Child to present to the *daimyo*. The ruler had never seen an oil painting before and was extremely impressed by it. As was customary on receiving gifts from strangers, he and his mother and his household prostrated themselves before the picture. Anjiro returned to Francis and reported how he and his gift had been received; it was a sign, Francis' companions said, that grace had touched these hearts, the pagans had honoured a representation of the Holy Mother and the Divine Child. Francis was not so sure; it might have been more of that etiquette and ceremonial which, in this land, seemed to hedge and hide hearts and souls.

Don Francisco

For some weeks Xavier did nothing but study the language, but Anjiro was not the best of teachers and Francis found that he could not make himself understood in Kagoshima, neither could he understand. Suddenly anxious about the adequacy of the translations made with the help of Anjiro, he began again to recast the prayers, the catechisms, and the commandments. For almost six weeks he gave all the time, all the concentration, all the power of his intellect to this work. He was beginning to realise that he had underestimated the vastness of the task he had set himself in evangelising Japan. Already he had seen a little of the practice of the various religions in Kagoshima. On the night before they landed, while the junk hove to in the bay, he had noted the coloured lanterns bobbing about in the streets and roads outside the town and enquired of Anjiro the reason for the illuminations; it would be too much to hope that, unawares, these people were honouring Our Lady's Assumption.

Anjiro said that it was the eve of the great feast of *Bon*, the annual commemoration of the souls of the ancestors. The people were going outside the city, bearing brightly coloured lanterns, to meet the spirits of their forebears. When one came to the spot where one imagined these souls to be assembled, one bowed, offered rice or ver-micelli—poor people proffered drinks of water from the hot springs—and conversed, saying: "Come home and be welcome! We have not met for a long while. You must be weary; pray rest and eat." Then, when the spirits had been given an hour to rest and refresh themselves, they were escorted with lanterns back to the abode where they had lived when in this present life. For two days the souls were feasted and then they were conveyed to the hills again; after having been so well fed, the ancestors would be able the better to face the ten million thousand leagues' journey to Paradise, which a disembodied soul took three years to reach. But, Francis asked, what became of the food? Would not the Japanese, a reasoning people, wonder when they saw the rice and vermicelli remain at the meeting place—the banquet untasted in the ancestral home? Anjiro was a bit nonplussed. The food was always consumed; none of the banquet remained; nobody had dared to stay to watch the spirits eat the food; such rudeness to one's ancestors was unthinkable. The *bonzes* alone went about to note when the spirits had finished their repast; when the souls took the food and money left for them, the *bonzes* then told the family that they might safely enter the room where the feast had been spread. There never was anything left. If Anjiro had the suspicions which Francis—long accustomed to the trickery and impositions of the Indian Brahmins—entertained, he said nothing.

After six weeks an invitation came for the foreign *bonze*. Francis and his companions were invited to the castle of the *daimyo*. There, in a squat fortress not unlike the castle of Xavier, they were received with great courtesy. Through doorway after doorway, along narrow corridors and up cedar-wood staircases they followed their guide until they emerged on a small verandah, leading to a little, sunny room with light-coloured wooden walls, sliding paper doors and bright straw matting on the floor. Here waited the *daimyo*, seated on a dais, his silken robes standing out stiffly from his erect body, his two swords crossed in his girdle, his swordsmen and attendants about him, some standing, some prostrated. After many and ceremonious greetings, he motioned Francis and the others to seat themselves. All present then seated themselves cross-legged and waited in silence. At a signal from the *daimyo*, a tripod, kettle and a porcelain bowl were brought in, and, with deft but unhurried movements, a dish of *cha* was prepared. Francis, taking his cue from the rest of the company, watched, without showing the slightest interest, the method of infusing the powdered herb known as *cha*. When the steaming beverage was ready, menials lifted into the centre of the apartment lacquered cabinets where the utensils for the *cha* drinking were kept. Tiny china cups, not much bigger than thimbles, were then filled with the beverage and handed to the *daimyo* and his guests.

Although the Europeans did not like this scalding drink, they had been well coached by Anjiro beforehand and knew that they must drink it as though it were the most delicious wine. Indeed, to invite a guest to drink *cha* was, for a Japanese *daimyo*, equivalent to an invitation from some Spanish nobleman or wealthy merchant to join him in partaking of the choicest wines in his cellar.

Still bearing in mind all Anjiro's instructions as to the etiquette to be observed on such an occasion, Xavier and his companions, most uncomfortable as they squatted, Japanese-fashion, on their heels, went through the *cha* drinking ritual, staring silently before them as did the *daimyo* and the entire company.

The *daimyo* was gracious. Surprised that Francis had travelled six thousand miles to preach a new religion, he gave him permission to expound the doctrines freely. His swordsmen had interrogated Anjiro and found that the Portuguese greatly venerated this shabbily robed *bonze* from their part of the world. The Japanese held the Portuguese in high honour, in that they were a warlike people, having made many conquests in the East. It would be very much to the advantage of the port of Kagoshima if more Portuguese ships and merchants could be attracted there—the *daimyo* would become wealthy and strong like those other *daimyos* in Bungo and Hirado in the north, and be in a better position to fight them. If he favoured this Christian *bonze*, the Portuguese would let him buy some of their wonderful weapons that spouted forth fire and death; his armourers would copy the firearms and his soldiers would be the best equipped in Japan. If the Portuguese knew that their holy man was in Kagoshima, they would follow him to this port. Yes, Francis might preach freely in the *daimyo's* lands.

This permission secured, Francis ventured to make a beginning. He would try out his new plan; instead of beginning with the children, the uneducated, the uninfluential, he would go to the *bonzes* and the rulers. He would begin with the *bonzes*.

Hardly had he returned from the audience with the local *daimyo* than word was brought him that the Robber had died while his junk was still in the harbour. Remembering that the man's wife and property were being held in Malacca against his return, Francis hastened to write the Governor there, telling him that the pirate had faithfully fulfilled his contract and asking him to look after the widow, to provide for her return to her own people, and to compensate her suitably for the loss of the man who was her only protection and support.

There were different monasteries of *bonzes*, some filled with black-robed, some with grey-robed monks. One might have thought oneself back in the monasteries of Rome, Paris or Lisbon. To the monasteries near Kagoshima Francis betook himself, bringing the good tidings to those Japanese whom he knew the ordinary people held in esteem. The black-robed *bonzes*, in particular, were venerated by all; they never ate meat or fish nor drank rice wine; one meal of herbs, fruit and rice was their daily nourishment. Their temples were clean and fragrant, a welcome change from those of Indian Buddhists; and their carpenters excelled in constructing and ornamenting these places of worship. The monks were themselves good husbandmen, tilling the mountain valleys, sowing, irrigating, reaping their rice harvests in terraces that ran, step by step, up the hillsides. Several times daily, their temple drum summoned the *bonzes* to *sutra* chanting, with its ritual of book and fan. Though Francis had heard that the Buddhists in Japan were split into various sects, he did not, at the beginning, endeavour to differentiate between them; to him they were all pagans, unbelievers, whether they belonged to the Zen creed, that favoured by the feudal lords, or to the Lotus, or the Pure Land Buddhists. Then there was the older religion, Shintoism, the strange mixture of nature and hero-worship which Buddhism had, by the sitxeenth century, practically supplanted. And there were the most pronounced Buddhists, the out-and-out unbelievers for whom Nirvana was utter annihilation, for whom there existed no Creator, no next life, no heaven or hell.

With the abbot of a monastery of these radical Buddhists, Xavier became very friendly. This abbot rejoiced in the name of "Heart of Truth"; he was cynical, truthful and ready to answer the many questions Francis asked him—unlike the other *bonzes*, who asked innumerable questions but answered none. Their creed, the abbot told Xavier, was: "Nothing exists; all is delusion." Once when Francis enquired as to the subject of the meditations the monks made a hundred times each year, squatting on their heels in the position Japanese seemed to find so restful but which was a torture to Westerners, the abbot smiled. "Some," he replied, "are adding up how much they collected in gifts at the feast of *Bon;* others are thinking about their food and clothes; others again of their amusement; you may be sure that not one is thinking of anything important."

One approached the Japanese slowly, obliquely. "When a sailor goes on a voyage," said Francis, carefully choosing his words, "which hour does he prefer—when he is mid-ocean, or when he is in sight of port?" The Abbot replied slowly, "I understand what you wish me to say, but that is not my case. It is in vain to ask me such a question, for I know nothing of the port towards which I sail." And Francis, listening, heard in his words the echo of hopelessness that, as the years go by, reverberates in the minds and hearts of all thinking and sincere pagans.

October came and went, a blaze of chrysanthemums. The rice harvest was gathered. The cold, wintry fogs began to blow in from the sea; days of fog were followed by terrible storms, and in the November mornings it was not unusual to see ice floating in the land-locked bay of Kagoshima. Bitter winds whistled through the cracks of the paper doors in the hut where Francis and his companions huddled about the charcoal brazier which was inadequate to warm the place. If one closed the outside wooden shutters the room was too dark for studying. And the winter air still rose through the porous floor matting and insinuated itself through every slit where the summer sun had shrunk the boards in walls or floor, leaving a crack. The hut, being raised on supports, allowed the wind to penetrate above and beneath and all around. To keep warm, it was necessary either to go to bed or to keep moving. Francis noted that the Japanese themselves chose the latter course; they wrapped up well and went to plough and plant their wheat and barley, their beets and radishes in the muddy fields. When he had finished writing the letters to Europe, he would get out and about; even the cold would be preferable to this endless sitting on one's heels, while one's backbone ached and ached. His companions had not complained; they were as anxious as he to accustom themselves to the manners of the Japanese and valiantly persevered with the native diet—a frugal meal of rice and vegetables once a day, a drink of warmed water morning and evening, and the ceremonious *cha* drinking in the afternoon. The latter was most difficult in the beginning as they tried to accustom themselves to the beverage with the strange tang; but, after some time, they found that it had certain refreshing powers.

The letter writing took a week. Brother Fernandez and Father de Torres—the Spaniard who had first met Francis on his voyage home from the New World—wrote some of the letters, Francis dictating, now to one, now to the other, as he paced up and down the little hut. Father Gomes and the brethren at Goa got four letters, and an epistle almost as long as that sent the previous year went to the Dutch Father who was bound for the iniquitous port of Ormuz. And there was a letter to the Governor of Malacca.

The Dutch Father was ordered to leave Ormuz and proceed to Japan with two other Fathers from India. To Father Gomes, Xavier wrote a personal letter with the postscript:

> For the love of God Our Lord I beg you to take great care so to comport yourself that all the brethren in the Company may love you. I also earnestly entreat you to write to me and tell me how are things with your soul. Write to me in detail about your interior life; you know how happy it would make my heart to hear that you are making progress towards perfection. And how I would rejoice to hear not only that all the brethren in Goa and throughout India are

loved by you but also that you have endeared yourself to all!

He was still uneasy about Goa. In the midst of the long
letter he broke off his accounts of the Japanese and the
plans for visiting Kyoto and the Emperor to beg the
brethren to abide in the love of Christ:

> I beseech you to have love for one another, not
> allowing bitterness to grow; turn some of your zeal
> into brotherly love and some of your desire to suffer
> for Christ into brotherly forbearance and patience,
> and for the love of God conquer all dislikes and
> animosities that might stifle the growth of this divine
> love.

Three weeks later, hearing that there was a Portuguese
ship at Hirado, a harbour to the north of the island, Francis wished to see if there were any letters from Goa. Leaving his companions behind, he set off, despite having been
laid low with fever—the old enemy—for the two previous
weeks. The Portuguese, delighted to see *el Santo,* fired
guns and played music when they saw him, giving him an
ovation which greatly impressed the *daimyo* of that area.
Reasoning that the tall Christian *bonze* must be someone
of exceeding importance in Portuguese eyes, he invited
Xavier to his fortress. As in Kagoshima, he gave permission for the new religion to be preached, and Francis immediately recited what he had memorised during the long
weeks of study—the Triune God, Omnipotent, Omniscient,
Eternal, Immutable, All-Perfect, All-Lovable; the Crea-
tion, the Fall, the Redemption; the Incarnation, Death,
and Resurrection of Christ, His Ascension into Heaven;
the means by which men may obtain salvation through
Jesus Christ Our Lord. When he had finished he lifted his

eyes, for when speaking he had kept them lowered, the better to rivet his attention on the God of whom he spoke, the better to remember all that he had with such difficulty memorised. Not an eye moved; not one face showed a vestige of interest, scorn, amusement, hate—nothing; he might as well have raised his voice to the stones on the road from Kagoshima. True, Anjiro had said his people would not become Christians at once; they would ask questions, reason, think slowly before taking the step. But in Kagoshima the converts, so far, were few and far between; and, although the *bonzes* had asked thousands of questions, some of them had been extremely silly questions and made one wonder were the *bonzes* the learned men Anjiro had said they were or mere mockers. What colour was the God of the Christians? Was He gilded? Did He seat Himself on a lotus leaf? And the soul—what was its appearance, colour and material? Why was man born with a propensity for evil? The endless questions, however, had one good effect: those queries that were repeated oftenest showed him the main difficulties of the race with whom he was now dealing. One had to explain reasonably the compatibility of the existence of evil with God's omnipotence, and to show carefully the necessity for the Incarnation; when this was done the battle was half won.

After a few weeks spent at Hirado, Francis returned to Kagoshima. As he walked along the icy roads, his thoughts went back to the sun-baked shores of the pearl fisheries, to the balmy islands of the southern seas, where his converts had come, not in ones and twos, but in scores and hundreds. There he had fished with nets. In Japan it was rod and line fishing, and the fish were wary, hard to tempt, no matter what bait one used.

His first Christmas in Japan was spent in Kagoshima.

How poor and sombre appeared the celebration of the
Christian feast in the icy hut! Hardly was the festival
over before Francis again visited the local monasteries.
All through Japan he had noted that the people were
given to the most bestial and unnatural sins of the flesh,
and the monasteries, he had discovered, were hotbeds of
such vice. He decided to visit the monasteries again, this
time like John the Baptist before the tetrarch, denouncing
the *bonzes* and their evil ways in scathing language. Some
laughed, some sat as though they had not heard the words
of the foreign devil, some went apart and whispered to
one another.

Spring came slowly, beautifully. The air bore whiffs of
camphor leaves, of plum blossom, of cherry and orange
blossoms. Poets nailed their lines to the wreathed trees.
The mockingbird sang. And the *daimyo* who, in the beginning, had showed himself so friendly, grew colder and
colder to Francis and his friends. The foreign devil had
fooled him: the Portuguese passed Kagoshima for the
northern port, where the rival *daimyo* lived. When the
people went out to see the first blooms on the azaleas and
the rhododendrons, they found the spring poems of the
poets replaced by notices saying that the Christian *bonzes*
were forbidden to preach and the people of Kagoshima
were forbidden to listen.

For the feast of Corpus Christi, which, in 1550, fell on
June 5th, Francis preached on the Blessed Sacrament. He,
with Father de Torres and Brother Fernandez and the
little band of converts, celebrated the *festividad del Corpus* with joy. Inevitably, the thoughts of the Spaniards
turned to their own land. Father de Torres remembered
Valencia and the great procession that would wind its
way from the Hieronymite Monastery of San Miguel along
the dusty road, past the turrets and battlements of the

Gate of the Mountaineers, and on to the Apostles' Door of
the Cathedral. Valencia would bank its streets and *patios*
with roses and lilies and carnations today; in the squares
palms and cacti would stiffly stand—the palms, lines of
giant sentinels; the cacti, deformed dwarfs. And, in the
Cathedral, *Nuestra Senora de los Desampardos,* Our Lady
of the Forsaken, would wait and smile, knowing that
when the procession and Benediction were over, many
would come to pray before her image, gleaming in the
dark of the little side chapel. Brother Fernandez remembered Córdoba, that town of leathers and carpets, of silks
and velvets, where this day the merchants would vie with
one another, spreading their most beautiful rugs and carpets on the streets, hanging balconies and window shrines
with their brightest silks, their richest satins. He wondered if those who now owned the big silk business which
was once the property of Juan Fernandez would remember to send special bolts of white Bruges satin to drape
the altar in the Cathedral for the Exposition. Francis
Xavier thought of the villages and towns of Navarre, in a
hundred and more of which the Basque sword-dancers
would be forming up to dance their stately intricate measures before the Blessed Sacrament as it was borne through
the streets. The dancers, like David of old, would dance
with all their might before the Lord; and the singers, following, would sing canticles and hymns, and in Xavier,
Pamplona, Sangüesa, and all the churches of his native
province, the praises of Our Lord would resound as valley
after valley, hill after hill, echoed to the singing and the
chimes of many bells.

In this land of flowers Brother Fernandez had little
trouble making an outdoor altar for Benediction. Trails of
wisteria, banks of azaleas, and lovely flowering shrubs
were the silks and satins with which he draped and made

beautiful the place where the procession would pause, where the Lord would bless Kagoshima and all Japan.

Many people, curious to see this outdoor ceremony, came to watch the Christians. Some *bonzes* from the nearby monasteries were present. Noting his augmented congregation, Francis, at the conclusion of the ceremonies, decided to avail himself of the occasion to give a discourse on the Blessed Sacrament. He began with the words of Christ: "I have many things to say to you but you cannot bear them yet." Slowly, carefully, begging God not to permit him to make mistakes in the difficult Japanese language, he told the gospel story of the sublime mystery of the Blessed Eucharist. It heartened him to note that the *bonzes* at the back of the crowd were paying great attention to his words. Perhaps—at last—his words to them were bearing fruit.

A few mornings after, Brother Fernandez showed him pools of blood at the entrance to their hut; blood was smeared on their door; there were scraps of blood-stained garments strewn about. What did it mean? Had someone been murdered during the night? They had heard no cry, no running footsteps. Soon they knew. Anjiro, pale and trembling, told of how the *bonzes* had spread the story that they were cannibals; they had heard, they said, that foreign devil say so in his sermon a few days before. They had understood that much of his sermon: he had said, "Unless you eat the flesh . . . and drink the blood." Already they were stirring up the people. The blood-stained rags, the door smeared with blood, had been their doing.

The child whom people said Xavier had raised from the dead, the blind man who had seen, the leper who had been healed, the great catch of fishes, all these wonders the *bonzes* had explained by pointing to Francis and saying "he hath a devil." They urged the *daimyo* to banish the foreigners. Now that it seemed quite definite the Portuguese were not going to use the port of Kagoshima, the *daimyo* was quite willing that Francis should undertake the journey he had wished to make several times in the past year, the journey to Kyoto to see the Emperor. Each time he had asked, the *daimyo* had courteously but firmly refused. When Francis had requested the previous year to be sent by sea to Kyoto, he was told that it was the typhoon season; when he asked to go by land, he was told that the roads were too unsafe and that the wars in the north would make it more dangerous still for a traveller, particularly a foreign traveller, in Japan.

Now, in the autumn of 1550, Francis and de Torres and Fernandez were told a junk was waiting in Kagoshima harbour. They might go to Kyoto. They might visit the Emperor. And the *bonzes*, standing by, laughed. The *daimyo* gave his word that those of his subjects who had become Christians might continue in their new religion. Francis thanked him. Leaving Anjiro—Paul of the Holy Faith—in charge of the hundred Christians of Kagoshima, Francis Xavier, de Torres, Fernandez, a Chinese and a Tamil, not availing themselves of the junk waiting on them, set out on foot for Hirado, where, several months before, the Portuguese ship had been anchored. On their way, they passed the monasteries of the *bonzes* on the hills to the north of the town. Stones and curses were flung at them as they went by.

The Portuguese were again at Hirado and were delighted to see *el Santo*. This time the preaching of the Fathers was more fruitful; so numerous, indeed, were the conversions in the area that Francis decided to leave Father de Torres behind, to look after the increasing number of Christians as well as to attend to the spiritual needs of the Portuguese whose ships seemed to be putting in there more frequently than ever. Father de Torres sadly watched Xavier and Fernandez leave for Kyoto. For once, Father Francis had written no letters to Goa, to Malacca, to Europe, though a boat was about to leave. When, later on, he heard news of the two travellers, de Torres took it upon himself to write:

> You may imagine how I felt at seeing them go, knowing the dangers and fatigue ahead of them, for they left here just as the Yamasse—the wind from the eastern mountains—began to blow, and when the first frosts and snows of this cold land began. But you know Father Francis! Such is the fire of the love of God within him that neither snows nor frosts nor fears nor dangers can deter him from spreading the gospel. When they went by water, they had to hide in the holds to avoid being enslaved by pirates; when they went by land, their plan was to attach themselves as lackeys to certain gentlemen of Japan; and, wearing turbans like the other Siamese grooms, they had to run all the way, covering ten leagues in this manner. They suffered great misery from the cold and the hunger, and in the inns, at the end of each day's journey, they found no way of drying or warming themselves. In the deep snow their sandals soon became useless and fell away, so that their bleeding feet made bloody tracks in the snow. And crowds of boys and a rowdy rabble followed them, mimicking their speech, calling them names and pelting them with stones and filth . . . With all this they never ceased preaching and confessing our holy faith. This will give you some idea of what Father Francis has had to endure to plant the seed of the gospel in Japan.

CHAPTER 13

In February, 1551, Father de Torres welcomed Francis and Fernandez back from Kyoto. Their clothes were in tatters, and they themselves worn and ill-looking. Father Francis had a fever. For several days their food had been a handful of dry rice—the thousand crowns brought to Japan by Xavier having been long since dispensed in alms. But Father de Torres was as overjoyed to see them as they were to be reunited with him. Again there was a Portuguese ship in the harbour, and when the news spread that *el Santo* had returned from Kyoto, the captain hurried ashore. Finding Xavier and Fernandez shaking with ague, he helped Father de Torres to get them to bed, fetched medicines from his ship and sent a physician to attend to the sick men and to bind up their wounded feet.

After a few days the two travellers were up and about again and able to tell the tale of their quest for the Emperor. First, they had journeyed five hundred miles to Yamaguchi, the second largest city in Japan, a town of fifty thousand souls. On their way there the Yamasse was blowing in their teeth as though it would blow them back all the way to Europe. They had heard of that evil east wind, saturated with salty vapours, but its effects had to be experienced to be believed. For days ahead one felt it

257

coming; its ominous whine depressed the blithest heart; it brought with it leaden skies that spread themselves like a pall not only over the landscape but over the minds of men. In Yamaguchi they had preached and taught in every street and square for two months; but they made only three converts—a man and his wife and an aged nobleman. The people had no respect for anyone dressed so shabbily as Xavier and Fernandez and hooted them from street to street. The children were their worst perse-cutors, gathering in mobs and yelling at them "O God! O God!" as they had heard Francis say each time he be-gan the so carefully memorised Japanese prayers. It took them both a long while to realise that their imperfect pronunciation had given the word an evil meaning and that this was what the children yelled at them.

A very powerful *daimyo* ruled Yamaguchi. His court and his city were degenerate, given over to the most de-grading sins. Occasionally the two foreigners were al-lowed into the luxurious homes of the *samurai* or into the populous monasteries, not because the owners wished to hear the gospel, but because they hoped for an hour's amusement looking at the Big-Heads, the Bulge-Eyed, the Raw-Skinned, the Loud-Lunged, the Elongated—for these and many other names were the titles they gave the two Europeans, whose physical characteristics were so differ-ent from their own. Finding that modesty and humility won nothing but disrespect for themselves and their gospel among these people, Francis, after a few days, decided that it was time to turn the tables. The two Spaniards, who had long before mastered and forsworn their natural pride, now hit back, giving as good as they got. Fernandez, who had become more proficient than any in his command of Japanese, was ordered to translate the Spanish invectives and thunderings of Francis and to

deliver them with sternness and vigour. Poor Fernandez!
When he noted the *samurai*, each with the carved jade
hilts of two swords protruding from a jewelled belt, his
heart died within him with fear. But he obeyed Father
Francis though he felt that his death-knell sounded in
every word he uttered with such assumed bravery. He
was Francis' mouthpiece, boldly telling the noblemen that
they and their *daimyo* and the *bonzes* were the filthiest
scum of a city whose people were "filthier than pigs,
lower than dogs or any brute beasts," by reason of the
vices to which they were addicted. But the words and
warnings fell on stony ground. A week before Christmas
they left Yamaguchi and journeyed another three hundred
miles northward, crossing icy rivers, plodding knee-deep
in snowdrifts, mocked, stoned, abused and even spat
upon. That was the time they had to turn lackey, running
thirty miles through slush and snow behind the paladin
of a nobleman, until they reached Kyoto.

Despite Francis' exhaustion and weariness, he had
leaped for joy at sight of Kyoto. Again and again he had
thrown an apple he was carrying into the air, catching it
as it fell, now in one hand, now in the other, playing
pelota, as it were, on the very walls of the city of the
Mikado, the Son of Heaven. Here was his goal. Here dwelt
the Great Voo—the sublime Emperor, Go-Nara, descend-
ant of the Sun-Goddess. Once Go-Nara was won, the rest
of Japan would follow. Brother Fernandez could not help
but remember that they had heard very little of the Emperor from anyone since they came to Japan. It was always the *daimyo* of this or that area whose name was
quoted as synonymous with authority. It was Anjiro who
had told them that the Emperor, if he became Christian,
would be followed by all his subjects. But Anjiro had told
them many other things of his country, which had not

fallen out as forecast. However, looking at Xavier's radiant face as he gazed down on the sea of black roofs, on the towers and temples that stood up here and there, like ships in that dark sea, on the snowy mountains that ringed the imperial city, Fernandez put away his forebodings and rejoiced with his friend.

When they entered Kyoto, they found a city whose streets and buildings showed every evidence of having been much battered in street fighting. The buildings unscarred by war were drab and dilapidated, a great contrast to the elegant city of Yamaguchi, which they had left in mid-December. They did not know that, although Go-Nara—Lord of the sixty-six kingdoms of Japan, the Great Voo, the Mikado, the Most Sublime Emperor, the Son of Heaven—could boast unbroken descent from the Sun-goddess, he was at this time only a nominal ruler. Even the Shogun of whom Anjiro had spoken so much as the Commander-in-Chief of the imperial armies and hence the real ruler—the power behind the throne—had, at the moment, no power. He was but a boy of fifteen, and the real power was in the hands of the *daimyos* who were always warring with one another.

Mystified at the deserted appearance of Kyoto, Francis and Fernandez wandered about the smoke-blackened ruins, noting how the temple and pagodas had been used as fortifications, asking questions from passers-by who seldom answered; finally discovering that, for the past year, Kyoto had been a battlefield in a local war in which rival nobles and rival monasteries had reduced the city to its present state. But the Emperor still resided there. He lived in retirement, never leaving his palace, for to touch his foot to the ground would defile one of such hallowed lineage. Every day his women brought him new garments; each meal was served in vessels fresh from the porcelain furnaces, vessels which were broken immediately after the Great Voo had used them. For so greatly venerated a ruler, Go-Nara seemed very poor. Anyone could go and peer through the thousand cracks in the walls of his broken-down palace; robbers could rifle the imperial orchards with impunity; pedlars stacked their packs on breaches in the walls and haggled with the hungry wives of the Great Voo who handed out their jewels, their embroidered kimonos, their fans, and gewgaws for a few sweet potatoes. When Francis saw others make so bold, he resolved to try to get an audience with the Emperor.

Not being a pedlar or a robber, he went to the entrance gate, where an official asked him for a stiff entrance fee—the Emperor was glad in these hard times to make a little out of selling his autograph and specimens of his calligraphy. The foreign *bonze* would have to pay the Emperor and also the sentry at the gate. But Francis had spent the thousand crowns given him in Malacca; he had given all to the poor of Japan; though the Great Voo qualified for the title of beggar, Francis had no alms left. "Any presents?" the official enquired. Yesterday's visitors had brought a peck of pepper; the ones of the previous week ten gold bars. A moon ago a man had brought a bushel of peacock's feathers. Had they not brought anything? Not even a lacquered cabinet or box? Not even a bolt of brocade?

Too late Francis and Fernandez remembered the presents the Governor of Malacca had insisted that they bring. The arquebus, the musical instrument with seventy notes, the mirrors, the crystal vases, the Portuguese dresses, the bale of cloth-of-gold, the spectacles, the chiming clock—all left behind, but where? They had forgotten about them since the day they had taken them on the Robber's junk. They would have needed them at the Emperor's court had he been as powerful as they thought; they needed them twice as badly now that they found him to be poverty-stricken and old. Bitterly disappointed and annoyed with themselves for making such an error in tactics, they began preaching in the streets. But Kyoto was still in the throes of civil war; temple bells clanged, not for prayer, but to give warning of approaching bands of armed *samurai* and *bonzes* from the hills; men and women gathered at street corners, not to listen to the foreign devils who stood telling their new Christian religion, but to talk about the war and the claims of the various *daimyos* and the strength of the armed bands descending on the city. The only ones who stayed by Francis and Fernandez were the children; taking their cue from their elders, they shrieked and yelled *"Ijin! Ijin! Foreign devil! Foreign devil!"* at the two men who must be preaching a very low, mean religion to be so poorly and shabbily clad.

After eleven days, Francis and Fernandez, seeing that nothing could be achieved by remaining in Kyoto, decided to go to the nearby harbour, where a junk was about to sail south. They boarded it and covered some of the return journey by sea; the rest of the way, through a land colder than any they had yet touched, was a severe trial; Francis' hands and feet became covered with chilblains. Yet he and his companion had been happy. Now and then, in lonely places, they had met little children unlike those in the cities and had made friends by giving them a little fruit or nuts from their own scant store of provisions. Xavier had blessed them. A few times they had found infants, newly born, thrown forth into the snow to perish. With what joy Francis melted some snow between his hands and baptised these dying infants, waiting until the

soul went back to God and then returning the frail body—
for so brief a time the temple of the Holy Ghost—to the
earth! With love and yearning his heart went back to
them, the Snowdrops of Heaven his hands had planted in
mountain passes and desolate waste-lands of that dreary,
cold country between Kyoto and Hirado. They were the
only milestones to mark his progress in Japan. How few
. . . how far between . . .

Well, Francis told Fernandez and Father de Torres, if
the journey to Kyoto had done nothing else, at least it had
sent some souls to Heaven to intercede for them and
Japan. And it had shown them that both Emperor and
Shogun were titles, nothing more. The *daimyos* were the
powerful ones in this kingdom; they were the ones to be
approached. The missionaries had also learned that the
Japanese would not respect a preacher coming like a poor
man. One should go to them in rich apparel, taking costly
presents for the *daimyo* of the place—which reminded
them of the presents brought from Malacca. Did Father
de Torres remember what became of them? Yes, he had
some of them in his charge—the sacred vessels and some
of the presents; but other presents had been left at Kagoshima in the care of Anjiro. Father Francis' robes of office
were there. Xavier was almost about to ask *which* robes
when he remembered that he was Papal Nuncio, Legate
of the Successor of St. Peter, Ambassador of King John of
Portugal to the kingdoms of the Far East. The Tamil,
Bernard, was bidden take two of Father de Torres' excellent Christians and journey to Kagoshima for the bales
containing the other presents and Francis' robes. While
he was gone, the Portuguese in the harbour were asked if
they could supply any material for new robes, not the
ordinary, poor serge, but some rich black material—brocade, the best that could be found. If *el Santo* had asked

for the King of Achin's necklace the Portuguese would have attempted to get it for him, even if it meant bearding the Barbarossa of the East in his Sumatran fortress. A bale of finest black brocade was at once unearthed, no one knew where. A Japanese seamstress was set to sew, to model new brocade soutanes from the tattered faded ones that had seen more wear than was good for them. The Fathers sent for the ship's barber and submitted to his ministrations; for the greater honour and glory of God they valeted one another, laughing heartily at the stiff soutanes of brocade that made them look like Chinese mandarins in wedding attire.

Soon Bernard returned from Kagoshima with the bales, the contents safe and sound. The Japanese were honourable; one could not leave so much valuable luggage behind in other parts of the East and hope to find it intact on one's return. Bernard had bad news. It concerned Anjiro—Paul of the Holy Faith. The *bonzes,* knowing that he had been left in charge of the Kagoshima Christians, had threatened him, frightened him; and Paul, the man who had inspired Xavier to come to Japan, had run away, no one knew whither. The Christians of Kagoshima were without a shepherd, but they were cleaving to the faith; they were fervent and met once a week for prayers and the reading of the Passion and the instructions Francis himself had written for them. Francis had confidence in Paul and knew he would return when the *bonzes* got over their fit of malice. Possibly, he was communicating with the Christians by stealth. And the Christians of Japan, though few, were the best converts of any in Asia; once convinced, they readily received Baptism; once Christians, they evinced an interest in and an enthusiasm for the faith that was most consoling to him who had begotten them in Christ. Xavier knew they would remain steadfast;

he was sorry Paul had run away, but it was only a temporary defection and he would return to his post. He did not know that Anjiro was now one of a band of corsairs coasting up and down the Yellow Sea, venturing up the Yangtze River. Paul, who had preached to others, had himself become a castaway.

When the camphor buds perfumed the air and Passiontide drew nigh, Francis and Fernandez set off again for Yamaguchi, taking with them the presents, the robes of the Nuncio, the ambassadorial regalia, the documents certifying that Francis was the Ambassador of Portugal.

No small sensation was caused in Yamaguchi when the strangers who had come some months before in rags and tatters now arrived in plum-blossom time, dressed in fine clothes, showing that they were the accredited representatives of the wonderful Portuguese, bearing rich gifts for the *daimyo*. The courtiers and *samurai* who had previously heard themselves stigmatized as filthier than the lowest brute beasts now crowded in to gaze at these marvellous gifts. The *bonzes* examined the wonderful spectacles with which an old man might regain the sight of youth. The mirrors passed from hand to hand. The *samurai* were shown how to handle and fire the arquebus. The *daimyo's* mother and womenfolk carried away the cloth-of-gold and the Portuguese dresses to their own apartments. The poets admired the crystal vases and the musical box that played of itself. Every time the clock struck the hour the whole palace gathered to listen to such a marvellous invention, and the *daimyo* sent word to his craftsmen that they were to note carefully the workings of the arquebus and the clock and set to work at once to copy—and, if possible, better—these useful objects. When the final present, the cut glass decanters and the fine wines, was unfolded, Francis made just as much a ceremony of decanting and pouring the wines as the *daimyo* of Kagoshima had made of the *cha* drinking on the occasion of their reception by that worthy.

The presents were the wonder of Yamaguchi and earned much respect for their bearers. The *daimyo* sent Francis a large purse of gold and another of silver, but Francis returned the money, greatly surprising the *daimyo,* since no *bonze* had ever yet refused money. Sending again to enquire what he could offer "the heavenly Pilgrim"—for this, he had been told, was the title which other peoples of the East had given the Christian *bonze*—he was asked for permission to teach the Christian religion. Xavier immediately received not only freedom to preach but a disused pagoda, with land attached. There he and Fernandez took up residence; there the Holy Sacrifice was offered.

The feast of cherry blossoms came and went; the tree-peonies bloomed. In the sunny days of June and July Francis sat in the Street of the Nobles, on the parapet of a well from which many came to draw water. And to all who came seeking to alleviate the thirst of the body, he offered the water of life. Crowds came to hear him; *bonzes,* Buddhist and Shintoist; nuns, *samurai,* nobles, merchants, craftsmen, asking endless questions, elaborating every answer. There was no time for prayer, no time for eating or sleeping. All day the crowds came to the well in the Street of Nobles, all night they thronged the pagoda, leaving Francis and Fernandez no privacy; with difficulty Fernandez regulated their hours so that Father Francis might manage to fit in his Mass and Office.

As Anjiro had foretold, there were no converts for a while. The people questioned, listened, questioned again, went away to think, returning in a while with further questions. One day, Fernandez was preaching when a passer-by spat in his face. Fernandez paused only to wipe his face and continued with his discourse. In the crowd, on that same occasion, was a man who had come day after day to contradict everything Francis said; the behaviour of Fernandez so impressed him that he followed Francis back to the pagoda that afternoon and became the first member of the Christian community in Yamaguchi. After him there came a steady trickle of converts—not many, compared to India and the other lands of the East, but the five hundred souls baptised in Yamaguchi were of a spiritual calibre second to none. Among all the five hundred the best was a poor, one-eyed showman, who found that the Street of the Nobles was a good place to sing ballads or to parade his tricks and jokes, in those times. He kept very close to the Christian *bonzes*, who brought him such trade. He could not help overhearing their teaching and he liked the tall Father Francis; when they returned to the pagoda in the evenings he ran alongside singing a snatch of song, strumming his stringed instrument, showing a conjuring trick, sometimes asking questions on the subject of the day's sermon, questions so shrewd that Francis was amazed at the man's intelligence and took more than usual pains to give answers satisfying to so keen an enquirer. Before long the street entertainer became a Christian; he placed himself and his unusual gifts at the service of Xavier, attracting the people to the well every day by his buffoonery and wit, helping Francis and Fernandez to manage the crowds, aiding religion with mimicry and repartee.

The feast of *Bon*, the feast of Lanterns, came and went; the lotus was in bloom; red-leaved maples bent, Narcissus-like, above the turquoise waters of tranquil pools. Francis realised, with a little surprise, that he had written only one letter since he came to Yamaguchi; the previous spring he had penned a—for Francis—unusually brief letter to the Fathers in Goa, telling how things were going in Japan. He recounted the various objections to the faith met with among the learned people of Yamaguchi, the principal point against Christianity being that if such were true, how was it that the Chinese—whose wisdom and civilisation the Japanese held in the highest esteem—had, in all that nation's long and honourable history, heard nothing of Christ or His gospel.

At the end of August, Francis got word that some Portuguese merchants awaited him in the port of Funai on the northwest shore of Kyushu, where he had first landed. The message was terse: the captain, one of the da Gama family, said that he bore letters from Goa which would show Francis that his presence was urgently needed in India. The very brevity of the message was ominous; da Gama would have said more if he thought Francis should have pondered the reasons for and against returning. In Yamaguchi, the fields were white to the harvest. "One man soweth and another reapeth"—how true were the words of Our Lord! Sending a fast messenger, the sower summoned Father de Torres and left him and Fernandez in charge of the five hundred baptised and five hundred catechumens of Yamaguchi.

On the day of his departure a crowd waited to escort him from the pagoda to the well in the Street of Nobles, where he was to say a few words of farewell. The one-eyed showman sang a sad little ballad specially composed for the occasion. The plum blossom had bloomed and faded, the cherry trees' bridal veil was gone; sadly the wisteria loosened its blue sash; the ranks of the irises flung their bright spears away; the perfume of no flower remained to make fragrant the wintry air, but forever in Yamaguchi would the name of Francis Xavier, the heavenly Pilgrim, be remembered and revered. The Christians knelt for his blessing. The pagans, remembering the wonderful presents this foreign *bonze* had brought their *daimyo*, stood round in attitudes of respect. Francis braced himself for the farewells. His whole life seemed to be a series of farewells: farewell to Xavier and his family, to Paris and the schools and his comrades; farewell to Rome and Ignatius, to Lisbon and Rodriguez; farewell to the pearl-fishers, to the old priest at St. Thomas' shrine at Mylapore, to the islanders in the great archipelago; farewell to Goa; farewell to Malacca. At each farewell his warm heart broke a little. Each goodbye was death in miniature. And now, farewell to his best Christians, to those whom he called "his own dear ones."

"In this life," he said, endeavouring to master his emotion, "you will have to bear troubles, persecutions and dangers. It is the surest road to heaven. I leave you Father de Torres and Brother Fernandez as your good guardians. They will do all they can for you; they will help and instruct you; but remember, put your trust in God alone."

They closed in on him for his blessing; mothers held their infants up—infants who might yet to their children's children say, "I saw the heavenly Pilgrim. I saw Father Francis." With difficulty the *samurai* converts who were to escort him to Funai extricated him from the crowd; all wished to accompany him a part of the way, but a wave of his hand was sufficient for them to understand that he did not wish it. Not even Fernandez—good Fernandez who had come through so much since he left his Córdoba silks; not even de Torres—the gallant conquistador who had never gone back to the wealthy estates he had won in New Spain but had come to make conquests for Christ in this land at the end of the earth. "I recommend you both, and all these to God Our Lord, now more than ever," he said, the tears coursing down his face as he embraced his brethren. "He will give you all the strength you need. He will know how to take care of you."

The two Spaniards gave him the old Spanish farewell: *"Vaya Usted con Dios.* Go with God." And he strode away, shouldering the pack containing the Mass vestments and sacred vessels. The *samurai* would have carried the pack, but Francis could not allow anyone else to carry it: it contained holy things.

Although he himself did not notice it, his step had lost its spring and his old agility was gone. The journeys of the previous winter had left their mark on him, and the months spent sitting cross-legged by the well had stiffened his joints. It took two days to come in sight of Funai, and at a village six miles from the port he had to give in. One of the Japanese hurried on to tell the captain of the ship that the Father had fallen ill; his feet were swollen and his head was paining him; it might be better to send a horse for him. Da Gama, much concerned, got together a party of merchants, who at once procured horses and set out to meet *el Santo*. They met him, being helped along by his two *samurai* converts; tired and ill, he carried a heavy pack which he would not relinquish. They felt greatly ashamed at being mounted and well dressed, while Father Francis limped and looked as shabby as ever; dismounting, they saluted him, and knelt for his blessing. He would not mount a horse, so they took turns at linking him along between them.

When da Gama saw the strange cavalcade approach, he flew all his flags, ordered his trumpeters to blow, sent his longboats to the shore for Francis and had the artillery fire more than two hundred salvoes. Such a display greatly surprised the Japanese, who at once enquired about the personage whose arrival was celebrated with such honour. Francis was too ill to notice anything beyond the noise

the trumpets and the cannon made, a torment to his
aching head. But he was grateful to da Gama. He lay in
bed and the ship's physician bled him and applied burnt
feathers to his nostrils and washed his temples with
vinegar. By degrees he recovered. In the evening, the
daimyo of that area, who had heard the trumpets and
artillery and feared that a pirate had come to Funai, sent
to enquire what had happened. The people of Funai, who
had been immensely impressed by the reception given the
honourable foreign *bonze,* reported to their ruler that the
Portuguese had received a great Christian *bonze* and the
noise was their welcome to him. At once an invitation was
sent to Francis to visit this *daimyo,* who was known as
King of Bungo.

The next day, the King of Bungo sent a palanquin for
Francis, but Francis decided to make his visit on foot.
The Portuguese, wishing to demonstrate the respect in
which Xavier was held in their dominions, insisted on
escorting him to the *daimyo* in royal fashion. To please
da Gama, Francis donned his full robes of office—a new
brocade soutane, a surplice with priceless lace, a green
velvet stole embroidered with gold and silver thread. The
longboats took off, with silken banners streaming in the
wind, with trumpeters and hautboys playing alternate
fanfares. By the time they reached the landing place a
huge crowd had gathered. Then the ship's officers, in full
uniform, formed up behind him as the servants of Eastern
monarchs were wont to do. They carried five gifts for the
daimyo; one had a pair of black velvet slippers, another a
Bengal cane chased with gold; a parasol, a Japanese
translation of the catechism, bound in white satin, and a
statue of the Blessed Virgin, wearing a shawl of violet
damask, completed the items for presentation. Da Gama
himself, very gorgeous in black armour damascened with

gold, ornamented with mascaroons, and holding in one hand a toque all ablaze with jewels and feathers, walked before Francis, holding a baton, as though he were a steward.

The young *daimyo*, a man of twenty, hearing of this distinguished company on its way, prepared an equally honourable reception. At the fortress gate, the *samurai* of Bungo staged an exhibition of military exercises; in the first reception hall a child of six recited a special poem of welcome composed by a court poet at short notice; in the second reception hall ranks of nobles prostrated three times in salutation. The visitors proceeded through the orangery and through the court of the *daimyo's* brother, who also recited a hastily prepared speech. Finally they came to the *daimyo*, who insisted on prostrating himself before the Very Honourable One of the Honourable Portuguese.

The young King of Bungo had a rather unsavoury reputation. It was rumoured that he had murdered his father, mother, and infant brother to ascend the throne. But he was favourable towards Francis, giving him permission to preach to his people—a permission of which Xavier took full advantage; so much so that the Portuguese complained that they could never see *el Santo* save when he returned to the ship at midnight, so exhausted that they insisted on his snatching a few hours' rest before dawn found him on his way ashore again.

So many became Christians that the local *bonzes* decided to stage a religious debate at which their famous holy *bonze*, the most learned in all Japan, would confront and overwhelm the Christian teacher. Great interest was taken in this debate which lasted several days and was open to all who cared to listen. The *daimyo* thought Francis very imprudent to attempt to engage in argument with this abbot, the most wonderful scholar in his kingdom. But Francis accepted the challenge and refuted his adversary, though, probably, his answers seemed as illogical to the abbot as the latter's questions seemed absurd to Xavier. One result of the debate was to incur the hatred of the *bonzes;* and this, more than anything else, convinced the Portuguese that the great Buddhist scholar and thinker had really got the worse of the argument. The *bonzes* did not dare attack Francis for fear of the Portuguese; but they vented their spleen on the *daimyo,* refusing to open the pagodas or offer the customary sacrifices to the idols; not even the alms of many wealthy citizens would make them emerge from their monasteries, where they threatened to immure themselves until the new *bonze* was sent away.

The *daimyo* was nonplussed, his subjects fearful lest the unpropitiated gods visit them with earthquakes, tidal waves, wars and other evils. While Father Francis prayed that God might show him what to do, word came from Yamaguchi that a *samurai* had led a revolt against the *daimyo* of that city—the same whom Francis had denounced for the unnatural vices of himself and his courtiers. In the heat of the fighting the *daimyo* had locked himself into his palace, killed his wife and son, fired the beautiful building to prevent its countless treasures, including Francis' presents, from falling into enemy hands, and committed hara-kiri.

A secret messenger brought letters to Francis saying that Father de Torres and Fernandez were safe, but had gone into hiding for the time being. The Christians were well and steadfast in the faith. The rebels were sending for the brother of the King of Bungo to become their new ruler. It was wonderful, de Torres said, how God had held

273

them all in His hand, as it were, during this bloody affair;
not a single neophyte had suffered.

Da Gama did not feel too happy. He had no doubt but
that the *bonzes* had been behind the revolt in Yamaguchi.
Who knew but that a similar rebellion was brewing in
Bungo? The young King of Bungo had not gained his
kingdom without making many enemies among his own
kith and kin. Concluding his business, the captain informed *el Santo* that they were leaving. There was a farewell visit to be paid to the *daimyo* and, if Father Francis
still wished to arrange for a church to be built in Bungo
for the new Christians there, an admirer of his, one
adventurer who had sailed with the captain, a fellow
named Mendes Pinto, would lend the money. Francis
would be wise to accept the offer at once, before Pinto
changed his mind or gambled the gold—gold not honestly
earned either, the captain would swear.

The *daimyo* parted from them on cordial terms, sending a Japanese envoy to make a trade agreement with the
Viceroy of Goa. Trade with the Portuguese meant riches
untold, and riches meant power; for, to make wars on
neighbouring and rival *daimyos*, one needed money to pay
one's *samurai*. The King of Bungo promised Francis that
in his dominions and in those of his brother in Yamaguchi
the Christians would be protected and the Christian
bonzes given every help and encouragement. And da
Gama, listening, hoped that the Portuguese in Goa would
make, and honour, that trade agreement; he could swear
that the young *daimyo's* enthusiasm for Christianity depended wholly on that business deal.

They walked back to the landing place. It was already
night and the stars were up. Francis stood for a moment
on the shore, taking his bearings from the planets. Somewhere in the far northeast was Kyoto, where the shadow-

Emperor dragged out his miserable existence. Two days' journey to the north lay Yamaguchi, with his dear ones, the thousand neophytes, and his beloved brothers, de Torres and Fernandez. Somewhere in the west lay Hirado, and far away to the south Kagoshima; perhaps two hundred Christians in Bungo, the same in Hirado, the same in Kagoshima. Two years and three months he had been in Japan and his labours and sufferings there had been great; and, in the end, barely sixteen hundred Christians . . . He was an unprofitable servant, he told himself. He sent his blessing in the direction of each of the missions and a special one to Fernandez and de Torres. In a few years he hoped to be back, bringing with him Japanese priests from Goa and Fathers from Europe, highly educated and most intelligent men, the sort he would tell Ignatius were needed in this land of intelligent, active-minded people. Then he knelt and kissed the ground. As he rose, he felt how stiff his limbs were; he was getting old—forty-five years and a half—still, not old enough for one's joints to stiffen, for one's muscles to ache so. Slowly he walked to where the longboat waited to bring him to the galley.

CHAPTER 14

On the first day of the Christmas moon of 1551, a storm blew up from Formosa, catching the ship that was sailing south for Malacca mid-way between the Ryukyu Islands and the coast of China. They tacked sails and ran before the wind. On the second day, the ship rolling and plunging violently in mountainous waves, they lightened their load, throwing everything movable, even the stove used for cooking, overboard. Xavier helped, like everyone else, and was up front, helping to cut away a portion of the poop, when a shout, "Men overboard!" brought everyone running to the side. The hawser that secured the life-sloop had snapped and the boat and some men who were working on her had been swept away. The captain tried to manœuvre the unwieldy caravel about but only put all in danger of being swamped. There was no sign of either men or boat. They were lost, da Gama said; nothing could live in that sea. He would have to abandon hope of rescue and endeavour to save the ship by continuing to keep before the storm. But Xavier asked him to wait, to send a man to the masthead to see if the sloop were in sight. An old sailor, standing by, shook his head and remarked on the hopelessness of sighting the sloop.

"O you of little faith!" cried Francis. "Do you think that

the Lord has less power than He had? Trust Him and His Mother. Have I not promised to say three Masses in the Church of Our Lady of the Mount in Malacca? I am sure they will save the boat and the men." To please *el Santo,* the captain sent a man up to the lookout; but after half an hour he reported that there was nothing to be seen but the crests of angry waves.

"Come down," said Xavier, "but, never fear, the boat will be back to this ship, as the daughter to her mother. Will you oblige me," he said to Mendes Pinto, the Portuguese adventurer standing beside him, "by heating a little water for me. I feel very ill."

Alas, the stove and the water casks had all gone overboard when they had lightened the ship's load. "My sins would not allow me to do him that one little service," said Pinto afterwards, telling the story.

"My head aches dreadfully," said Xavier, causing everyone to turn and look at him. He who never mentioned his sufferings had, twice in a few moments, complained of his headaches. "I am dizzy," he said, and reeled unsteadily. Pinto caught him. "No wonder Your Reverence feels ill," he said, "you have been here on deck all yesterday and all last night. Come into my cabin and rest a little." He helped Xavier into the cabin, and, bidding his Chinese servant wait on the Father, returned to the deck. Some hours passed and the servant came to him. "*El Santo* did not lie down nor sleep," he informed Pinto; "he has been kneeling on the bunk praying all the time since." Pinto would have liked to go back and tell Father Francis to sleep and rest, but he felt strangely happy and comforted to know that in such a storm, they and the poor fellows gone down with the sloop were being prayed for.

At sundown, Xavier, wan and haggard, dragged himself out on deck again.

277

"Any sign of the sloop?" he asked.

"Not a sign," said da Gama. "Father, those poor fellows are at the bottom of the sea by now."

"I beg you, send the man up the mainmast again," requested the priest.

To please *el Santo*, da Gama himself climbed aloft with the seaman. They looked in all directions, then shouted down that there was not a sign of the sloop or the missing men. Xavier knelt on deck and rested his aching head on a block of wood for a minute. Then he prayed aloud: "O Lord, by Thy five sacred wounds have pity on us and save the souls astray in the sloop." After repeating these words a few times, he seemed to sleep, his head still on the block of wood. Suddenly the seaman on top of the mast shouted: "The sloop! The sloop!" Everyone but *el Santo* looked in the direction where the lookout pointed and there, not a gunshot away, was the sloop, with the fourteen men and the boy—the captain's nephew. The joy that overcame them was unbearable; no one cheered; no one shouted; all, with one accord, wept like children. The sloop having come alongside, they hauled in the companions they had thought lost. The last to be lifted ashore said, "Don't leave Father Francis behind in the boat. Give him a hand up. Had he not been with us, we were lost."

"But he never left the ship!" cried the others. "He has been sleeping on deck for quite a little while."

"No; he came to us and sat amongst us in the boat," insisted the rescued men. "Just a little while back. When he came we feared no more."

Those who had seen him in the ship and those who had seen him in the boat at one and the same time suddenly ceased speaking. Pinto remembered the Achinese pirates and how *el Santo*, though far away, had witnessed the victory. He and da Gama and the sailors and the men who

278

had come back from the waves all went to where Xavier was lifting his head from the wooden block, having wakened from his sleep. They tried to throw themselves at his feet, but he forbade them sternly and, going away, hid himself in the captain's cabin. A little while later the captain's nephew rapped rather timidly and called through the keyhole: "Please, Your Reverence, my clothes are in the cabin and I want to change out of these wet ones." Trying the door he found it unlocked and slipped in quietly. *El Santo* was sleeping peacefully on the floor. The boy changed his clothes and was about to leave the cabin as quietly as he entered when the Father spoke: "Tell your uncle to praise God for His goodness, and say that he is to make ready to sail south again; the storm is almost ended. And tell the two Mohammedans who were in the sloop that I will see them now."

The Mohammedans were waiting outside the cabin door. They wanted to be instructed and to be baptised in the Christian faith. The souls astray in the sloop had found salvation.

Early in December they anchored at Sancian, an island at the mouth of the Canton River, about six miles off the Chinese coast. Their caravel was badly damaged and they had to wait to have it repaired before sailing for Malacca. Fortunately, two Portuguese ships were already anchored there, one captained by Diego Pereira from Malacca, who had always been a good friend of Xavier's. Pereira was trimming his sails, preparatory to setting out for home. He would be more than honoured if Father Francis would transfer to his ship, the *Santa Croce;* if they did not make Malacca in time for Christmas, they would do so for New Year. Mendes Pinto decided to remain with da Gama. The goods bought in Japan would find a ready market in Siam, he told Francis. The wealth of India was nothing to the

wealth of Burma and Siam; there were good trading cities
in those parts, too, and if Father Francis wanted further
lands to convert, Pinto thought there must be as many
millions of pagans in those countries as in India. And as
for China—China must have tens of millions. Of all the
countries to which Pinto's adventures had taken him,
none had equalled China.

Xavier had thought that no foreigner could enter
China. How then, he asked, had Pinto managed to enter
that land? Mendes Pinto had been in the company of a
merchant friend—no need to tell *el Santo* that he and his
friend had been merchants in name, buccaneers by trade
—and they had taken a chance and put in at various ports.
They had ventured inland more than once and had many
strange adventures. It would not do to tell Father Francis
about the robbing of those tombs near Nanking; he would
think it sacrilegious, that robbery of the silver the Chinese
used to line the coffins of the great. To be sure, they had
been surprised before the deed was done and had had to
fly for their lives and sail out to sea where, that night,
Pinto's friend had been drowned in a typhoon. Pinto's ship
ran aground in the Gulf of Nanking and then he and his
companions made the acquaintance of the real China, for
they tramped from town to town and from city to city—
going even to the gates of Peking, where the Ming Emperor lived. When *el Santo* concluded his business in India
and returned to Japan, he needed only to ask at the various ports for Mendes Pinto and the latter would himself
accompany His Reverence to the great Empire of China.
Indeed, if the Father were back in Malacca by the middle
of the following year, more than likely he would find
Pinto there then, and they could journey together to Japan
or China or both countries. Meantime he commended

himself to the prayers of Father Francis and begged a farewell blessing.

During the voyage to Malacca, Francis again and again thought of China. He remembered how the Japanese had always ended their discussions with him: they invariably asked, "If what you say is true, why do the Chinese not know about it?" They thought the Chinese the oldest and wisest people on earth. Instead of going to the Emperor first, hoping to convert the Japanese through him, Francis told himself now that he should have gone to the Chinese first. He had been ill-advised by Anjiro; and he had wasted much time learning, the hard way, the real Japan. Ever the optimist, he began to plan all over again. This time he would begin with China. He would journey to Peking, to this Emperor of the Ming dynasty, this ruler who was no shadow, who delegated none of his power to *daimyos;* he would go to this country not torn by wars of rival lords as were Japan, Burma and Siam. Highly elated with his new plan, he confided in Diego Pereira, who thought it a very good plan and told Francis that many Portuguese were rotting in the Canton jails—the worst prisons on earth— and had managed to smuggle letters to him. He heartily wished that cordial relations could be established between Portugal and China. The only hope of setting these poor wretches free, the prisoners themselves had said in their letters, and the only way foreigners might obtain permission to enter China, was to send a well-appointed embassy, laden with rich gifts. Francis listened enthusiastically; it should not be too difficult, he told his friend, to induce the Viceroy at Goa to send an ambassador to Peking. Pereira himself would make an excellent ambassador; and Francis would go in his train and get permission to preach in China, while Pereira could negotiate for the removal of the ban on foreigners and for the release of his countrymen from prison. For the rest of the voyage they planned the venture. Francis would approach the Viceroy and write King John. Pereira would order a cargo of the richest merchandise in Malacca and have all in readiness for their departure the following year.

Malacca presented a sorry appearance, having been besieged by Javanese and Sumatran pirates for several months. A large portion of the town was razed. The pirates, when finally routed, had poisoned all the wells on the outskirts of the city, and in consequence, a plague was raging. The good governor, Pedro da Gama, came to welcome Francis; accompanying him was his brother, Alvaro. Alvaro had little to say. He was remembering the time Martin da Sousa had thrown him into the dungeon in Mozambique, unjustly accusing him of treason. This was the priest who had walked to the ship with da Sousa —walked away, leaving Alvaro in that hell-hole. Well, da Sousa was no longer Governor of Goa. But Alvaro was coming to replace his half-brother as Commandant of Malacca. This Francis Xavier, about whom there was so much talk in Goa and elsewhere, did not impress Don Alvaro very much. Evidently, the priest was not too particular about the company he kept. Diego Pereira might be a wealthy man but what was known of his Portuguese background or of his antecedents? Nothing; for the simple reason that there was no background, there were no forebears to be proud of. The fellow's speech gave him away: uneducated; a plebeian, for all his money; another of the rabble who had worked their way out and amassed riches rapidly while Don Alvaro and other captains had risked their lives making it safe for them to do so.

Pereira was enthusiastically unfolding the plans for the mercantile and spiritual conquest of China. Pedro da Gama thought it an excellent idea; even Don Alvaro unbent to admit that such an idea had its possibilities. Already he saw himself leaving a deputy commandant in Malacca while he sailed for China, the Ambassador of his King and country. Already he was reckoning the trading profits such a venture might bring him. It was quite a good idea, he told Father Francis, before he took his departure to visit the garrison.

In Malacca waited something that, if Francis had been asked to name a gift for himself, would have been his choice of all the gifts this world could offer. It was a letter from Ignatius. A letter from Ignatius, from whom he had not heard for four years! Ignatius—in whose continued silence another might have imagined estrangement, disapproval, waning friendship! But no, the Captain of Pamplona did not change. With tears Xavier read the letter, right down to the last line, which told him how much he meant to Ignatius: "All yours, in such manner that I cannot ever forget you. Ignatius."

Over and over again he read the news from Europe. There was so much Ignatius had to tell, so much encouragement and consolation he had to send the labourer bearing the burden of the day and the heat. Ignatius was not without his own troubles. It had taken time and tact to counteract Bobadilla's ill-timed lambasting of the Emperor Charles. And Rodriguez, despite warnings, seemed to have allowed the patronage of John III to go to his head a bit; he was enrolling novices by the dozen and the score; already there were between three and four hundred in Coimbra—good young seminarians, of that Ignatius had no doubt, but definitely not being trained in that obedience set down in the Constitutions. One year he was begging to be sent to India or Ethiopia, the next to Brazil. Ignatius had sent for him to come to Rome, and the King of Portugal had written saying that he thought it advisable for Ignatius to remove Rodriguez from Portugal. Any day now, Ignatius said in his letter, he was due in Rome and Francis Xavier would please pray, on receipt of this news, that Ignatius might be enabled to deal with Rodriguez without causing him too much hurt—Xavier would remember old Rodriguez as a regular touch-me-not. It would not be easily settled, this matter, though Ignatius thought of making two Provinces of Spain and putting Rodriguez in charge of one, while sending Diego Miron to Portugal. It was difficult to know what was best to do. One thing was sure: much prayer and thought were needed before coming to a decision.

Ignatius reported that the Society was spreading rapidly. There were foundations in Sicily, France, Cologne, Vienna, Naples, Tunis, Ethiopia, besides those Francis already knew of, and some that had come to nought but where the Fathers hoped to try again, such as Ireland. With houses, works and numbers multiplying, the cares of the Founder multiplied. At Candlemas—a few days before Ignatius wrote—Francis Borgia, the Duke of Gandia, had made ready to leave Rome, where he had spent a few months with Ignatius; he was gone back to Spain, to Oñate, where recently a Jesuit house had been established; there he would make the public renunciation of his dukedom and receive Holy Orders. Ignatius himself had been ill, so ill that he had wished to be relieved of the position of General, but the Fathers with one exception had all voted for him to continue bearing the burden of the Society's cares. He was well again and had been able to be up and about when Francis Borgia left. These and a hundred other details Ignatius told his friend. Rome was strange at present, what with the rebuilding of St. Peter's and the amount of scaffolding that was up about the Basilica. The new Pope, Julius III, had had a heavy year's

work during his first year as Pontiff. It had been a Jubilee
year. The new Order, founded by Master Philip Neri, who
was a very good friend of Ignatius—and a most delightful
fellow, always in good humour, like Francis himself—had
made its mark during the Jubilee, caring for the needs of
poor pilgrims. Philip often called round to see the Jesuits
and they visited him. Some jokers said that soon no Jesuit
in Rome would have a button left in his gown, Neri having
a habit of twirling them absentmindedly as he talked to
anyone. The influx of pilgrims had been great, and the
crops failed and only the energetic and prompt action of
the new Pope had averted a famine. He had sent fast
couriers to the King of France and to the Emperor and
got permission to import corn from Provence and Spain.
This action and the revoking of the flour tax had made
Julius III popular from the beginning. But Francis would
remember that Julius was one of the del Monte family, a
family opposed to the Church reform that had just been
inaugurated. He would need to pray for the Pope and the
Church. Some of the Cardinals who had been active in
the cause of reform were already protesting and refused
to attend the banquets, bull fights, races, gaming and
other entertainments that the Pope patronised and attended so frequently. The keeper of the Pope's ape had
been adopted by one of the del Montes, given a princely
income and raised to a cardinalate. It was an anxious
time. Francis would pray for all in Rome as his friends
were praying for him. Francis *did* pray, even as he read,
but each time he read the letter only one line stood out as
though written in gold—"All yours, in such manner that I
cannot ever forget you. Ignatius."

· · · · ·

Pereira could not travel to India, but he got *el Santo* a

passage on the *Gallega* and, with his customary generosity, gave Francis a parting present of three thousand crowns. On January 24th, 1552, Francis landed at Cochin. He had been almost three years absent, and, from the letters received in Japan, as well as from items of information gleaned in the course of conversation with various Portuguese officials met in Japan and Malacca, he had reason to believe that things were not well with the Society in India. It was reassuring to receive good news on landing; the Father in charge of the Cape Comorin mission came to render an account of his stewardship. There were now forty thousand Christians at the pearl fisheries, and several Fathers, all fluent speakers of Tamil, were there, working in fields where Xavier had ploughed the first furrows.

In Cochin there was a regular outcry against the Jesuits. A church, the property of a confraternity in that town, had been lent to the Fathers some years previously. In the absence of *el Santo*, Father Gomes, Rector of Goa, without as much as a by-your-leave to the Cochin Brotherhood, appropriated the property altogether. Ignoring the rights and protests of the Confraternity, he was proceeding to have the church replaced by a new college when, providentially, Xavier arrived back from Japan. The only way, Francis decided, to deal with such a vexatious situation was to repair the damage immediately. So he went in person to the Brothers of the Confraternity, apologised humbly for the wrong done them by a member of his Company, restored them the keys of their chapel and begged pardon of the whole city of Cochin for the scandal given by this outrageous affair. So moved were the Brothers of the Confraternity that they immediately insisted on presenting their church to *el Santo*, to use as he would.

There were letters to be despatched from Cochin, letters to King John, complaining of the cruelty of some of his officials to the natives, and of one captain in particular. A letter went to Rodriguez and another to Ignatius, telling him the sort of recruits required for Japan—men of tried virtue, but also learned men, well able to argue; men with a good knowledge of astronomy, since the Japanese set great store by those who could explain such things; men of great bodily strength and robust health, able to resist cold well. After telling Ignatius of his plans and preparations for China—already he had made good progress in the study of Chinese—he begged for two special missionaries: one to be Rector in Goa, the other to be a spiritual Father to the whole Indian province. He was touched at the wish Ignatius had expressed in his last letter to see him again before the close of life. God knew how Francis reciprocated that wish. What a joy such a reunion would be! How he would clasp to his heart his Father in God!

In the middle of March he arrived in Goa. He had sent an order on ahead to Micer Paul to dismiss from the Society two Fathers who had refused to obey an order to go to Malacca. All his worst fears regarding the administration of Gomes had been realised. During Xavier's absence the Rector had promoted himself to the position of Vice-Provincial; he had ignored and hampered gentle Micer Paul, claiming that his own appointment by Rodriguez superseded any regulations made by Xavier. He had tried to run the College on European lines, and his overbearing manner with the students resulted in a general runaway of most of the native students one night. Then, in a rage, he had expelled the innocent remainder and filled the place with Portuguese students, sons of Goanese merchants and officials. The Fathers in Goa did not know whom to obey: Micer Paul said Xavier had left him in charge; Gomes said that Rodriguez had appointed him.

When Francis arrived at the gate of Holy Faith College, about fifty Fathers, brothers and novices, awaited him. Micer Paul and Gaspar Berze, the Dutch Father, recently recalled from Ormuz, were there; only the Rector was absent. Micer Paul told Xavier that they had a young brother dying in the infirmary. How he had lasted so long, no one knew; he kept saying that if he could but hold on to life until Father Francis came he would recover. As Micer Paul spoke, Francis was already striding to the infirmary, where he blessed the dying man and read a gospel over him. And, from that moment, the brother began to recover.

A clean sweep was made in Holy Faith. All the Portuguese students were told that they need not attend on the morrow nor on any future date—Holy Faith was a college for native students preparing to work in the various Indian and Eastern missions. A letter was there from Ignatius, appointing Xavier Provincial of the newly established Indian province. His first task was to dismiss Father Gomes from the College and from Goa, sending him to a small Portuguese settlement in the hill country six hundred miles to the north. Father Gaspar Berze, who had done wonderful work at Ormuz, was made Rector. Native students were hunted up and invited back. A hundred and one details of college and community organisation were seen to. And all the time, the ardent heart was straining at the leash, longing to be away to China, and after that to his beloved Japan. Letters had to be written to all the mission stations, with advice for all the Fathers there. Micer Paul and other old friends in Goa thought Xavier very worn and were shocked to see that his hair had gone white; they tried to make him eat, but he suffered so much from a stomach complaint that all he could take was an egg flip. Yet, he prayed as fervently as ever; as was always his way before setting out on a new enterprise, he retired from the world as much as possible for a few weeks before leaving for China, fortifying his soul for the coming adventure. Micer Paul watched him walk in the gardens of Holy Faith, his eyes uplifted, as was his custom, an expression of intense delight suffusing his whole countenance. The man was literally afire with the love of God. People said that his habitual attitude—keeping the *loba* a little lifted out from his body on the left side—was due to the intense heat of that holy furnace, Xavier's heart.

Father Francis was due to leave Goa on Holy Thursday, April 14th. He said Mass, gave Holy Communion, and preached in the College chapel that morning and afterwards carried the Blessed Sacrament to the Altar of Repose. But the wind was contrary and they had to wait until Easter Sunday. It was the Easter of 1552, exactly four years since that Easter when he had sailed for Japan. The ship put in at Cochin, where there were still some matters to be attended to. Another priest had been captured by the Badagas on the fishery coast and had died shortly after being rescued by his converts; he had to be replaced. A letter had to be sent to Goa, asking for funds for the new College in Cochin. After a week in Cochin they sailed for Malacca, past the pearl fisheries and Cape Comorin and Travancore, past the shrine of St. Thomas and out across the Bay of Bengal where sunsets were glorious, sunrises more glorious still. Francis, looking west where India lay and raising his face to Heaven, smiled with happiness. He remembered the old dream in which he used to carry the Indian on his back. Since he came to the East he had never dreamed that dream but—*Madre de Dios!*—not in a dream, but in truth, he had carried the

289

Indian and not only the Indian, but the Malayan, the island savage, the Japanese. And now he was going to shoulder the Chinese.

After the usual storm they reached Malacca, then ravaged by the plague. China had to be put out of mind for a few weeks while Francis tried to do what he could. He had huts erected along the seashore, to serve as temporary hospitals, the existing hospital being entirely inadequate for the numbers of the plague-stricken; he himself attended on the sick, spending his days and nights in the main and auxiliary hospitals.

In Malacca a wholly unforeseen persecution awaited him. Don Alvaro, the new Commandant, having discovered that he was not being sent as Ambassador to China but that a mere merchant like Pereira had been appointed to lead the embassy, immediately proceeded to do all in his power to stop Pereira, the embassy, Xavier and all from going to China. The brocades and tapestries and pictures, all specially ordered to impress the Emperor in Peking, lay, tied in their wrappings, on the wharf. Xavier's three companions, a Portuguese brother named Ferreira, a Chinese youth—one Antonio—and a Malabar named Christopher, wondered what was the cause of the delay. They had reached Malacca in May and now, in July, they were still there. Some said that Don Alvaro did a bit of private smuggling and that the embassage would have ruined that profitable trade. Seeing that Pereira meant to sail, with or without permission, the Commandant had the rudder taken off his galley. Father Francis had to intervene to save bloodshed.

If he had been possessed by the devil, Don Alvaro could not have hated Xavier more. When Francis wrote, reminding him that he was Papal Nuncio and had power to excommunicate him for hindering a missionary enterprise, Alvaro spat on the floor, crying, "That's what I think of your credentials! Where are they, anyway? Show me the papal brief." Alas, Francis, never dreaming that such papers would be required, had left the letters of Pope Paul III in Goa. He told this to Alvaro, who spat again and yelled aloud, so that all might hear, "Perverted hypocrite! Forger of papal documents!" Malaccans, anxious to be on good terms with the new Commandant, took up Don Alvaro's accusation and followed Xavier about the streets, hurling insults and abuse at the man who, only two months before, had nursed them through the plague. Forgotten was the wonderful expedition against the Achins; nothing was remembered save that this was a man not in the good graces of Don Alvaro. Alvaro had reviled him, so the crowd reviled him. He could not go from his hut at the hospital to Our Lady on the Mount without hearing the most scurrilous epithets shouted after him in the streets. Soon, the persecution became so intense that his friends besought him to remain indoors. From that time on, he spent his nights in the church, prostrate before the Blessed Sacrament or the Lady altar; in the mornings he offered Mass for Don Alvaro, adding the collect *Deus, Pacis:*

> O God, who lovest and keepest peace and charity: grant to all our enemies true peace and charity, and grant them remission of all their sins; and by Thy might deliver us from all their guile. Through Our Lord Jesus Christ, who with Thee and the Holy Ghost liveth and reigneth one God, world without end. Amen.

Towards the end of June Alvaro said that Xavier might go, but without Pereira. There was to be no embassy, and to make sure no attempt would be made to fit a rudder to the *Santa Croce* and slip away at night time, the Commandant confiscated the ship, all Pereira's goods, all the gifts purchased for presentation to the Emperor in Peking, leaving Pereira and those of his friends who were financing the venture absolutely ruined. Some of the ill-used merchants came, in tears, to Xavier, telling him of their misfortune. Not so Diego Pereira. Noting how Alvaro was dismissing, one by one, the men whom the owner of the *Santa Croce* had already hired for the voyage and replacing them with his own men—several of whom were ring-leaders of the mobs who daily pursued *el Santo* in the streets—Pereira divided the little money he had left among such of those on the ship who he thought would be of use to Francis, ordering them to provide for the Father's needs on the voyage, as long as the money lasted.

Don Alvaro's men were in high good humour. They hoped to make a good profit out of the trip to Canton. The pepper and other goods purchased by Diego Pereira were of the rarest quality and the crew intended to make the voyage highly rewarding to themselves. The "impostor" could make his way to China alone, Don Alvaro had said; there he would probably get his deserts. A touch of the tortures inflicted on Europeans caught entering China would soon teach this Francis Xavier a thing or two about the Dragon Kingdom. Mendes Pinto and other friends of *el Santo* were anxious and miserable. Pinto had had experience of Nanking jails—irons on wrists, ankles and neck; lice and vermin numerous enough to devour a man. Before that, Pinto had been taken prisoner in a country village several miles from Nanking, where the peasants had tied his hands behind his back, beat him almost to death and then put him into a cistern where he was in water to his waist; the water was full of leeches and, when he made his escape next day, he was covered with sores from head to foot. Pinto was horrified at the thought of Father Francis going to China with no European in his company. At the last moment he tried to obtain Don Alvaro's permission to go on the *Santa Croce,* but the Commandant threatened to clap him in irons if he attempted to join the ship. Pinto retired, an unhappy man. He spent the afternoon wandering about Malacca enquiring as to the possibility of getting to Canton by another vessel. He could not travel with *el Santo* but he might yet manage to overtake him before he landed in China.

Meanwhile Don Alvaro was carefully reading through some letters; they were letters Xavier had been writing and Alvaro had taken care to intercept them before forwarding them to Goa.

One was to the Superior of Holy Faith College. It concerned a Portuguese who was living with a native woman and who refused to have the union regularised; Father Francis thought that there was perhaps some canonical impediment which the man was hiding; he hoped that Father Gaspar would do what he could to obtain the necessary dispensations from the Bishop of Goa. Not a word of the papal briefs. Alvaro snorted. He had been right; all the fine talk of Xavier's about the excommunication and all the claims to be Nuncio Apostolic were so much froth. The second letter, dated three days later, was to the same Father Gaspar Berze. Don Alvaro's lips curled as he read:

> Would that God had allowed that Don Pedro should be Governor of Malacca this year also—then Diego Pereira's embassy to the Chinese empire, on which we had fixed our hopes so much for an extension of God's kingdom, would certainly have prospered better. How differently his brother, Don Alvaro, has acted towards me, in depriving me of the

293

means of sailing for China, in confiscating the vessel placed at my disposal by the Governor! I greatly fear that the Divine Majesty, so grievously offended by his injustice, will visit him with far severer punishments than he expects or imagines.

Next day, the *Santa Croce* sailed. The Vicar of Malacca, wishing to be on good terms with both *el Santo* and the Commandant, asked Francis if he would go and bid farewell to Alvaro. "I bear him no ill will," was the reply; "but the only place I shall see him again is in the Valley of Jehosophat." A crowd of friends waited to see him depart. To their consternation he took off his sandals and beat them off the rock, shaking the dust of Malacca from his feet. They remembered the words of the gospel: "Amen, I say to you, it shall be more tolerable for the land of Sodom and Gomorrah in the day of judgment than for that city."

Diego Pereira stood on the height above Our Lady of the Mount, watching the *Santa Croce* cross the harbour bar. There went his fortune, his ship, his friend. He had done as Father Francis had requested; he had not added to Xavier's heartbreak by going to say farewell. His tears blinding him, he went to the church and, clambering to the bell-tower, tolled the bell slowly, mournfully, like a passing-bell. As he pulled on the rope, he went over in memory that last letter, every syllable of which was engraved in his heart:

. . . My sins have been so many and so great as to have stood not only in my way but in yours; God knows how I have wished to serve Him and you . . . I am now going aboard ship, to escape all those people who come to me in tears, saying that the failure of the embassy has ruined them. May God forgive him on whom lies the responsibility of so many and such great misfortunes.

I beg of you not to come visit me—you to whom I have been the cause of so much misfortune and grief —the sight of you would only increase my unhappiness. Yet I trust that this calamity may eventually turn to your advantage: I have written the King, asking him to reward worthily your zeal for the spread of the gospel. I have ceased to meet the Commandant, who has so unceasingly opposed a voyage that would have been so fruitful for the faith. May God forgive him! I grieve for him, for he will have to suffer worse punishments than he imagines. May Our Lord preserve your health and may He guide, direct and accompany my present endeavours! Amen. From our house at Malacca, on the point of embarking in your ship, the *Santa Croce*.

Francisco

.   .   .   .   .

Don Alvaro tried to concentrate on his card game; now and again he stopped and spat on the ground as though to rid his mouth of a bad taste. He, like the others at the gaming tables, had heard women talking outside the open window about the departure of the ship.

"And what," asked one, "did *el Santo* say when the Vicar asked him was he not coming to bid the Commandant farewell?"

"He spoke very gravely," said her friend. "He said that Don Alvaro would see him no more in this life; but that he would await the Commandant before the judgment seat of God, where Don Alvaro would have to render an account for the deed he had done in preventing the spread of the gospel."

No one of those at the card table pretended to have overheard the conversation, Don Alvaro least of all. And, out to sea, on the deck of the *Santa Croce* Francis Xavier stood, his face turned towards Our Lady of the Mount, his hands outstretched, praying for his enemy. When he had finished, he sang the *Salve*. Antonio, his Chinese boy, was unable to join him in the hymn; the Portuguese seamen, sullen, grumbling, went about their various tasks, pretending not to hear; but suddenly from the prow, a fine resonant voice took up the chant; it was the man at the helm, the pilot—not one of Don Alvaro's men, but a faithful servitor of the wronged Diego Pereira. When the *Salve* was sung, Francis Xavier turned his back on Malacca and his face towards China.

CHAPTER *15*

IN THE middle of the sixteenth century the letters of Father Francis Xavier were being eagerly read by his brethren and friends in Europe. From Rome and Coimbra copies of the missionary's letters went to the Jesuit houses all over the Continent. Other missionaries made ready to follow the trail blazed by *el Santo;* already, at the latter's request, a Father had been despatched to Japan, there to labour with Father de Torres and Brother Fernandez. Little did the newcomer dream that the polite Japanese, who received him with such etiquette, had recorded his coming in their chronicles in the following not very flattering terms:

> Nine foot in stature, his head small compared to his body, his countenance red, his eyes brown and a long nose. Looked at from the side, his shoulders were seen to droop; his mouth extended to his ears, and his pure white teeth resembled those of a horse. He had fingernails like the claws of a bear. His expression was one of deep humility, his voice like the cooing of a dove. When he raised his arms aloft one could almost imagine one was faced by a bat with outspread wings. He was a most hideous sight.

Thus did West appear to East.

297

Don Francisco

At Lisbon six Fathers waited to sail for Brazil, to begin in the South American dominions of Portugal the work established by Xavier in the East. Three others were preparing themselves to enter the lands of the Negus in Abyssinia. No less keen were those whose missions took them to Germany, Scandinavia and other lands lost to the Church through the heresies. There was no lack of vocations; every house was packed to capactiy; not a few of the aspirants had come from the court of Portugal and from the universities—the accounts and example of Xavier moving many a courtier and student to set aside earthly honours and to work for the greater honour and glory of God.

Some of the letters found their way to the little castle of Xavier. Don Martin, the Doctor of Navarre, took particular care to forward copies of those that came to Coimbra. A friend of Don Juan de Jassu y Xavier frequently sent excerpts from the letters received in Lisbon, which a secretary of the Spanish Ambassador at the court of King John was proud to transcribe. From Rome, too, Ignatius, mindful of the time he had been made welcome in Xavier, sent frequent bulletins and copies of the latest letters received from Don Juan's brother in the East.

On the first Friday of December, 1552, Don Juan was reading the latest of these letters to his second wife, Lucia. It was late in the afternoon and the nip of frost was already in the air; in the hall a fire of pine cones crackled. Doña Lucia, stitching away as she listened to her husband, promised that she would name the child for Father Francis—it *was* a little miracle in a way, she being childless for the early years of their marriage and no longer young, and now, when she had almost given up hope, God had heard her prayers, or rather Father Francis' prayers. Don Juan read on, though the daylight was waning fast. Doña Lucia laid aside her sewing and stared into the bright fire, seeing in its ruddy caverns Malacca and Japan and India and all the strange places where *el Santo* was known—*el Santo* who had once been a boy in this same hall, who had once been to Doña Maria as Lucia's unborn child was now to her. As Don Juan folded the letters, remarking on the briefness of the winter evenings, a shuffling on the stairway announced the approach of someone very old, very stiff in the limbs.

"Guillerma should be as old as the fog, as old as the hills," the captain of Xavier told his wife as they watched the old woman drag herself down the stairs from the oratory to the hall where they sat. She was the oldest person in the seven Basque valleys, a place where longevity was the rule, where centenarians were quite common. Don Juan thought Guillerma must be well over a hundred years—he had heard his mother say that the old nurse had attended on his grandmother when Aunt Violante was born. Lucia could depend upon it that when her time came, Guillerma would be pottering about somewhere. And, indeed, she would be a good one to have present. Had she not assisted at the births of the two *Santos* of the family—Doña Madalena of Gandia and Father Francisco, far away in the Orient? There would be no need for Lucia to worry: other women as old and older had come through their ordeal easily enough; his mother had been much older at the time of Francisco's birth.

Guillerma stood in front of them, bent almost double on her stick. The knuckles of her gnarled old hands stood out like little nuts; her almost toothless gums mumbled and mumbled. She gesticulated in the direction of the little oratory of St. Michael.

"It's rosary time," said Doña Lucia. "She wants us to say the Rosary in front of *el Cristo*."

"It's Friday," commented her husband; "it's only on Fridays she acts like this. Except the first time— You remember, she began these rosaries for Father Francis in Holy Week, on his forty-sixth birthday. Then on Good Friday and every Friday since. This is the thirty-third Friday."

Guillerma was begging them to accompany her. They followed the old woman down to the oratory. In the half-light, *el Cristo* of Xavier truly portrayed One who bore all human infirmities—One who carried the sorrows of all mankind. Guillerma was weeping the slow tears of the aged. When the Captain of Xavier proposed that they recite the sorrowful mysteries of the rosary, she fumbled for the sandalwood beads Francis had brought her from Compostela a generation before. The Captain and his wife said the prayers in *castellano,* Guillerma in Basque. And all the time her tears flowed—for what, she could not have told. She had heard many of Father Francisco's letters read aloud, the letters that friends had sent to Xavier, to tell where he was and what wonders he was doing. There had been no letters this long time. And, all this year, since Passiontide, a great grief oppressed her on Fridays. She had no doubt but that her nursling, if not actually shedding his blood for Christ, was in such trouble and grief that he shed tears—tears, the lifeblood of the soul. The rosary being finished, the Captain and Doña Lucia went away. But Guillerma remained, passing the Compostela beads slowly through her stiff fingers, sighing and weeping as she gazed on the crucifix and thought of Father Francisco. It was Friday, December 2nd, 1552.

On the same first Friday of December, 1552, Francis Xavier lay dying in a hut on Sancian Island off the coast of China, at the mouth of the Canton River. At the end of the previous July he had landed at Singapore. There he

had written the usual batch of letters. Two to Diego
Pereira to cheer him in his troubles and advise him to
turn to God, who alone could console the most afflicted;
two to Father Gasper Berze; one to another Father, and
one to a Japanese convert in Goa College. From Singapore
they sailed for China and most of his time on board went
nursing his three helpers, Brother Ferreira, the Chinese
boy and the young Malabar, all three of whom were prostrated by fever and needed constant attention. At last they
reached Sancian. No Portuguese ships might go any closer
to the mainland. Indeed, while at Sancian the Portuguese
had to be always ready to weigh anchor; the mandarins
in Canton, only six miles away, angry at this illicit trading
on their very doorsteps, had sometimes swooped down
upon smugglers, dragging many an unfortunate European
to those prisons where, chained flat to the ground in fetid
corridors and galleries, overrun with vermin, men died—
luckier ones soon, the others later. Francis knew of the
Chinese jails; he knew that he himself—if he succeeded,
with his imperfect knowledge of its language and customs, in entering this land—was almost certain to end up
in one of these dungeons. If so, he could at least console
the other poor prisoners. If he succeeded in getting into
the interior of the country, he would try to get to the
Emperor.

On arrival at Sancian the Portuguese lay brother, terrified at the stories he had heard from the seamen of the
dreadful imprisonment, of the awful deaths by torture to
be met in China, told Francis that he could not go any
further. He was told to take the next ship back to Malacca
with a letter to the Jesuit Father in charge there, asking
him to regard Ferreira no longer as one of the Society;
the Brother lacked certain essential dispositions for one
of their calling, but he might be quite suitable for some

other Order, and the Father was requested to look after him. The next disappointment was the Chinese boy, the interpreter, Antonio. Eight years in Goa had made Antonio forget his mother tongue. When a few smugglers came out to Sancian in a Cantonese junk, Antonio could not understand them nor they him. Another interpreter was hastily hunted up, but he, on reflection, thought the venture too dangerous; he had no wish to end up in the prisons of China. The only one to be depended upon now was the Malabar, Christopher, and whenever Father Francis looked at him he sighed deeply and said, "Ah, Christopher! Christopher!"

But even though no one went with him, Francis would venture alone into the great Dragon Empire. Meantime, during September and October, there was work to be done on the island of Sancian. He offered Mass daily, heard confessions, taught catechism and prayers. One arrival on Sancian was George Alvares, the Portuguese captain who had come to him at Malacca at the end of 1547, telling him about Japan and introducing Anjiro. Also in Sancian was another Portuguese adventurer named Pedro Velho. He had been among those who formed the escort of honour in Japan, only a year before, when Francis had gone in state to visit the King of Bungo. This last captain was a confirmed gambler and tried to while away the tedious hours on Sancian by dicing or playing chess for stiff wages. It was the first time *el Santo* had smiled since they left Malacca, the few seamen of Don Pereira said when they disembarked from the *Santa Croce* and found Father Francis standing behind the gamblers, smiling as Pedro Velho told the company of how the Father had advised him to mortify himself for the good of his soul—of how he had actually offered him a discipline. This was such a good joke that the gamblers ceased rattling dice to laugh. Pedro made his excuses and walked away with *el Santo.*

"You did not tell them how you gave me a generous alms every time you felt you should have taken the discipline," Father Francis said.

"What a thing to tell! If the truth were known, probably you have been flogging yourself for me every time I gave you an alms."

"Go back to your companions; they are calling you," Xavier said. "I want to talk to this group of slaves. I wish you would sell me into slavery in China like them."

"Heaven forbid!" ejaculated Pedro, piously and earnestly. "No, no, Father Francis; however you get into China, we are not going to allow you to go as a slave. Don Alvaro's men might; but not George Alvares or myself."

Francis sighed as he went towards the slaves. It was quite a problem, getting into China. If he had been half as good a swimmer as he had been a runner, he would have ventured to swim those six miles some night. It was most tantalising to be so near journey's end and yet so foiled in covering that last little distance, to have travelled half the world's circumference and yet be halted two leagues from the goal.

He discovered a girl cowering among the slaves—an Arabian, a Christian girl with a Portuguese seaman for protector. Francis' heart went out to the couple, so helpless, so menaced. A knife in the night would soon deprive the Arab girl of her only guardian. What fate lay before her then, a lone maiden—and a comely one at that—on an island with a shifting population of adventurers, slaves and traders! He decided that she should be married to the seaman who had brought her there. All Portuguese, even seamen, expected dowries with their brides. So Father

Francis returned to the gamblers, where Pedro Velho, perched on a bag of spices, was intent on his game.

"Pedro. Pedro."

"Yes, Your Reverence."

"Pedro, will you please give me three hundred *crusados?*"

"This is a bad time to ask me for money, Father Francis," said Pedro, "just when I'm trying to make a bit."

"All times are good times for doing good, Pedro."

"Well, since I won't take the discipline, I suppose you won't take a refusal from me. And at the moment, these fellows are out for all I have. If I don't watch out, they'll make a beggar of me. I can't afford to be talking, even to *Santos*. Take the key off my neck and help yourself out of my chest."

Francis took the key and went to Pedro's hut, got the dowry for the Arab girl, solemnised the marriage, and continued with his instructions to the slaves. Later that evening, Pedro Velho came to him for the key of his chest.

"I had a good day, Father Francis," he confided. "I gave two of Don Alvaro's captains a proper skinning, cleaned out their chests and won two bushels of pepper that one fellow hoped to trade with and three pecks of seed pearls off the other. Come to my hut and have a stoup of wine with Alvares and myself. You look a bit feverish this evening. You haven't been flogging yourself for Pedro Velho's sins again, I hope?"

Xavier accompanied him to the hut. He wanted to ask Alvares to keep an eye out for Anjiro, Paul of the Holy Faith, when in the China Sea. Some said Anjiro was a pirate there. He would tell George to look out for his first Japanese convert. He had other things besides to say to George and Pedro. That Chinaman—the fellow with the

junk who had agreed to take Francis to the mainland some
night for the outrageous fee of two hundred *cruzados'*
worth of Malaccan pepper—the Chinaman was a long
time turning up. And if he did turn up, he was quite
capable of pocketing the passage money and then failing
to keep his part of the bargain. So George had said; but
then, both George and Pedro were against his going to
China.

In the hut they told him that they were leaving next
day. They would take that last batch of letters he had been
writing, to Diego Pereira and the Fathers in Malacca and
in Goa. George tried again to dissuade him from making
the attempt on China. It was madness, the captain said.
Would the Father not make up his mind to sail with them
for Malacca and Goa next day? They would be honoured
to take him. But Xavier shook his head. It was no small
thing, he told them, to be able to offer the Holy Sacrifice
at the very gates of China. Who knew what graces were
being showered down on that Empire by reason of the
Divine Victim being immolated without the gate! He
would wait. The Chinaman might yet come.

Pedro, taking the key from *el Santo*, went to his chest.
There in the bag, were the three hundred *cruzados* he had
told the Father to take.

"Did you help yourself to that money, Father Francis?"
he asked, trying not to appear excited.

"Yes. I took three hundred *cruzados* from the green
bag. I am afraid I may have left you short. That was all
the money there. I was glad to hear you won at the gambling since, though I don't like to hear of the others'
losses."

"But, Your Reverence, my winnings are all in this purse
I carry about with me, and there are still three hundred

305

cruzados in the bag in the chest. Are you sure you emptied it?"

"Yes. I gave the money as a dowry to an Arab slave girl whom I married to a Portuguese this afternoon. And I promise you, Pedro, in the name of God, that your purse will never be empty; you will never know need."

El Santo seemed in a strange mood this evening, both captains thought. They felt rather upset to be leaving him here on this island; Don Alvaro's men on the *Santa Croce* were not inclined to do much for him—probably afraid of their Commandant in Malacca, who had given them their instructions when leaving there.

"Can we do anything for Your Reverence besides delivering these letters?" asked George.

Xavier shook his head. Sorrowfully, they accompanied him to the poor shelter of boughs thatched with straw, and knelt for his blessing. They would leave very early, before dawn. They asked to be remembered in his Mass.

In the morning their sails were far out in the bay. Anxiously, Francis scanned the horizon to see if there was any sign of the bamboo-masted, lateen-sailed junk of the Chinaman. It was mid-November and the cold fogs, heralds of approaching winter, were beginning to roll over the island. Food was scarce and Sancian was a barren spot; the few Chinese who had ventured from Canton to sell chickens to the Portuguese stayed away when they saw that George Alvares and Pedro Velho had gone. Antonio, the Chinese boy, had to go to the seamen of the *Santa Croce* and beg food for himself and his master. The night of the new moon, when the Chinaman was to appear, came and went. But no sign of either junk or Chinaman. The moon grew; the days and the nights passed, but the smuggler from Canton came not.

On November 21st Francis was struck by the enemy

that had so often before lain in ambush—fever seized him. So ill did he feel that he did not resist when Antonio insisted that he go aboard the *Santa Croce*. All the night of Tuesday, November 22nd, a stiff wind set the ship rolling and he felt his fever grow steadily worse. Besides, Don Alvaro's men did not make him very welcome. Even to this distant coast and in his last illness the hatred and rancour of one man followed him. In the morning he asked to be put ashore again. One of Diego Pereira's men presented him with a pair of warm trousers. Antonio asked the Captain if they might have some food; he received a handful of bitter almonds. During the day, Pereira's men, anxious for *el Santo,* came ashore and found him lying a little way up the beach, burning with fever. They were no physicians, but they did as they had seen physicians do at such times: they bled him; then the fever became worse. On Thursday and Friday, they bled him again, sadly conscious that they were poor surgeons. On both occasions he fainted after the blood letting.

It was then he became delirious. Preaching away in strange languages unknown to Antonio, unknown even to the Portuguese seamen, he lay there, gazing up to Heaven as usual, with the same expression of delight lighting his face as always when he looked upwards. Thousands of miles away, Michaelangelo was standing, looking up at St. Peter's, still wrapped in miles of scaffolding. He was forever looking up, men said. He had lain on his back for years painting the ceiling of the Sistine Chapel. He looked up because his heart could not bear to look down—to gaze upon the infamies, the sordidness of the men of his time. When Xavier looked up, it was not because the sight of human misery was too much for him; rather was it because he held his heart up, a chalice that God might constantly replenish, a cup forever brimming over with "compassion for the multitude."

Antonio, listening to the clear voice speaking, now in one language, now in another, caught a Latin phrase here and there which his few years in Goa College enabled him to understand.

"Have mercy on me, however great my sins and my shortcomings."

"Jesus, Son of David, have mercy on me."

"Mother of God, remember me."

For eight days, *el Santo* suffered, alone, absolutely denuded of human help. Don Alvaro's men kept to the ship. Some of Diego Pereira's few men had returned with George Alvares' ship; the pilot, who wondered how Father Francis was and why the Malabar and the Chinese boy were not returning to report, was warned to stay at his post. At any minute the Chinese mandarins might sally down the river mouth and the Portuguese would need to make a quick getaway; the man at the helm must stay at his post, the captain said. And, anyway, it was easy to explain the absence of Father Francis and his boys: some smuggler had slipped in at the farther end of the island and the Father was away to China.

On Thursday, December 1st, at midday, the Chinese boy noted, with pleasure, that the Father had recovered himself a little. For the last three days of November he had lost speech and the power of recognition. Now, both were restored to him. Frequently he repeated the holy name of Jesus. Again and again he murmured, "Most Holy Trinity, Father, Son and Holy Ghost!"

On Friday, December 2nd, Xavier turned to the young Malabar, Christopher. Regarding him fixedly, he sorrowfully shook his head, saying three times, *"Ay triste de ti! Alas, for you I grieve!"* Not many months later Christopher, fallen into evil ways, was murdered. The Malabar rose and wandered disconsolately up and down by the shore. Antonio could have rolled himself in his mat and slept, as he had done on the previous nights, but he felt moved to watch by the Father, who seemed to him in danger of death.

Far away, in Xavier, old Guillerma, bent with the weight of her hundred winters, watched and wept before the crucifix in the oratory of San Miguel; and, as Friday changed to Saturday, she began to doze, being overcome with weariness. Sometime between midnight and dawn she bestirred herself. It was Saturday, a day for the glorious mysteries of the rosary. She continued her self-imposed vigil, the beads of the sandalwood rosary Francis had brought her from Compostela passing through her bony fingers, the slow, rheumy tears of the aged trickling down her sunken cheeks.

· · · · ·

He was dreaming again. That Indian—who was at once an Indian, a savage of the islands, a Malayan, a Japanese, a Chinaman, a renegade Portuguese—was fastened on his back. The weight was prostrating. And he had to carry his burden, the burden that was Asia, a long, long way. Still, he had never refused to shoulder any of the loads that God had seen fit to lay upon him, so he set off in the darkness of night, carrying his brother, the man of the Orient, to God. Now and then he stumbled, his heart pounding under the strain, sweat pouring off him as he exerted himself. Across the mountain passes of Japan, following the tracks of his own bloodstained feet, noting how the souls of the baptised infants he had buried in the snowy wastes were shining like bright stars, guiding him all the way to Yamaguchi. There he blessed Father de Torres and Brother Fernandez and the other workers but recently arrived in those faraway fields so white to harvest. But he could not linger in Japan nor leave his burden down, for he bore on his shoulders a man—millions of men, men for whom Christ died, men for whom God became Incarnate in the Virgin's womb, men for whom He suffered and died.

So he was away again, south to the teeming islands, to the Isles of Hope in God, to Ternate and Amboina and Morotai, smiling upon his faithful catechists in the villages, his brethren in the Portuguese settlements. On to Malacca, where he toiled once again up to Our Lady of the Mount and, looking out on the town and the harbour and the hinterland, blessed all. After Malaya, India. It was a long journey to St. Thomas' shrine at Mylapore. The man on his shoulders was a dead weight as he trudged the burning sands at Travancore; past the pearl fisheries, where his beloved Paravas sang the Litany of Loreto as they guided their frail *catamarans* through the breakers to the oyster-banks. From Cape Comorin to Cochin and Goa, and then that nightmare voyage back round the Cape of Good Hope; fighting back bouts of seasickness, enduring the pair of hands that clutched his neck, he sailed past the sweltering Guinea Coast, right up to Lisbon.

But he had further to travel and he had friends to see. So it was on again over the Pyrenees, over the Alps to Rome and Ignatius. There he was, the old Pilgrim, sitting at his desk, the leg that had been short since Pamplona stretched out so that he might, now and again, rub the painful site of the old fractures. Ignatius was writing a letter, pausing occasionally to exclaim "Sinner that I am! My poor soul! My wretched soul!" The letter was to Xavier, recalling him to Rome; it was necessary that

Francis—whom Ignatius wished to succeed him as General of the Society—be with his Father in God for the remainder of the latter's life, which was not likely to be prolonged. Xavier sighed as he turned away. How ill he had fulfilled Ignatius' commission to enkindle and inflame the whole world! The East was still cold despite his efforts to cast fire upon it . . .

He shivered and the boy, Antonio, drew the sleeping mat closer about him. Noticing a change on the face of *el Santo,* the solitary watcher lit a blessed candle and held it in the dying man's hand . . .

It was dark in the crypt at Montmartre and he held a taper; it was fitting to hold up a little flame when making one's oblation to God Our Lord. He renewed his vows of poverty, chastity and obedience. In 1534 he had thought his surrender to have been something, now it seemed nothing—nothing at all; but God loved even such infinitesimal offerings. God was so great, so good . . . He trudged again through the muddy streets of Paris. Strange professors passed down the Rue de Chiens between the filthy Montaigu and the Ste. Barbe; other students' voices rang out in the Mule and the *Pomme de Pin.* He could catch the refrain:

> Claquin of Brittany, where's he gone?
> Where's Auvergne's Duke, the Conte Dauphin,
> And the late lamented Alençon?
> But where, ah, where's brave Charlemagne?

He would have liked to sing a line or two but his throat troubled him; and he was gasping with the weight on his back as he wearily faced southward. The stars were clear over Xavier, that little fortress in Navarre around which the wintry blasts blew chill on this night when Francis came home, his Indian on his shoulder. He sat once more in the window embrasure listening to Don Miguel translate the *Aeneid:*

> *O nimium caelo et pelago confise sereno*
> *Nudus in ignota, Palinure, iacebis harena!*
> Oh, all too trustful of the smile of sea and sky
> On an unknown shore, naked, O Palinurus,
>   shalt thou lie!

Once again he paused at *la Peña del Adios*, that height on the road to Sangüesa from which one could see not only Xavier and the six Sierras but, far to the North, the snowy peaks of the Pyrenees. No longer lithe-limbed—as when on a September morning in 1525 he had swung himself about in the saddle on this very spot to gaze back at the torn towers and ruined battlements of his home—but bowed beneath his load, he looked back for the last time. Now, as then, he fancied he saw, through eyes that blurred, his mother's lone figure silhouetted against the morning sky, leaning against the Homage Tower as she waved farewell . . .

He shivered again and Antonio tried to draw the meagre coverings closer round the thin shoulders. The Yamasse that had been blowing down the Straits since the last day of November was searching Sancian for the one it had come to torment. It cut through the raffia matting that patched the hut, lashing with its thousand thongs on the prostrate, helpless figure lying there. The Chinese boy crossed himself. He knew that the wind-demons rode the Yamasse; doubtless they had come to persecute and torture *el Santo* in his last hours. If only there were someone to keep him company; if only the dawn would break! But all was dark and no sound broke the silence save the sea, fretting and moaning under the onslaught of the Yamasse, and the laboured breathing of Father Francis—the death rattle in his throat. Antonio steadied the guttering candle and noted that *el Santo* was staring fixedly beyond the candle flame, straining forward like a runner whose race is almost won.

Antonio was not mistaken, for Don Francisco de Jassu y Xavier was nearing the end of the road; he was approaching the *Portico de la Gloria*. His dimming eyes saw it away to the west and his heart grew glad, though his body was crushed with the weight of the man he carried. Only for that Indian, he would have run to the *Portico*, as he felt his limbs grow supple again and the strength of a wondrous youth course through his veins. But he had loved the Indian too long and carried him too far to let him go now—in sight of the goal. Bracing the strong sinews of his soul, he bore this charge entrusted him by God the last few steps of the road . . .

Antonio supported his shoulders and held the candle steady.

In his numbing hands Xavier felt, not a candle, but a pilgrim stave; for him, the darkness beyond the candle-flame was Compostela, the Field of the Star. With great gasps he dragged himself on, his load unbearably heavy now. Thus he came to the base of the *Portico*, where the animal-headed demons yelled forever into the silent stone unspeakable blasphemies and imprecations; some, pig-eared, vulture-beaked, gnawed the worm that never died; others—humpbacked, gaping-mouthed toads—grinned obscenely as they unwillingly upheld the weight of the great Cathedral. Beyond the Great Judge the damned grimaced and gnashed unyielding teeth; they were the accursed, lost forever, immobilised in stony torments . . . Don Francisco passed them by, intent only on bearing his Indian to God. He passed the prophets—turbaned Isaias, smiling Daniel, sad-eyed Jerome; he passed on to the agate column where the stone kings mounted the last pre-Christian centuries . . . And there, at the fulness of time, her arms open and waiting, stood the Sinless Mother of God, the Compassionate Mother of men. Before her Francis stopped. He would give her his Indian, so that her unspotted hands might present him to God. Swinging his burden from his shoulder, he marvelled that it should suddenly have become so small and so light. Looking upon the man—the millions of men—he had carried, he found only a little Child, a Child for whom His Mother's arms were outstretched, for whom her quiet eyes smiled . . . And, with one accord, the ancients, the Evangelists, the elect, the angels and archangels played harps and viols and psalterions that made sweet music in the ears of Xavier . . . Raising his eyes to the Judge, he saw the hands of Christ, radiant with wounds, lifted to His Heavenly Father . . .

"Into Thy hands, O Lord, I commend my spirit . . . Let me not be confounded for ever . . ."

They were the last words Antonio heard. It was not yet dawn on Sancian, but bright shafts shone on the *Portico de la Gloria* as the heavenly Pilgrim, Francis Xavier, entered into the joy of his Lord.

Feast of the Annunciation, 1952

BIBLIOGRAPHY

ALTAMIRA Y CREVEA, Rafael: *A History of Spanish Civilisation* (London: Constable, 1930).

ARTECHE, Jose de: *San Francisco Javier* (Zaragoza: Hechos y Dichos, 1951).

ARTETA, Valentin, S.J.: *El Castillo y la Villa de Javier* (Zaragoza: Hechos y Dichos, 1952).

BAUMANN, Emile: *Trois Villes Saintes* (Paris: Grasset, 1912).

BELLOC, Hilaire: *Characters of the Reformation* (London: Sheed & Ward, 1936).

——: *The Great Heresies* (London: Sheed & Ward, 1938).

——: *Hills and the Sea* (London: Methuen, 1906).

——: *Paris* (London: Methuen, 1902).

——: *The Path to Rome* (London: Allen & Unwin, 1916).

——: *Places* (London: Cassell, 1942).

——: *Towns of Destiny* (New York: Robert M. McBride & Co., 1932).

BERTRAND, Louis, and Petrie, Sir Charles: *History of Spain* (London: Eyre & Spottiswoode, 1934).

BLUM, Andre: *The Last Valois: Costumes of the Western World, Vol. 8* (London: Harrap, 1951).

BOXER, Charles Ralph: *The Christian Century in Japan* (Cambridge: Cambridge University Press, 1951).

BRENAN, Gerald: *The Literature of the Spanish People* (Cambridge: Cambridge University Press, 1951).

BRIGGS, Everett: *New Dawn in Japan* (New York: Longmans, Green & Company, 1948).

315

BRODRICK, James, S.J.: *Saint Francis Xavier* (London: Burns Oates, 1952).

——: *The Origin of the Jesuits* (New York: Longmans, Green & Company, 1940).

BROU, Alexandre, S.J.: *Saint Francois-Xavier*, 2 Vols. (Paris: 1912).

BUCHAN, John: *Japan* (London: Hodder and Stoughton, 1923).

CAMPBELL, Thomas J., S.J.: *The Jesuits, 1534–1921*, 2 Vols. (London: Encyclopedia Press, 1921).

Catholic Encyclopedia: "Pilgrimages," "Compostela."

CATHOLIC RECORDS PRESS, Exeter: *Japan's Martyr Church* (Exeter: 1942).

CELLINI, Benvenuto: *Memoirs of Benvenuto Cellini, A Florentine Artist; Written by Himself*, translated by Anne McDonnell (New York: E. P. Dutton & Co., Everymans Library Edition).

COLERIDGE, Henry J., S.J.; *Life and Letters of Saint Francis Xavier* (London: Burns Oates & Washbourne, 1890).

COLLIS, Maurice: *The Grand Peregrination* (London: Faber & Faber, 1949).

——: *The Land of the Great Image* (London: Faber & Faber, 1943).

CROS, Louis M., S.J.: *Saint François de Xavier de la Compagnie de Jésus: son pays, sa famille, sa vie* (Toulouse: 1874).

——: *Saint François de Xavier: sa vie et ses lettres*, 2 Vols. (Toulouse: 1900).

DAVIES, Trevor: *The Golden Century of Spain—1501–1621* (London: Macmillan, 1937).

DIRECCIÓN GENERAL DE TURÍSMO, Madrid: Data concerning various localities in Spain.

EDICIONES JUVENTUD DE ACCIÓN CATÓLICA: *Santiago de Compostela. Guia* (Madrid: 1948).

ESCALADA, Francisco, S.J.: *San Francisco Javier y su castillo* (Pamplona: 1917).

FIDEL MESAS DE GRACIA (Fotografias y Edicion): *Santiago de Compostela, Ano Santo 1948* (Madrid: 1948).

FINLAYSON: *Michael Angelo, the Man.* (London: G. Putnam Sons, 1936).

FÜLÖP-MÜLLER, Rene: *The Power and Secret of the Jesuits* (London: G. Putnam Sons).

GALLOP, Rodney: *A Book of the Basques* (London: Macmillan, 1930).

GASQUET, F.A.: *The Eve of the Reformation* (London: John C. Nimmo, 1900).

GOODIER, Alban, S.J.: *Saints for Sinners; The Failure of St. Francis Xavier* (London: Sheed & Ward, 1936).

GRISAR, Hartmann, S.J.: *Martin Luther, His Life and Work* (Westminster, Md.: The Newman Press, 1950).

HEATH, Sydney: *In the Steps of the Pilgrims* (London: Rich & Cowan, 1950).

HOLLIS, Christopher: *Saint Ignatius* (London: Sheed & Ward, 1931).

———: *Erasmus* (Milwaukee: Bruce Publishing Company, 1932).

HOONAERT, R.: *Saint Teresa in her Writings* (London: Sheed & Ward, 1931).

HOWE, Sonia: *In Quest of Spices* (London: Herbert Jenkins, 1946).

HUGHES, Philip: *History of the Catholic Church. Vol. 3: Aquinas to Luther* (London: Sheed & Ward, 1940).

LAVAL, Père R. Gay, O.F.M.: *Les Clarisses* (Paris: 1912).

LEWIS, D. B. Wyndham: *Emperor of the West Charles V* (London: Eyre and Spottiswoode, 1932).

———: *François Villon* (London: Peter Davies, 1928).

LOJENDIO, Luis M. de: *Gonzalo de Córdoba (El Gran Capitán)* (Madrid: Espasa-Calpe, S.A., 1942).

MADARIAGA, Salvador de: *Christopher Columbus* (London: Hollis & Carter, 1949).

———: *Hernán Cortés* (London: Hodder & Stoughton, 1942).

MARTINDALE, C. C., S.J.: *What are Saints?* (London: Sheed & Ward, 1932).

MAYNARD, Theodore:*The Odyssey of Saint Francis Xavier* (Westminster, Md.: The Newman Press, 1951).

Don Francisco

MS 16th Century: *La Vida de Nuestra Madre, Sor Magdalena de Jaso y Javier* (Kindly lent by the Poor Clares of Gandia, Valencia, Spain).

National Geographic Magazine: Issues containing articles on India, Japan, Malaya, Siam, Burma, Ceylon and the Islands of the East Indies (Washington, D. C.).

Newton and others: *Travel and Travellers of the Middle Ages* (London: Kegan, Paul, 1926).

PASTOR, Ludwig Von: *History of the Popes*, Vols. X, XI, XII, XIII (London: Routledge, 1894–1933).

PIDAL, Ramôn Menéndez. *The Cid and his Spain,* translated by Harold Sunderland (London: John Murray, 1934).

——: *The Spaniards in Their History* translated by Walter Starkie (London: Hollis & Carter, 1950).

PLATTARD, Jean: *Life of François Rabelais,* translated by Louis P. Roche (London: Routledge, 1930).

PLATTNER, Felix Alfred, S.J.: *Jesuits Go East* (Westminster, Maryland.: The Newman Press, 1952).

RAIT: *Life in Medieval Universities* (Cambridge: Cambridge University Press, 1912).

RASHDALL, H.: *Universities of Europe in the Middle Ages,* 3 Vols. Powicke and Emden Edition. (Oxford: Oxford University Press, 1936).

RIX, E. M.: *The Testament of Ignatius Loyola* (London: Sands, 1900).

ROBERTSON, Arnold H.: *Missionary and Mandarin* (California: University of California Press, 1942).

ROSE, Stewart: *Saint Ignatius of Loyola and the Early Jesuits,* 2 Vols. (London: Burns Oates and Washbourne, 1891).

SCHURHAMMER, George, S.J.: *Vida de San Francisco Javier* (Bilbao: 1936).

——: "San Francisco Javier y Navarra" (in *Príncipe de Viana,* No. XXIX).

——: "Inbentario de los vienes que quedaron en Javier" (*Príncipe de Viana,* Nos. XL and XLI).

SEDGWICK, Henry Dwight: *A Short History of Spain* (London: 1925).

Don Francisco

Sitwell, Sachervell: *Spain* (London: Batsford, 1950).

Starkie, Walter: *Grand Inquisitor: Being an Account of Cardinal Ximenez de Cisneros and His Times* (London: Hodder & Stoughton, 1940).

Strange, G. le: *Romancero: A Collection of Spanish Ballads* (Cambridge: Cambridge University Press, 1920).

Ubillos, P. Guillermo, S.J.: *Vida de San Francisco Javier, Apostol de las Indias y del Japon* (Madrid: Apostolado de la Prensa, S. A., 1949).

Valverde, Jose: *Santiago de Compostela: Guia de sus Monumentos e itinerarios* (Santiago: 1950).

Veilliard, Jeanne: *Le Guide du pèlerin à Saint-Jacques de Compostelle* (Macon, France: 1938).

Walsh, William T.: *Isabella of Spain* (London: Sheed & Ward, 1931).

———: *Philip II* (London: Sheed & Ward, 1938).

———: *Saint Teresa of Avila* (Milwaukee: Bruce Publishing Company, 1943).

Xavier, Adro: *Huellas en la Arena: San Xavier en la India.* (Madrid: Sociedad de Educacion Atenas, S.A., 1952).

Yeo, Margaret: *The Greatest of the Borgias* (London: Sheed & Ward, 1936).

———: *Saint Francis Xavier, Apostle of the East* (London: Sheed & Ward, 1931).

A NOTE ON THE TYPE

IN WHICH THIS BOOK WAS SET

This book is set in Caledonia, a Linotype face created in 1939 by W. A. Dwiggins, which is by far one of the best book types created in the last 50 years. It has a simple, hard-working, feet-on-the-ground quality and can be classed as a modern type face with excellent color and good readability. The designer claims Caledonia was created by putting a little of each of Scotch Roman, Bulmer, Baskerville and Bodoni together and producing a lively crisp-like book type. This book was composed and printed by the York Composition Company, Inc., of York, Pa., and bound by Moore and Company of Baltimore. The typography and design of this book are by Howard N. King.